Transforming Ethnomusicology

Transforming Ethnomusicology

Political, Social & Ecological Issues

Volume II

Edited by

BEVERLEY DIAMOND

AND

SALWA EL-SHAWAN CASTELO-BRANCO

OXFORD

UNIVERSITY PRESS

OXFORD
UNIVERSITY PRESS

Oxford University Press is a department of the University of Oxford. It furthers
the University's objective of excellence in research, scholarship, and education
by publishing worldwide. Oxford is a registered trade mark of Oxford University
Press in the UK and certain other countries.

Published in the United States of America by Oxford University Press
198 Madison Avenue, New York, NY 10016, United States of America.

© Oxford University Press 2021

Library of Congress Cataloging-in-Publication Data
Names: Diamond, Beverley, 1948– editor | Castelo-Branco, Salwa El-Shawan, editor.
Title: Transforming ethnomusicology : Political, Social & Ecological Issues /
[edited by] Beverley Diamond, Salwa El-Shawan Castelo-Branco.
Description: New York : Oxford University Press, 2021. |
Includes bibliographical references and index. |
Identifiers: LCCN 2020032783 (print) | LCCN 2020032784 (ebook) |
ISBN 9780197517550 (v.2 ; hardback) | ISBN 9780197517567 (v.2 ; paperback)
| ISBN 9780197517581 (v.2 ; epub) | ISBN 9780197517598
Subjects: LCSH: Ethnomusicology. | Applied ethnomusicology.
Classification: LCC ML3798 .T735 2021 (print) | LCC ML3798 (ebook) |
DDC 780.89—dc23
LC record available at https://lccn.loc.gov/2020032783
LC ebook record available at https://lccn.loc.gov/2020032784

DOI: 10.1093/oso/9780197517550.001.0001

1 3 5 7 9 8 6 4 2

Paperback printed by Marquis, Canada
Hardback printed by Bridgeport National Bindery, Inc., United States of America

Contents

Acknowledgments

The field of ethnomusicology now has many professional societies that provide opportunities for academic exchange. When Salwa was elected president of the International Council for Traditional Music (ICTM) and Beverley was elected president of the Society for Ethnomusicology (SEM), both in 2013, however, we recognized that these societies hardly ever met together and we started a conversation about a collaboration. Within the ICTM, the idea was to create a new meeting format, named the ICTM Forum, that would join the ICTM with sister societies. Since the Limerick meeting with SEM, the ICTM has organized two other fora in collaboration with other scholarly societies (SEM was again involved with the third of these).

Longtime friends, we realized in 2013 that there had never been a joint meeting sponsored by the two largest academic organizations for ethnomusicology and we were determined to change that. We were exceedingly grateful that our colleagues at the Irish World Academy of Music and Dance at the University of Limerick stepped up as hosts for the event and we owe tremendous thanks to Colin Quigley and Aileen Dillane for ably co-chairing the Local Arrangements Committee. We formed a Program Committee of Senior Scholars on which Gage Averill and Samuel Araújo played key roles in formulating the topic of the joint symposium: Transforming Ethnomusicological Praxis through Activism and Community Engagement. Given that topic, we ensured that a number of public sector musicians, activists, administrators, Indigenous scholars and cultural animators were also involved. SEM executive director Stephen Stumpfle and ICTM secretary-general Svanibor Pettan provided generous assistance at every hand. Of course we are each extremely grateful for support at our own institutions for various projects we have undertaken. At the Research Centre for Music, Media and Place (MMaP) at Memorial University, Meghan Forsyth offered exceptional assistance and Graham Blair did his usual expert design work for the symposium. At the Ethnomusicology Institute of the Nova University of Lisbon (INET-md), Gonçalo Antunes de Oliveira was tireless in providing administrative support. We were also grateful for financial assistance from both ICTM and SEM, from the Irish World Academy of Music and Dance, and from the Social Sciences and Humanities Research Council of Canada. We met September 13–16, 2015, for what proved to be an inspiring and lively exchange. The initially planned meeting overlapped for one day with the annual meeting of the European Society for Ethnomusicology, thus extending the reach of the event and the input of scholars with diverse experiences and institutional backgrounds.

We appreciated ongoing advice from Senior Editor Suzanne Ryan at Oxford University Press in conversations that began at the Symposium itself. It was Suzanne's idea that "the book" be two volumes rather than one tome and we agreed that this was a good format decision. We also thank Norman Hirschy and Sean Decker for ably expediting the publication, along with their team of designers and copy editors after Suzanne's departure from the Press in 2020.

For both of us this project has been an important milestone in our careers. We are grateful for the many—too many to name, but among them colleagues, students, and community members—from whom we have learned so much about being conscientious and socially responsible ethnomusicologists. We have seen the field change a great deal and have been extremely lucky to be able to contribute to the communities and institutions where we have worked.

Of course, we are equally grateful for the support of family and feel that we have each been really fortunate to have partners who truly understood our work as ethnomusicologists and supported us in so many ventures. Beverley's partner, composer Clifford Crawley, valued her work and supported her in many ways even while struggling with illness throughout her SEM presidency. Salwa's life mate, physicist Gustavo Castelo Branco, has been a constant emotional and intellectual support for this and other academic projects.

The road to the publication that you now have in hand was quite long but rewarding at every turn. We feel privileged to have had the opportunity to work with distinguished colleagues whose work was intellectually stimulating and personally inspiring.

Ethnomusicological Praxis

An Introduction

Beverley Diamond and Salwa El-Shawan Castelo-Branco

A Historical Moment

Ethnomusicologists are no strangers to real-world issues. Engagement with communities and individuals is a requisite for the sort of detailed ethnographic work that is central in the majority of work in the discipline. Indeed the International Council for Traditional Music's "Declaration of Ethical Principles and Professional Integrity" states this very eloquently and clearly:

> Our work with others and the potential impact of our work upon others requires us to work for the benefit of those around us through the creation of new knowledge as well as by means of direct action, engagement, and the application of knowledge. We strive not only to do no harm, but additionally to design our research, teaching, and other activities to bring benefit to those who collaborate with us directly in the study, research, and dissemination of music and dance and associated scholarship. We recognize that our duty of care for those with whom we work most directly is privileged over and above demands or expectations emerging from individuals or organizations outside that immediate context. (ictmusic.org/governance/ethics)

We are called upon to face the challenges of the individuals and communities with whom we work but we also contribute to shaping cultural policies and politics through our work with national and international institutions, to studying colonial histories, and to engaging as activists in a variety of political, social, and environmental causes. For decades, then, ethnomusicologists worldwide, like scholars in other humanities and social science disciplines, have been addressing how best to engage with a wide array of systemic and socially challenging issues. These issues are more often thought to be the purview of other disciplines and yet our research has revealed significant, though sometimes marginalized, insights and strategies for positive change. In light of this, "transforming" in our title obviously has two connotations, one in which "ethnomusicology" is being

Beverley Diamond and Salwa El-Shawan Castelo-Branco, *Ethnomusicological Praxis* In: *Transforming Ethnomusicology*. Edited by: Beverley Diamond and Salwa El-Shawan Castelo-Branco, Oxford University Press (2021).
© Oxford University Press. DOI: 10.1093/oso/9780197517550.003.0001

transformed as a discipline and another in which ethnomusicologists are contributing to social change.

While the major academic societies in the field have individually encouraged such research and reflection, prior to 2015, they had rarely collaborated to consider such matters. This anthology emerged from collaboration that began in September 2015, when the Society for Ethnomusicology (SEM) and the International Council for Traditional Music (ICTM) organized a joint forum[1] to push ethnomusicological praxis further and to consider new directions. The European Seminar in Ethnomusicology was able to arrange their annual meeting to overlap with the forum for one day. Hence, not just two, but for one day, the three organizations met together. The format combined the deep-delving, single-topic explorations of SEM's pre-conference symposia characterized by exciting cross-sector exchanges, with the intensive international colloquia on cutting-edge themes that ICTM regularly supports. Both academics and public sector activists were featured. Ample time was scheduled for discussion, time that far exceeded discussion space in most tightly scheduled academic conferences. The forum was described as a space to be safely vulnerable. As such, like all "unsettled" spaces, it was a first step to new conversations. Keynote presenters and selected other speakers were invited to develop papers for this anthology, and they found many ways to deepen and extend the issues.

Ethnomusicologists have long done research that engaged with many social and cultural institutions and issues that affect musicians and all citizens unevenly. These range enormously in scale and scope. Some of us work with or within institutions that gaze to the past, many of them, such as museums and archives, formed originally as part of imperial and colonial enterprises. Others envisage various cultural futures, often in the face of challenges to cultural sustainability. These may range from international agencies such as UNESCO, to work with national and regional heritage organizations, or local projects. Some, such as creative cities initiatives are utopian while others, such as cultural projects of recovery after war, natural disasters, or forced displacement, seek the means to hang on to survival itself. Some ethnomusicologists work on cultural institutions that offer vastly uneven benefits to cultural "workers" including artists; these include intellectual property regimes or legal structures of legitimation or censorship, among others. Many ethnomusicologists study and take action where possible on social structures of marginalization: persistent racialized and hetero-normative social imaginaries and policies, constructs of legitimacy and privilege that underpin racism, sexism, and class inequities. Those of us who work in universities struggle to ensure that pedagogies are rethinking and not replicating these problematic social structures. We recognize that we must be vigilant about the ways our institutions are complicit in sustaining industrial, governmental, or military regimes that exacerbate inequity. We recognize that music itself is often framed naively, that sound may indeed serve destructive as well as constructive social processes. We struggle to understand a complex array of emerging global challenges, among them: increasing conflict and violence, spiraling economic inequity, natural disasters and environmental devastation, the unprecedented mobility of individuals and communities, and the impact of such mobility on human health and well-being.

Praxis, Music Studies and Approaches to Social Inequity and Marginalization

We specifically did *not* identify this volume as "Applied Ethnomusicology"—though some of the authors claim that affiliation. Rather, we offer a critical discussion of a range of socially engaged approaches as well as their deep historical roots which we consider fundamental to the ethnomusicological endeavor. To elide such things as Marxism, feminism, Indigenous studies and work on the sustainability of music and dance heritage—to name only four—denies their specificities and historical contingencies. The connection between the theories that help to explain and connect local experiences, knowledges, situations, or phenomena with various needs for action in the real world is what defines praxis. Praxis has a long and multifaceted intellectual history.

Most trace the philosophical origins of the concept of praxis to Aristotle who argued that "being" was an interweaving of contemplation, doing, and acting in society. Catriona Hanley (http://www.bu.edu/wcp/Papers/Acti/ActiHanl. htm) summarizes key distinctions: "*Theoría* in Aristotle is the activity of contemplation of necessary objects, while *praxis* and *poíésis* require knowledge of contingent objects. Whereas *poíésis* is an activity of making, aiming at a goal that is distinct from the action involved in the achievement of the goal, the goal of *praxis* is achieved in accomplishing the very action itself." She notes that Heidegger shifted the emphasis from the actuality of life to "possibility" while also prioritizing *praxis* (making) over *theoria*. While praxis has come to be linked to Marxist theory, the Frankfurt School, and Gramsci by many scholars, its philosophical basis is broader, encompassing work by Arendt, Sartre, and Kierkegaard, among others.

Research on structures of inequity and marginalization may be rooted in Marxist theory, feminism, anti-racist scholarship and studies of intersectionality, as well as participatory action research. This brief introduction cannot, of course, offer a comprehensive overview of music scholarship in each of these. Rather, we present examples and music-specific issues that we regard as significant and point to instances where ethnomusicologists have added new dimensions and nuances to praxis that originated in other disciplines or where the subject of "music" casts the issues in specific ways. The papers in this volume rethink and extend the boundaries of praxis in ethnomusicology.

As is well known, Karl Marx's intellectual life was shaped by his concerns about class struggle and the capitalist economic bases that create and exacerbate inequities. In music scholarship, Marxist-influenced analyses of music as a commodity have most often focused on popular music. Unlike the critiques of Max Horkheimer and Theodor Adorno, who disliked popular music and regarded its mass production as a means of dulling individual and social consciousness, however, ethnomusicologists and other music scholars have demonstrated how music production raises distinctive issues that cannot be so easily dismissed. The relations of production are exceedingly diverse and complex.[2] As Timothy Taylor writes in his study of commodification processes: "Capitalism isn't as monolithic as it comes across in many of his [Adorno's] writings, people aren't always duped by the cultural industries, music isn't always a commodity, and, if it is, isn't always a commodity in the same way. If we have learned one important thing from the Marxian study of culture after Adorno—from Raymond Williams—it is that the world is always in flux, that processes, even the most draconian effects of American capitalism, cannot be captured with snapshots of particular cultural moments, or examinations of a single work or two" (2012, 5).

In ethnomusicology a pioneering project was the anthology *Music and Marx* edited by Regula Qureshi. In her introduction she observes the growing number of "critiques of gender, race and class" and notes that "their collective engagement raises issues of power and hegemony that are increasingly concerned with global capitalism and its impact on people as much as on music" (2002, xv). Her own work examines capital in relation to feudal systems—a label she applies to (pre—and post-colonial) India. Qureshi draws on Marx's distinction between use value and exchange value, examining how use value is similar to cultural capital, beyond materiality. Among other contributions in her anthology, is Adam Krims's (2002) exploration of commodity fetishism which shows how musical styles (such as hip-hop) obscure and often exploit the actual economic contexts in which they originated. More recently, Peter Manuel (2019) has written a valuable updated overview that traces ethnomusicological contributions to our knowledge of music's modes of production (from feudalism to neoliberalism), as well as sonic articulations of socioeconomic class, and resistance to hegemonic structures.

Since Qureshi's publication, attention to globalization, particularly with regard to popular music and the rapid spread of the world music industry, has proliferated (Perrone and Dunn 2002, White 2012, Taylor 2012, Matsue 2013, to name only a few) and has also turned to globalization and the neoliberal phase of capitalism. Such studies as Peter Manuel's wide-ranging presentation of "cassette culture" in India (1993) and his daring analysis (2002) of the parallels between capitalist social values and the development of closed forms (song form, sonata form), Tim Taylor's multivalent theorization of music consumption practices (2012), or David Hesmondhalgh's ethics-based approach to capitalism and media (2017) demonstrate how varied Marxist-influenced music scholarship has become. Scholars of globalization (such as Steven Feld 2000) observe that music studies of the 1990s were polarized about the extent to which industrial capitalism controls not just the circulation and spread but also the valuation of world music. Stokes's overarching account of music and globalization (2004) demonstrates, however, that local values, structures and cultural initiatives, as well as the nature of musical sociality itself, challenge generalizations.

The relationship of economically driven inequities on migration has been studied by numerous scholars, among them Toynbee and Dueck (2011), and Anna Morcom (2013). Morcom demonstrates the unevenness of micro industry practices in Nepal, practices that are both capitalized and outside capitalism. Some studies (e.g., Meintjes 2003, Hilder 2017) examine power-laden interactions of production itself—in the recording studio, for instance—as microcosms of race/gender/class relations, rather than on the exchange value of the products of music. Also focusing on local production, Stobart (2010) reveals that, in Bolivia, piracy (characterized either positively or negatively in different sectors) has challenged the power of the large-scale, multi-national music industry. Many ethnomusicological studies demonstrate the wide range of attitudes that coexist among musicians, some valuing social intimacy and rejecting commodization while others learning very well how to work within commercial markets.

Some ethnomusicological initiatives move away from issues of commodification to focus on the impact of economic disparity more generally. The relationship of economic marginalization and human rights (e.g., Stillman, Ramos & Ochoa, and Helbig, all in Weintraub & Yung 2009), on one hand, and cultural sustainability (Grant 2014, Schippers & Grant 2016) on another, are among topics of concern. Other studies by Aaron Fox (2004) and Montero-Diaz (2017) examine constructs of class, the first in live contexts, and the second via digital media. An important initiative was a set of papers on music and poverty published in an issue of the *Yearbook for Traditional Music* guest edited by Klisala Harrison (2013).

On issues of social justice, the boundaries between the sub-disciplines of music scholarship (e.g., ethnomusicology, musicology, music theory, music education) are especially blurred.[3] Feminism is a case in point. As many have noted, feminism and queer theory came late to both musicology and ethnomusicology. Perhaps because of the disciplinary attunement to cultural difference, however, ethnomusicologists have diversified and deepened feminist theory by examining how gendered ideas and practices are shaped by different social values and beliefs and subject to reshaping, even though asymmetrical power relations are widespread. Our work goes well beyond analyses of how feminism itself was shaped by national academic traditions (Moi 1985) as the pioneering personal history by Ellen Koskoff reveals in *A Feminist Ethnomusicology* (2014). While early feminist work focused on gender binaries as instantiated in different cultural concepts and musical practices, many studies noted how concepts are renegotiated in relation to sociopolitical change or intercultural encounter (e.g., Moisala & Diamond 2000, Koskoff 2014, Magrini 2003). The gendering of listening remains an understudied area although as early as 1994, Cusick proposed an approach to queering listening practices and acknowledging how the "love" of music actually could inform analysis. More recent work in music, as in other disciplines, has focused on more complex, nonbinary embodiments of music/dance as both text and social practice and on the historical specificity of gendered performance (Sugarman 1997, Buchanan 2006, among many others). Studies that historicize specific mobilizations of gender (e.g., Soviet uses of Bulgarian women's choirs abroad, about which Buchanan has written) or changing constructs of gender that negotiate shifts in governmental or religious policy (Kisliuk 1998, Morcom 2013, Sunardi 2015) nuance normative readings of gender and music in both everyday life and staged presentation. Cross-gender music/dance performance (Sunardi 2015) as well as research on queer performativity in cognate disciplines (Halberstam 1998) has opened new approaches to embodiment. The gendering of affect has been a central component of work by Hahn (2007). Wong (2015) has examined the sexist and racist constructs of eroticism. Though it is not usually a research focus, ethnomusicologists have sometimes written about the gendered nature of their own fieldwork experiences (Shelemay 1991, Hagedorn 2001, Moisala & Diamond 2000). Often influenced by Judith Butler's analysis of "performativity," ethnomusicologists in recent decades have examined sound as a dimension that performs, negotiates, or resists binary structures on and off stage. Sugarman's overview (2019) of music-related gender research and queer theory is a valuable update.

Music and race has an enormous literature and is often linked with other systems of marginalization such as gender and class. Increasingly, sound-oriented scholarly studies have considered the intersectionality of such systems. A President's Roundtable at the Society for Ethnomusicology in 2014 devoted to the topic of music and power, for instance (see Berger et al., *Ethnomusicology*, 58, no. 2 [2014]) engaged with intersectionality. Maureen Mahon (2019) recently extended the analysis of critical approaches to race that she offered in that panel. Academic societies strive to move beyond talk to action. "Minority cultures" have become a strong focus in the culturally diverse ICTM, while the SEM has instituted many "diversity" initiatives over several decades.

Two influential ground-laying works are Radano and Bohlman's *Music and the Racial Imagination* (2000) and Josh Kun's *Audiotopia: Music, Race and America* (2005). The majority of studies of music and race focus on blackness, especially but not exclusively in the United States and Caribbean. The inflection of racial constructs through the globalization of Black popular music as described in Paul Gilroy's *Black Atlantic* (1993) influenced subsequent studies of the world music industry (see, e.g., Pacini Hernandez 2004, Hayes 2010, White 2012). Monson (2003) introduced the concept of diaspora in relation to complex sociopolitical differences in racialized musical contexts. She has also focused on state diplomacy in times where racism at home is strongly challenged, in her study of Black musicians abroad during the US civil rights movement (2007). The colonial roots of race-based, classed, and gendered constructs of the human voice with reference to nineteenth-century racial constructs of Indigenous and Afro Colombians have been analyzed compellingly in Ochoa Gautier's *Aurality* (2014). In national contexts, many music scholars have explored the racial shaping of specific genres: zouk (Guilbault, 2003), hip-hop (e.g., Rose 1994, Mitchell 2001, Helbig 2014 and others), salsa (Waxer 2013), or bachata (Pacini Hernandez 1995). In the Americas, whiteness has sometimes been a focus in both musicology and ethnomusicology; see Oja (2009) and Montero-Diaz (2017), for instance. Rao's study of Chinese opera in America (2011) addresses white constructs of Asian stereotypes.

In Europe, different political circumstances have shaped music studies of racism. Music's role in articulating the linking of racial or ethnic purity with constructs of anti-Semitic national identities has been studied by Bohlman (2004, 2011), Móricz (2008), and others. The racism that underpins attitudes toward marginalized groups such as the Roma who have been particularly skilled as music performers has been addressed by Pettan (2003, 2010) and others. Racialized listening has been addressed recently by Kheshti (2015) and Stoever (2016). Postcolonial racism has been addressed by many; Griff Rolleson's intersectional study *Flip the Script* (2017) is one important contribution focusing on the often racialized genre of hip-hop in Europe.

For many, action-oriented strategies can best be determined through Participatory Action Research (PAR), an approach that questions elitist control of knowledge production. It began as a movement pioneered by Colombian sociologist Orlando Fals Borda (1991, 2006). Noting that "*forms and relationships of knowledge* production should have as much, or even more, value than forms and relationships of material production" (1987: 337) he describes the focus on method as follows:

This experiential methodology for life and labour implies the acquisition of serious and reliable knowledge upon which to construct power for the poor and exploited social groups and their authentic organisations. In this connection, *people's power* may be defined as the capacity of the grass-roots groups, which are exploited socially and economically, to articulate and systematise knowledge (both their own and that which comes from outside) in such a way that they can become protagonists in the advancement of their society and in defence of their own class and group interests. (1987: 330)

The modes of PAR "research" include but expand on conventional qualitative and quantitative methodologies by ensuring that research aims and methods are formulated by communities themselves. Communities, then, determine appropriate means to address problems they face; in collaboration, researchers might conduct surveys, document and gather data from assemblies and both informal and formal performance events, or recover history by tapping oral traditions and interviews. Of particular importance for ethnomusicology is the emphasis on cultural dimensions ignored in other social sciences, dimensions such as art, music, drama, sports, beliefs, myths, story-telling, and expressive, creative, or recreational modes. This method was spread further by the influential philosopher and educator Paulo Freire (2005). The necessarily long-term nature of the interaction involved in collective PAR research is reflected in the important work of Brazilian ethnomusicologist Samuel Araújo and the youth with whom he works in the favela of Maré in Rio de Janeiro. Araújo and the Grupo Musicultura often coauthor publications, a practice that is influencing other ethnomusicologists to share authority. Many scholars use elements of PAR, working with communities to determine the social needs, research goals and methodologies of research, but Araújo is notable for his commitment to the *longue durée* of PAR in a way that few other music scholars have been. While there is, we argue, some naiveté in many studies that regard "participatory music making" as a de facto equivalent of participatory action research, we applaud projects that direct music making and/or media making to address such things as poverty and sub-standard living conditions (see, e.g., Frishkopf 2017, Araújo 2013).

Heritage Praxis and Sustainability

We now turn to heritage praxis, which has a long and multi-faceted legacy of institutional work and community engagement in ethnomusicology. A ubiquitous global phenomenon in late modern societies, heritage[4] matters because as a form of intervention and a transformative process (Hafstein 2014), the ways in which it is used has "consequences for the individual, community, national, and global understanding of self and other" (Smith 2012: 393). Ethnomusicologists have contributed to shaping and implementing state and international heritage regimes (Bendix et al. eds. 2012: 12–13),[5] and have done significant work toward the documentation, revival, safeguarding, and dissemination of music heritage and the recognition of its custodians.[6] This work has only recently begun to be acknowledged as an important part of ethnomusicological praxis and of the field's history. On the national scale, it entails the design and implementation of public policy and legislation on music heritage, though much of it is little known outside its national boundaries. It also involves the creation and management of museums, research centers, sound and audiovisual archives and other institutions that document, research, safeguard, and disseminate music heritage, provide training in field research and safeguarding measures, and promote collaborative research with communities on their music and dance practices (Berlin & Simon 2002, Murphy 2015, Seeger 2006, Seeger & Chaudhuri 2004, Pettan & Titon 2015). Ethnomusicologists have also disseminated heritage practices as concert and festival organizers, exhibition curators, authors of radio programs and educational materials targeted to the general public, and compilers and editors of influential collections of ethnographic recordings.[7]

Increasingly, ethnomusicologists promote projects that aim at repatriating recorded collections to their communities of origin and creating the conditions for communities to access, recollect, revitalize, and sustain their music heritage, privileging dialogue with the descendants of the documented tradition bearers, promoting networks of "forward-looking reciprocity" (Fox 2013: 552), fulfilling moral and ethical obligations toward communities of origin, and contributing to decolonizing the discipline (e.g., Corn 2012, Fox 2013, Gray 1997, Nannyonga-Tamusuza & Weintraub 2012, Treloyn & Emberly 2013; see also the chapters by Emberly & Davhula, and Treloyn & Charles, both in the present volume). Australians have been leaders in repatriating Indigenous recordings particularly since the establishment of the Australian Institute for Indigenous and Torres Strait Island Studies (AIATSIS) in 1989 as an archive devoted exclusively to Aboriginal materials.[8]

Ethnomusicologists also acknowledge heritage custodians through nominations to programs designed to honor their legacy[9] and the creation of opportunities for them to perform, record and transmit their knowledge to new generations (see José Jorge de Carvalho's chapter in this volume). Some also act as advocates and facilitators of community-based projects that aim at revitalizing and sustaining cultural heritage, and valuing cultural diversity (see Tan's chapter in Volume I). As heritage experts, in some countries ethnomusicologists are called upon to spearhead complex initiatives with positive and negative

dimensions such as the preparation of applications for the inscription of music
and dance practices on national heritage registers and on UNESCO's programs,
like the Masterpieces of the Oral and Intangible Heritage of Humanity, the
lists of Intangible Cultural Heritage (ICH) regulated by the 2003 Convention
for the Safeguarding of Intangible Cultural Heritage (UNESCO 2003), and the
Creative Cities Network, established in 2004. The preparation of applications,
their results, and the complex negotiation of different agendas of government and the heritage and tourist industries are sometimes wrought with
conflict, with consequences that can contradict the initial objectives. A few
ethnomusicologists have recently begun to critically assess their involvement
with such programs on the national level and within UNESCO, and the impact of heritagization on musicians, communities, music performance and associated artifacts, their ownership and meaning (Ceribašić 2019, León 2009;
Samson 2015, Samson & Sandroni 2013, Sandroni 2010, Stojkova Serafimovska
et al. 2016, Yung 2009).

On the international scale, several ethnomusicologists, some as official representatives of the International Council for Traditional Music (ICTM), an NGO in
formal consultative relations with UNESCO, have been involved in the development, critical discussion, formulation, and implementation of UNESCO's ICH
programs.[10] ICTM's Secretary-General (Dieter Christensen in 2001 and Anthony
Seeger in 2003 and 2005) collaborated in the evaluation of the applications to
the Masterpieces of the Oral and Intangible Heritage of Humanity program
(Seeger 2009, UNESCO 2001). Several ICTM members also contributed to
the configuration of the principles that undergird the highly influential 2003
Convention for the Safeguarding of the Intangible Cultural Heritage (UNESCO
2003), to the critical discussion on the concepts and terminology used therein
(Adrienne Kaeppler, Krister Malm in 2001, and Wim van Zanten in 2002, 2004,
2007 & 2009), and on ICH lists (Egil Bakka, László Felföldi, and Tvrtko Zebec in
2007).[11] ICTM officers were also involved in drafting the 2005 Convention on
the Protection and Promotion of the Diversity of Cultural Expressions (Krister
Malm) and served on several of UNESCO's bodies and committees, most significantly the Consultative Body of the Intergovernmental Committee for the
Safeguarding of ICH (Wim van Zanten, 2012, and Naila Ceribašić, 2013–2014),
and the Evaluation Body (Ceribašić, 2015).

UNESCO's ICH paradigm established by the 2003 Convention has had
a wide-ranging and diverse influence in many parts of the world.[12] It "provided a common language for talking about living cultural traditions" (Kurin
2017: 40). In fact, the concepts, as well as the spirit and letter of UNESCO's ICH
Convention, were adapted in legislation of many states, anchoring the design and
implementation of public policies, influencing heritage discourse more broadly,
and transforming the relationship between scholars, practitioners, communities,

and the state. In many cases, this has entailed the reconceptualization, transformation, and recasting of local practices as national and/or "global heritage," and as commodities for tourist consumption (DeCesari 2012: 409, Hafstein 2014, Kearney 2009: 13).

The imbrication of ethnomusicologists and other scholars in structures of power that impact on heritage—especially in the "dynamic triangulation" among the three constitutive elements in the "governmentalization of the global sphere" (Hafstein 2014: 55), namely, international authority, state and community—poses many challenges and has epistemological, methodological and ethical implications on fieldwork, research outputs, policies, institutions and communities of practice. The role of ethnomusicologists and other scholars in heritagization needs to be critically assessed, an endeavor in which a few ethnomusicologists are engaged (e.g., Ceribašić 2019, Murphy 2015, Seeger 2009). On the other hand, as Regina Bendix argues, "critical analysis ought not to disable the positive potential inherent to heritage-making but rather support the infusion of reflexivity in heritage decision-making processes" (Bendix et al. eds. 2012: 19) and in the role of scholars therein. Indeed, as several ethnomusicologists have argued, heritagization can contribute to the revival, valorization, and sustainability of heritage practices that were marginal, subaltern, or neglected (e.g., Howard 2012, Rees 2012).

Looking toward the future, a growing number of ethnomusicologists have been concerned about the long-term sustainability of heritage and other music and dance practices. Adopting an ecological perspective, recent studies explore the necessary conditions for the sustainability of music as a basis for culture policy, and for designing revitalization strategies in partnership with communities (see Titon's chapter in Volume I, Schippers & Grant 2016, Schippers & Bendrups 2009, Titon 2009).

Cultural Rights and Intellectual Property

Cultural and intellectual property and cultural rights, especially as they pertain to minorities and Indigenous peoples, have become a focus of ethnomusicological research and advocacy (Guy 2003, Kapchan 2014, Mills 1996, Seeger 1996, Weintraub & Yung 2009, Zemp 1996). The notions of cultural heritage and cultural property are sometimes used synonymously, though they constitute "parallel rather than identical modalities within the patrimonial regime . . . [and] are supplemented by intellectual property" (Bendix & Hafstein 2009: 5). Cultural property was first contemplated in UNESCO's 1954 Convention for the Protection of Cultural Property in the Event of Armed Conflict, also known as The Hague Convention. However, the issue of cultural property is not explicitly addressed in UNESCO's 2003 Convention. The World Intellectual Property Organization (WIPO), a UN agency dedicated to protecting intellectual property throughout the world, recognizes the rights that individual authors have over their literary and artistic work (copyright), but does not yet contemplate community rights. As has been argued by several ethnomusicologists, copyright legislation does not apply to collectively (re)created musical expressions, a common practice in communities throughout the world. The discrepancies between Indigenous customary law that views music as a form of relationality that requires "responsible access" and the Western world's focus on "ownership" are particularly divergent, as ethnomusicologist and law professor Trevor Reed (Hopi) has eloquently described (2019).

Within ethnomusicology, the ICTM spearheaded the debate on issues of ownership and copyright. A "Statement on Copyright in Folk Music" was published in the September 1957 issue of the Bulletin of the International Folk Music Council. The Executive Board of the Council appointed a Commission on Copyright and Ownership of Traditional Music and Dance in 1989 which was chaired by the then board member Krister Malm.[13] The commission was formed taking into account the interest of WIPO and UNESCO in addressing copyright for different forms of "folklore" and the work leading up to UNESCO's 1989 Recommendation for the Safeguarding of Traditional Culture and Folklore (Bulletin 75, 1989: 5). The commission was also charged with completing a survey of copyright legislation and concepts regarding the ownership of traditional music and dance. In addition, this was one of the themes of the 33rd World Conference held in Canberra (Australia) and the focus of several articles published in the Yearbook for Traditional Music, volume 28, 1996 (Mills 1996, Seeger 1996, Zemp 1996).

Ethnomusicologists and dance scholars also advocate for cultural rights and the freedom of music expression, denouncing censorship through research (Hall 2018) and the media, and fighting for freedom of expression and cultural equity through national and international organizations. Krister Malm is co-founder and member of the Executive Committee of Freemuse (https://freemuse.org), an independent international organization founded in 1997 advocating for and defending freedom of artistic expression that has denounced the censorship of musicians in many parts of the world. Where culture is concerned, however, there are always competing agendas surrounding performance. The public display of music and dance both constrained and mobilized in the interests of politically diverse authorities and projects. The work that ethnomusicologists, ethnochoreologists, and popular music scholars do in demonstrating these contended uses is socially important as complements to work that addresses cultural rights directly.

Human and Ecological Well-being

Rights are closely connected with health and well-being in human contexts. Music scholars are contributing to broadening the discourse about health and wellness, especially by insisting on the multiple dimensions that are biological, psychological, social, emotional and spiritual (Barz & Cohen 2011, Koen, 2008, 2018, Bakan 2015, de Nora 2014. The AIDS epidemic hastened important initiatives in Africa in particular. There and elsewhere, many have noted the impact of music on pain reduction and social support.

The huge range of music-related subjects associated with health and well-being cannot be adequately addressed here. Among this plethora of topics, aging has been one focus, with studies of older taste communities (Bennett 2018, Whiteley 2005, Ragot et al. 2002), as well as music and memory decline. Other work has related to music and mobility, music and psychological distress, or sonic vibration and healing.

The "music and wellness" scholarship has shifted over time from articulating the need to recognize "that the concept of disability saturates the cultural fabric" (Strauss 2011). Recent studies argue compellingly to dismantle normativity and hence respect differential physical and mental capacities (Wrazen 2016). Fields in which normativity has been challenged include studies of music and deafness that reveal how "listening" can be differently embodied and explained (Sawchcuk et al. 2018). Autism research has also been particularly important in this regard (Bakan et al. 2018).

The broadening of music praxis to "sound studies" within both anthropology and ethnomusicology has enabled multivalent approaches to the well-being of the earth itself and that of humans and other life-forms. Pauline Oliveros's "deep listening" training has been one widely lauded initiative, generating deeper knowledge of the sonic communication systems of environments and other-than-human beings (Allen and Dawe 2016, Minevich, Waterman & Harley 2013). McCartney (2016) has conducted longitudinal studies of changing sound as a result of environmental change and has also questioned the ethics of soundscapes studies. Feld's concept of acoustemology is an important advocacy for a broader inter-species approach to sound. He asks us "to consider the nature of human sonic interactions with all other species, with environments, with technologies. It [acoustemology] asks about the ethical and political consequences of an anthropocentric belief in an essential human nature, and engages how this idea aided imperialism and the domination of people, species, and places. It takes seriously the implications of these consequences for studies of music and sound" (2017, 94). This perspective aligns well with Indigenous approaches.

Two other ways in which recent ethnomusicology is contributing to sound ecology are through studies that address ecological precarity and to environmental activism. With regard to the former, Jeff Titon has provided leadership through a widely read blog on "sustainable music" (sustainablemusic.blogspot. com) and through academic publications (2009). See also Titon in this volume. Attention to ecology with regard to the materials used in the production of musical instruments is one aspect of the broader topic of ecology and is a topic of growing concern (Simonett 2016, Tucker 2016). In other contexts, as scholars have described, music is used to articulate public attention about environmental issues (e.g., Rees 2016, Manabe 2015, Frishkopf 2017).

Indigenous Studies scholars have long articulated how song and dance enact the broader ontologies of life on earth in the communities in which they work and/or live. Australian scholars pioneered this area of study (see, e.g., Wild 1981, 1984) and Andean scholars have also published actively on this issue. See, for example, contributions by Anthony Seeger and Bernd Brabec de Mori in a special topics issue of the *Ethnomusicology Forum* (2013). They have also worked with Indigenous singers and elders to articulate how music expresses relationships with the spirit world (e.g., Marett 2010). Indigenous-authored studies are understandably circumspect about sharing such knowledge. The ethical and theoretical implications of newer Indigenous-centered approaches are having an impact on music scholarship and pedagogy.

Indigenous Studies

Although it is often treated as an "area studies" initiative, the unique positioning in relation to colonialism and the global reach of Indigenous Studies[14] in recent decades, has ethical, theoretical, and methodological implications that must be considered in relation to praxis in ethnomusicology as in all scholarly fields. Indigenous Studies is the only form of praxis described here that addresses "settler colonialism"[15] centrally and the very concept of "property" addressed above. But while colonial oppression and deterritorialization defines the shared history/context of most Indigenous groups worldwide, Indigenous Studies also validate the authority, indeed the sovereignty, of the very local. The *sovereignty* of local beliefs, laws, and lifeways is central, even though global alliances and interactions among Indigenous people are widely recognized as tactics for addressing a wide range of issues, including many relevant to music scholarship. These include concepts of ownership and intellectual property, relationships in fieldwork, ontologies that recognize interrelations of human and other species, the very methods of music scholarship which have so often replicated those of "extractive" industries in the name of "collecting," to name a few important ones.

Concepts such as "collaboration" or even "decolonization" are being questioned as "moves to innocence" (Tuck and Yang 2012) that appease settler guilt without actually addressing the basis of settler colonialism as a system bent on taking Indigenous lands and ending Indigenous societies.

Because Indigenous-centered approaches have grappled with the divergent scale of praxis and because local knowledge is valued, the frequent collapsing of such differences in generalizations about "Indigenous" people and cultures is felt to be particularly egregious. As described earlier, respect for local knowledge is also valued in Participant Action Research, an approach to praxis that is widely used in Indigenous studies (though often still initiated by settler scholars). Just as PAR questions the control of knowledge production, Audra Simpson and Andrea Smith remind us that "native studies since its inception has steadfastly engaged the historical and political context that defines truth" and further acknowledges that because of these contingencies, what anyone regards as "true" is flexible and changing (2014, 3). Related to this, is what Indigenous scholars have labeled "eth-nographic entrapment" (Simpson and Smith 2014, Povinelli 2002): namely, the problematic representation of racial "others" as static and anti-modern and the expectation that Indigenous people must exhibit the "loss" of these traditional knowledges and lifeways.

Recent studies (Rifkin 2011, Mackey 2016) develop these and other aspects of the "structures of feeling"—particularly entitlement—that continue to animate settler colonialism. Rifkin asks, "How does that feeling of connection to this place as citizens of the state actively efface ongoing histories of imperial expropri-ation and contribute to the continuing justification of the settler state's authority to superintend Native peoples?" (2011: 342). Entitlement to land is central but the authors in Levine and Robinson (2019) have shown how entitlement also inflects practices of listening as well as research approaches. Robinson (2020) has discussed the concept of "hungry listening" that underpins much fieldwork. And the comparison of "collecting" songs and "extracting" natural resources has been reiterated by many. Indigenous studies aim to dismantle settler colonialism and to protect people and lands that are central to their existence and ways of being. Some see in such aims an implicit critique of Marxism as a Western development model. Concerns arise about the inaccurate "post" in postcolonialism, or about the homogenizing of local difference in contexts where "Indigenous" is expressed as a singularity. While scholars who work with Indigenous communities have always been asked how their research might benefit the communities, the theo-retical implications of such questions are now emerging in ethnomusicology in ways that are dynamic and exciting. The impact of colonial violence, particularly in the contexts of boarding and residential schools, has received close attention (Troutman 2009, Robinson & Martin 2016). Constructs of "modernity" have been discussed in relation to the colonial definitions of Indigeneity as outside modernity (Ochoa 2014, Levine & Robinson 2019). Related research examines the implications of technology for realigning histories and relationalities (Neuenfeldt 2007; Hilder et al. 2017) in the twenty-first century.

Reflections on Applied Ethnomusicology

Many of the praxis-oriented approaches discussed so far uncovered structures of thinking and feeling, structures of governance and education, roles and relations, that normalized lifeways for the privileged (usually white, European-descended, Northern Hemisphere dwellers) and critiqued concomitant structures of marginalization. Some of them have been directed toward action in the world. Increasingly, however, ethnomusicologists have wanted to move more explicitly to action, to contribute to social justice initiatives and social change. Much of the latter work self-identifies as Applied Ethnomusicology.[16]

Applied Ethnomusicology has existed—but on the margins of scholarly discussions and even scholarly consciousness—for a long time. Like anthropologists, folklorists, sociologists, and other social scientists, ethnomusicologists have always done community-oriented work and offered to help with projects that communities deemed important but in earlier decades, such work was regarded simply as a way of giving back. Many projects were done out of friendship but were rarely written about. Perhaps as a result, many contend that applied work has been undervalued in the academy. As a "conscious practice" (Sheehy 1992: 323), Applied Ethnomusicology has experienced a surge of energy in the twenty-first century, however, and has, as a result, instigated debate about best practices and analyses of the different social contexts that shape community-oriented work (see Dirksen 2012). The adjective "applied" has itself proved contentious (see Averill 2003); some prefer "activist," "engaged," or "socially relevant," while others argue that all ethnomusicology, and not just a sub-area labeled "applied," engages with or responds to social needs and community aspirations. A number of anthologies of Applied Ethnomusicology have now been published (Harrison, Mackinlay & Pettan 2010; Pettan & Titon 2015). They outline how applied ethnomusicology extends and complements other academic domains. With specific reference to the U.S. context, Titon identifies various kinds of activities or "interventions": cultural policy interventions, advocacy, education, as well as peace and conflict resolution; medicine, law and the music industry, museum and archive work (repatriation), journalism, environmental sound activism and ecojustice. With reference to other national contexts, Pettan echoes a number of Titon's themes but also describes the importance of attention to immigration and recognition of minority cultures, to conflict studies and peace building initiatives.

Ethnomusicologists have already made significant contributions to many of these issues. They have contributed new dimensions to the study of conflict and violence (see O'Connell and Castelo-Branco 2010). They have illuminated music's social roles in times of war (Pettan 2010, Ceribašić 2000), and in contexts of ongoing violence (Ramos & Ochoa 2009). Scholars have helped mobilize music after conflict as a vehicle for generating communication and possibly effecting agreement or for voicing dispute (e.g., Pettan 2010, Sweers 2015). But they have also uncovered how sound and music are playing roles in exacerbating dissonance (O'Connell & Castelo-Branco 2010, Pieslak 2015, Gilman 2016) or even causing injury and death, as is the case with no-touch torture (Cusick 2008, Daughtry 2015).

Awareness is growing about potential pitfalls and problematic assumptions that may tinge some "applied" work. The idea of "enabling" communities assumes a position of power for researchers that often reinscribes a Western-centric hegemony: it implies that researchers are "helpers" while assuming that community collaborators who may have historically been "wards of the state" in colonial contexts in particular (Coulthard 2007, 2014) need help. Furthermore, writing about field experiences is sometimes silent about situations in which researchers are quite helpless.[17]

As has been noted at (at least one) recent Applied Ethnomusicology gatherings, there has been a rosy cast to many Applied Ethnomusicology discussions and too little attention paid to the very difficult and often dangerous negotiations of power in fieldwork. While there have been accounts of vulnerability (e.g., Babiracki, Beaudry, Kisliuk in Barz & Cooley 2008), there are fewer instances of scholars who discuss political interference, although exceptions include Levin (1996). Some studies (e.g., Spinney 2006, Kisliuk 1998) have described power struggles between village leaders and missionaries, for example, but few have addressed the roles that ethnomusicologists may be called upon to assume and the real dangers that may be associated with those roles.

Introduction to the Papers

As the chapter summaries below describe, the papers in this anthology strive to understand the aims and uses of sound-oriented research and the roles of ethnomusicologists, together with collaborators, as activists and socially engaged scholars. Some chapters could easily be categorized within some of the dominant approaches to praxis outlined above, but many cross boundaries between approaches and this, we argue, is significant for future research. Gender, class, and race constructs as well as colonial histories are not always named as analytics but nonetheless inform many of the chapters, including those by

Muller and Öhman, Treloyn, Emberly, Dirksen, and Hofman. Institutional structures—be they governmental, legal, educational, or otherwise socially constructed—frame discussions by Seeger, Pettan, Shao, Hofman, McGraw, McDonald, Liebmann, Emberly, and Wong. In addition to Indigenous-centered approaches by Hamill, Roberts, Treloyn and Charles, and Emberly and Davhula, there is a strong ecological turn in several other chapters, most notably those by Hamill, Dirksen, Dillane and Langlois, Titon, and Frishkopf. Health (spiritual, social, psychological, and physical) is at issue in chapters by Shao, Frishkopf, Dirksen, and Hamill. The extension of sound studies beyond the realm of the human (Hamill), the re-storying of spaces (Tan), and the uses of new media to document environmental degradation and to lobby for change (Dirksen, Hamill, Araújo) are all extensions of earlier praxis approaches conceptually, representationally, and socio-politically. The revitalization, transmission and sustainability of heritage practices; the transmission of knowledge by heritage custodians, honored and integrated in revitalization projects and established institutional structures; and the repatriation of sound recordings and their use as catalysts for revitalizing social practices are addressed in the chapters by Tan, de Carvalho, Emberly and Davhula, and Treloyn and Charles. UNESCO's ICH programs are also critically addressed in Titon's chapter. Globalization and its economic implications are central frames in Hofman, Impey, de Carvalho, Frishkopf, and Shao. Applied ethnomusicology approaches range from the activist (Liebman) to research oriented work (Muller and Öhman). Araújo historicizes and uses Participant Action Research as does Tan. Projects described by these authors as well as Emberly and Davhula, and Treloyn and Charles further sustainability by engaging intergenerational participants. The chapters that follow, then, adopt various approaches to praxis, often influenced by more than one of the above-mentioned epistemological traditions, but framed by specific geopolitical circumstances pertaining to their work.

Before describing the individual chapters, we draw attention to the "position statements" of the authors. Rather than submitting conventional biographical notes, we asked the authors of this anthology to write about what moved them to do the engaging work they do. They responded with passion and candor. The statements reveal amazing experiences that underpin motivations, methodologies, and modes of explanation. While our biographies and professional trajectories are diverse, we share a deep commitment to fight for human rights and a more equitable society, social and political justice, fair labor conditions inside and outside academia, as well as cultural and environmental sustainability. We urge you to meet us as individuals through these extraordinary position statements.

The two volumes are complementary, and while the subtitles of each indicate some differences in their orientation, there are many thematic intersections across the two volumes as well. Volume II, which focuses on "Political, Social and Ecological Issues," begins with two chapters by Jeff Todd Titon and Michael Frishkopf that offer broadly based and unabashedly utopian visioning for creating a better world. Titon's metaphor of "sound communities" and Frishkopf's "social resonance" have certain common bases but also different reference points. They both urge us to think globally, presenting analyses of the philosophical underpinning of economic, social, and environmental relationality that has led to dehumanization and massive human suffering (as Frishkopf outlines).

Titon focuses on the economic dimensions of cultural production, exploring the multiple senses of a "sound economy" as both physical vibration and good health, resonance and presence. With a strong ecological emphasis, he suggests replacing Adam Smith's concept of the individualistic "homo economicus"— a concept that still has theoretical currency in economics—with "homo reciprocans" that recognizes the interdependence of humans, other beings, and environments. Familiar with Intangible Cultural Heritage programs, Titon argues that agencies such as UNESCO and WIPO who relate heritage to economic growth have developed programs with mixed results.

Frishkopf asks how music can "support social reintegration and rehumanization of social relationships." Drawing on Habermas's concept of "lifeworlds," he analyzes the malleable and adaptive qualities of culture. The projects he has initiated through the Music for Global Human Development (M4GHD) networks put Participatory Action Research paradigms to work toward healthier communities. He critiques "development" that ties to economic growth and metrics such as HDI (Human Development Index), arguing that the nature of music as participatory and unbounded should be central in development initiatives.

Two of the boldest critiques of systemic problems (ones with both local and global dimensions) that praxis-oriented scholars face are offered by Samuel Araújo and Ana Hofman. In this anthology, Araújo calls for rethinking the politics and epistemologies of knowledge production in ethnomusicology, arguing for the integration of "horizontal modes of knowledge production, individual or collective action and public policy-making and implementation." Critically assessing the field of Applied Ethnomusicology, he questions the epistemological, political, and ethical foundations of the distinction between "pure" and "applied" research. He also highlights the important intellectual contribution of Brazilian educator Paulo Freire and Colombian sociologist Orlando Fals Borda, and their commitment to radical sociopolitical change. Finally, Araújo urges us to discard "presumably politically correct terminology" and move toward an ethnomusicology that is "a committed, critical engagement with human difference that goes beyond false dichotomies between theory and practice."

Bringing perspectives from the Eastern European sphere, Hofman analyzes the material, social, and intellectual impact of economic changes within European universities, with particular but not exclusive focus on Slovenia. The problem of precarious labor—short-term, underpaid contracts for academics rather than secure, long-term jobs—is relevant more broadly, even though specific national differences are important to consider. Her chapter provides a multifaceted description of precarity and the "metrics" that universities increasingly use to evaluate scholarship, metrics that disregard some of the community-oriented projects done in "Applied Ethnomusicology." At the same time, she observes a widespread turn within the broader society that demands research that addresses social issues. This, in turn, often transforms academics into "knowledge providers" in projects driven by economic interests, redefining what "applied" work is and further reducing the possibility of sustained and deep reflection.

Dillane and Langlois reflect on the LimerickSoundscapes project they devised to promote active engagement within specific communities and locales. By offering community members agency and partnership as "citizen collectors," and with a keen eye and ear for privacy and confidentiality, they relate sound (broadly defined) to concepts of critical citizenship in the multi-ethnic, post-industrial city of Limerick, Ireland. Sonic attentiveness, they argue, is a tool for increasing social awareness and countering discrimination. The complex and changing nature of sonic awareness, as well as one's physical capacity to hear anyone's social position, are factors that shift over time on both micro (in the course of a day) and macro levels (over weeks, years, or centuries). They explore such factors as they engage in an ongoing conversation with local groups about what sounds are important for what reasons and at what times. They see value in "research" that strives to be a catalyst for action.

Taking care of place is central to the chapters by Indigenous scholars Chad Hamill (Spokane First Nation) and Australian Aboriginal scholar Rhoda Roberts. Hamill addresses ecological and environmental issues from a Spokane perspective, demonstrating how, in a "sacred geography," song interacts with the river that is the lifeblood of the Spokane people, but also describing a compelling parallel between the polluting of the river and the colonial measures of missionaries and others that aimed to obliterate traditional song. Like a number of other authors in this anthology, Hamill presents an alternative to conventional academic writing by rooting his presentation in a traditional story, a primary mode of telling history among his (and other) Indigenous people.

Roberts uses her high-profile position as the Aboriginal Advisor to the Sydney Opera House to ensure that Indigenous land-based beliefs and lifeways are respected by a broad intercultural audience at an elite arts institution. She describes various initiatives that have played a role in decolonizing audiences.

It is still a relative rarity in ethnomusicology to see co-authored studies that emanate from collaborations between a local expert and a visiting scholar. Two models—by Andrea Emberly and Mudzunga Junniah Davhula on one hand, and by Sally Treloyn and Rona Goonginda Charles on the other—are, therefore, important models. Treloyn and Charles takes issues of repatriation one step further, however. They contemplate the various stages and layers of "discomfort" that necessarily accrue to settler colonialism, and that demand recognition if endangered music is to be sustained. They build on Deborah Bird Rose's model of "deep colonizing" as a way of examining power relations of both the past and the present and of both the researcher from outside the community and local knowledge bearers who often feel obliged to collaborate. Focusing on the *junba* dance and song project, they reveal how they struggle to develop an epistemological framework that supports vitalization. Their vision goes beyond access to consider intergenerational transmission of song and dance knowledges as well as "relational accountability."

Andrea Emberly and Mudzunga Junniah Davhula present their work on the Dancing Domba Project, an initiative in Vhavenda, South Africa, that seeks to revitalize initiation schools. While some Venda cultural traditions have been sustained or energized, since "semi-independence" in 1969 and after apartheid, the initiation schools have declined because the structures of colonial institutions—especially the scheduled semesters of government or church-run schools—do not allow for instruction in isolation from the larger community, traditionally for long periods of time. The several age-related stages of instruction for girls teach healthy lifeways, age-related social responsibilities, and appropriate ways of venerating ancestral spirits. The project is, in part, a repatriation of John Blacking's *domba* recordings of the 1960s. In part it is a revisioning of the tradition so that, without violating restrictions associated with some parts of the rituals, aspects might be incorporated in school curricula, or public performances at festivals or other events.

The final two chapters turn to the ecologies and political structures of institutions. Andy McGraw provides an account of a music program he facilitated in the Richmond, Virginia, city jail and the ethical ambiguities arising from his overlapping roles as, on one hand, volunteer program organizer at the jail and, on the other, ethnographer of the institution and its actors. He examines the vague boundaries between applied and academic ethnomusicology, voluntarism and work, as well as personal and institutional ethical standards. An ethnomusicological approach to music in jails and prisons exposes ethical frictions between policies, methodologies, and the codes espoused by Institutional Review Boards (IRB) or other ethics review procedures/institutions. McGraw notes that the IRB's ethical guidelines argue that research should not change the lives of "human subjects." As an academic observing the criminal justice system and as an ethnomusicologist conscious of the transformative effect of music, McGraw questions if his personal and disciplinary ethics are in irreconcilable conflict with those of the IRB system.

The final chapter in Volume II describes a truly transformative initiative. José Jorge de Carvalho was at the center of a collaborative and theoretically innovative project developed at the Institute of Inclusion in Higher Education and Research at the University of Brasília that has expanded to other universities in Brazil and Colombia. Dubbed the Meeting of Knowledges, it provides a framework for holistic and integrative systems of knowledge within academia by inviting masters of traditional knowledges (Indigenous, Afro-Brazilians, and popular cultures) to teach regular courses and conduct research in science, technology, traditional music, dance, theater and related arts, and spirituality. The project emerged out of two distinct and complementary social and intellectual movements in Brazil: the struggle to meet quotas for Black and Indigenous students in universities, and the movement of a national network of agents, producers, and researchers on popular cultures that demanded public policies for the groups, communities, and masters of those traditions. The model established by this project represents a radical political transformation in ethnomusicology and in academia more broadly, changing the rules and protocols that define the discipline and our role as teachers, researchers and activists.

Future Possibilities

This anthology refuses the neat packages of some classic approaches to praxis theory. It offers some daring reflections on methodologies and considers ways that ethnography itself can be useful in real-life contexts. It examines concepts: among them, "collaboration," "property," and "well-being." It also looks inwardly at the histories of academic institutions and outwardly with an eye to the potential of daring, radical change.

We suggest that some of the strategies that underpin this anthology should be carried forward in future initiatives. These include, for instance: comparing the ways central concepts and theories have developed in different cultural spheres and national contexts as several authors in this anthology began to do (the Global South remains underrepresented in this anthology as do Indigenous contributors); learning from discomfort and vulnerability, both by honestly presenting our motivations and limitations, but also by cultivating more openness to different positionalities; evaluating the effectiveness of projects, practices, and institutions and their intellectual and political assumptions. Most important, we anticipate that further collaborations among academic and public sector organizations and international institutions will be an effective strategy to identify how best ethnomusicologists can contribute to understanding and resolving rapidly changing global and local challenges as they emerge.

Notes

1. The Forum was beautifully hosted by the Irish World Academy of Music and Dance of the University of Limerick. The Irish World Academy is known internationally for its commitment to community engagement and to exploring how the arts can contribute to social inclusion and to health (http://www.irishworldacademy. ie/research/research-groups/). The University of Limerick engages in Peace and Development Studies through a specialized research Center (https://www.ul.ie/ppa/ centre-for-peace-and-development-studies).

2. Adorno's writing on music has been compiled and translated into English. See Theodor Adorno, Richard Leppert and Susan Gillespie, eds., *Essays on Music: Theodor W. Adorno* (2002).

3. Hard evidence for this statement is virtually impossible to locate and so this is impressionistic but based on citational practices here and elsewhere.

4. Heritage and similar notions such as "tradition" or "patrimony" are in wide circulation in many contemporary global societies. Many national and international institutions such as UNESCO include a definition of heritage in their statutes. The notion of "heritage" and its modes of production has also been the subject of scholarly debate in the interdisciplinary literature on heritage and many scholars have pointed out the "difficulties involved in untangling the different values and meanings attached to ideas of heritage" (Roberts 2014). Drawing on current literature, we use the notion of "heritage" to refer to the discursive and performative production of selected "objects, places and practices" (Harrison 2013) associated with the past to which new value and meaning are ascribed in the present, with a vision toward the future (Harrison 2013; Kirshenblatt-Gimblett 1995 and 2004).

5. Anthropologist Regina Bendix defines the state heritage regime as "a set of rules and norms regulating the relations between a state-government and society" and the international heritage regime as having come about "through negotiations among actors on an international level" (Bendix 2012: 12–13).

6. Sheehy (1992), Seeger (2006), and more recently Pettan (2015) and Titon (2015) call for the recognition of the significant work of ethnomusicologists in public sector and applied ethnomusicology, much of it on "music heritage," and review the activities of some of its main figures and institutions in Europe and the United States. This work is referred to in several chapters of the *Handbook of Applied Ethnomusicology* edited by Pettan and Titon (2015); for examples, see the chapters by Murphy (2015) detailing the work of ethnomusicologists and public folklorists in government agencies in the United States and Boyu (2015) on the contribution of ethnomusicologists and other scholars to the discussion and implementation of cultural policy in diverse sectors in China. Several chapters in Howard (2012) refer to the contribution of East Asian scholars in shaping cultural policy, and in safeguarding and promoting "traditional music."

7. Since the institutionalization of Comparative Musicology in Berlin by Carl Stumpf and Erich Moritz von Hornbostel in the early twentieth century, ethnomusicologists have made, curated, and published ethnographic recordings, including extensive

written documentation. Sponsored and published by major institutions such as UNESCO, the Smithsonian Institution and the ethnological museums of Berlin, Paris, and Geneva, these recorded collections document music traditions from around the world, sustain scholarly findings, and introduce a wealth of musics to musicians and the general public.

8. The current Institute built on earlier initiatives since 1950. Other projects and institutions dedicated to repatriation and partially described in the above-mentioned references include: The Library of Congress Federal Cylinder Project; the Archives and Research Center for Ethnomusicology in New Delhi partly dedicated to the re-patriation of collections of musics from India held in archives outside the country for access to Indian scholars and institutions; the National Recording Project for Indigenous Performance in Australia; and the Center for Ethnomusicology at Columbia University repatriation project of the recordings made by Laura Boulton in 1946 of the Iñupiat to their community of origin in Barrow, Alaska.

9. Japan pioneered the recognition of culture bearers through its Living Human Treasures program launched in 1950, an initiative that was emulated elsewhere in East Asia and, in the United States through the National Endowment of the Arts National Heritage Fellowships launched in 1982 (Murphy 2015: 713). In 1993, UNESCO launched the Living Human Treasures program with the aim of "encour-aging Member States to grant official recognition to talented tradition bearers and practitioners, thus contributing to the transmission of their knowledge and skills to the younger generations" (https://ich.unesco.org/en/living-human-treasures).

10. The synthesis that follows on the contribution of members and officers of the ICTM to UNESCO's intangible cultural heritage programs is partially based on ICTM's 2015 report to UNESCO regarding its contribution to the implementation of the 2003 ICH Convention. We are also indebted to Naila Ceribašić, Anthony Seeger, Krister Malm, and Wim van Zanten for sharing their experiences as ICTM officers, experts, and consultants.

11. Several ethnomusicologists participated in the conference entitled "A Global Assessment of the 1989 *Recommendation on the Safeguarding of Traditional Culture and Folklore: Local Empowerment and International Cooperation*" jointly organized by the Smithsonian Institution and UNESCO held in Washington, DC, in 1999. This meeting was significant for establishing the importance of local-level control over the processes of safeguarding ICH (see Seitel 2001 for the proceedings), one of the key principles of UNESCO's 2003 Convention.

12. By 2017, UNESCO's 2003 Convention was ratified by 175 states parties: https://ich.unesco.org/en/news/the-2003-convention-reaches-175-state-parties-00255

13. We are indebted to Krister Malm, Don Niles, and Carlos Yoder for this information.

14. A United Nations document (2009) states that there are more than 370 million Indigenous people in at least ninety countries. Statistics are often lower than actual numbers for several reasons. Some Indigenous individuals or groups may choose not to identify or may not be counted according to specific governmental criteria. Definitions of Indigenous vary, although most agree that Indigenous references those with their own cultures and languages who were victims of colonialism and

imperialism, often enduring genocidal policies, deterritorialization, and extreme racism.

15. Wolfe (2006) defined settler colonialism as a particular type of colonialism where the colonial powers came to stay and thus had to try to eliminate the Indigenous populations who occupied the land they wanted.

16. Closely related and yet also distinctive is Applied Anthropology, which is discussed by Lassiter and Seeger in Volume I.

17. Several recent articles, however, have addressed this issue (see, e.g., Bendrups 2015, Treloyn & Emberly 2013).

1

A Sound Economy

Jeff Todd Titon

"We used to talk about good soil. Or about a good stand of trees. Or simply good land. Now we talk about property."—Philip Booth

The study of music as culture sometimes diverts attention from the economy of music and from the economic conditions upon which continuing musical exchanges rest.[1] Musical and cultural futures are profoundly dependent on and affected by disturbance and change to the economies of sonic communities and their regional and transnational bases. In this essay I examine the transformational implications of a sound economy. Throughout, I think of sound simultaneously as a physical phenomenon (sound vibrations), and as a metaphor meaning among other things healthy (as in a sound body), cohesive (as in a sound community), sensible (as in a sound reason), and linked (as in a sound connection). After summarizing sound as both a metaphor for, and a bodily means of, connection, and outlining some ecological characteristics of a sound community, formed interdependently through sound connections, I turn to the economics of a sound community. I consider the consequences of applying the neoclassical economic assumption of homo economicus[2] to musical exchanges within sound communities. I argue that UNESCO's cultural policy concerning traditional music—safeguarding it as an intangible cultural heritage (ICH) of particular, usually ethnic and regional, communities, and then encouraging those communities to regard it as property and market it as heritage for tourists—confuses cultural values with economic value and leads to unsustainable consequences. Instead, more effective strategies for resilience and sustainable futures are being enacted by applied ethnomusicologists in partnership with communities and intended to benefit their music cultures and goals directly.[3] When applied ethnomusicologists, collaborating with the leaders of tradition-bearing communities, revisit the older formulation, music in culture, we and our community-based partners may more easily be enlisted to extend social responsibility beyond cultural equity to economic justice.[4]

Jeff Todd Titon, *A Sound Economy* In: *Transforming Ethnomusicology.* Edited by: Beverley Diamond and Salwa El-Shawan Castelo-Branco, Oxford University Press (2021). © Oxford University Press. DOI: 10.1093/oso/9780197517550.003.0002

Applied ethnomusicologists engaging with contemporary musical communities confront the economic paradox that music is treated both as priceless cultural heritage and as a priced marketplace commodity. As cultural heritage that is beyond price, music instances an ecological rationality, interconnecting music-makers and the physical environment by means of sound energy. But as a priced marketplace commodity, music brings its makers into the economic rationality of costs and benefits, property and ownership, contracts and law. In this essay I discuss this paradox and concentrate on the differences between a sound economy exhibited through an ecological rationality that leads to fairness, versus an unsound one characterized by an economic rationality that leads to injustice. Because a sound economy is exhibited by a sound community and rests in sound experience, I also discuss these aspects of a sound ecology, or ecological rationality. Elsewhere I have been developing the experiential and communal aspects of a sound ecological rationality, as this remains an ongoing epistemological project to place sound, rather than text or object, at the center of being and knowing.[5]

This project is a thought-experiment with practical applications. In our new millennium, the goals of ecojustice, cultural equity, and individual well-being face the wicked problems of climate change and climate justice, ones that the instrumental rationality of science, technology, and engineering has been unable to solve. An economics that places self-interest above all else stymies collective political action: the Kyoto and Paris accords increasingly seem too little, too late. Ecomusicologists, environmental humanists, ecological economists, and environmental philosophers bring values and ethics into the sustainability discussion, with small but measurable positive effects on the environment. In the world of the arts, the heritage industry attempts to sustain endangered traditions. Yet scientific knowledge, cultural values, and sustainability strategies rest upon how humans regard ourselves (with others) as beings in the world, and upon how we know what we know. In other words, sustainability is at bottom an ontological and epistemological problem. A sound ecological rationality contrasts with our current instrumental, economic rationality and offers, I believe, an opportunity to reframe wicked problems such as achieving sustainability and well-being, and to devise solutions that will put humans and other beings on a path toward justice and fairness.

A sound ecology is based in sound's peculiar characteristics: vibration, resonance, and presence. In its function, sound announces presence: it communicates "Here I am." Traveling in longitudinal waves through air or some other medium, a sound connects two bodies, a sender and a receiver, that then vibrate at the same frequencies. Sound, as Thoreau wrote in *Walden*, is language without metaphor (Thoreau 1971 [1854]: 111). Two or more sounding bodies aware of each other constitute co-presence, the connection that is the basis for an interdependent community. Music, of course, is enveloped by the larger category, sound. What if one takes sound instead of texts or objects as the paradigmatic case for being in and knowing the world? Scientists experiment on objects; humanists typically interpret texts. My turn to a sound ecology asks what kinds of communities, economies, and ecologies one may expect if one takes sound rather than texts or objects[6] as the primary basis for experiencing and understanding the world and oneself within it (Titon 2015b, Titon 2020).[7]

The ideal type of sound community is a participatory, cooperative, diverse group whose exchanges of sound presence affirm identities and maintain cohesion. This sound community embraces a sound commons (Titon 2012). A commons is a resource that is not owned but shared, respected and managed by all those who make use of the resource and understand that everything and everyone is connected. Animals such as birds share a sound commons in which they communicate. Many sound communities enjoy a traditional music commons in which resources are shared and performances are not considered individual property.[8]

Sounding co-presence is a more general phenomenon of the communal world. It need not mean that both creatures emit sounds. The bee dance to tell hivemates the location of a honey source is well known; but that information is indicated more reliably by the dance-accompanying buzzing sounds they emit at low frequencies (Wenner 1964). A bird signals presence to its mate with its song. The mate must be able to recognize in the song the individual bird that is its mate. Birds are co-present to each other in song: they regulate their territorial boundaries by means of song. Sound helps birds keep order; it also keeps bird communities together. The so-called flight call keeps the flock together in flight. In human music, co-presence enables coordination so that people may sing and play together (Clayton, Sager &Will 2004). Whether it is a string quartet or a string band, making music together is enabled by co-presence, when two or more people are present to each other in sound (Schütz 1951: 76, 79). Learning to make music well with others means learning to hear not only one's own sound presence but also others' sounding presences. Beginning musicians have ears only for themselves.

A sounding co-presence among two or more actors leads to an interdependent community marked by and based in communication, that is, to a communication community. Of course, community may be based in other things as well as sound communication: a common interest or background, for example; or physical proximity, such as a neighborhood. Community is maintained through action, sound action among them. Ecological scientists as well as sociologists have outlined two ideal community types. Ecologists view communities either as tightly integrated, consisting of interdependent species; or as loosely grouped species that co-occur according to the individual responses of each species to variable environmental conditions (Vellend 2015). Ecologists may have let go of the "balance of nature" paradigm, the idea that nature moves toward a climax state of dynamic equilibrium; but they have not abandoned the foundational premise that organisms are interconnected with and interdependent on one another and their environments (Kricher 2009).

Classical sociology also viewed human communities as either tight-knit or loosely grouped. One need not resuscitate Tonnies's thorny Gemeinschaft/ Gesellschaft (community/society) distinction in order to observe that community remains a key, if controversial, subject, especially regarding virtual, internet-enabled social groups (Delhanty 2003: 167–185). When ethical and not merely empirical matters are at stake, it is useful to consider an ideal type of well-integrated community in which social exchanges are based in personal relationships, mutual benefits, and cooperation. Personal relationships, established and maintained through communicative acts including participatory music performance, take precedence over other kinds of relationships, such as legal or contractual ones. A sound community is connected through personal relationships. Within modern, developed societies, integrated communities (of varying degrees) may be found among families, neighborhoods, villages, and affinity groups. Indigenous societies that do not participate significantly in the developed, or developing, worlds also exhibit such communities; but these come under pressure insofar as their people modernize. On the other hand, the loosely grouped community is an entity, such as a city or corporation, that is bound together not by personal relationships, although personal networks do exist in such groups. Instead, members come together on account of coinciding self-interests. Exchanges are governed by legal and social contract. Instead of integration, individualism characterizes behavior in this ideal type of community; that is, individuals feel themselves in competition and place self-interest ahead of the good of the group. Communication, sound-based and otherwise, tends to be presentational more than participatory in such groups (Turino 2009). Individuals feel more alone in them. Sociologists note that modern, mass society is characterized by such groups. Of course, these community types represent more a spectrum than a dichotomy; persons in societies belong simultaneously to several social groups at different points on the community spectrum.

A sound, well-integrated, egalitarian and participatory community will display a sound economy. What may be learned about a sound economy from contemporary economic theory?[9] Mainstream (that is, neoclassical) Western economists assume that human beings behave rationally, in their individual economic self-interest, in order to maximize personal wealth. Such economic behavior is congruent with "economic rationality," the idea that resources (human, material, cultural, environmental) are economic assets best put to efficient, productive use (Edwards 2015: 162). Economic rationality functions most efficiently when legal and contractual arrangements take precedence over personal connections.

By starting with the individual and by asserting that it is human nature to maximize material wealth, as if this axiom were an empirical finding, neoclassical economists erect their science upon a presumption, not a universal fact. I prefer not to start an inquiry into a sound economy by assuming that humans are selfish, or by assuming that economic rationality is progressive. The first principle of a sound economy is that exchanges (market outcomes) are just, not that they are efficient or useful. As Daniel Finn points out, "Mainstream economics has long attempted to eliminate moral judgments from economic science out of a concern for objectivity. . . . All perspectives on economic systems, from left [progressive] to right [neoliberal] address certain basic common issues; and each, out of necessity, resorts to moral argument at least implicitly. . . . The overall question that is inevitably asked, at least implicitly, in any moral defense or critique of markets is: 'Under what conditions are the outcomes of markets just?'" (Finn 2003: 160, 137, 153).[10]

Suppose one looks more closely at neoclassical economics by considering how it is taught. A college textbook that has gone through seven editions from 1986 through 2006 claims that economics "is the study of how individuals, experiencing virtually limitless wants, choose to allocate scarce resources to best satisfy their wants" (Ekelund & Tollison 2000: 4). The authors state that "We are never satisfied with what we have," implying that human beings are greedy by nature (Ekelund & Tollison 2000: 4). The authors go on to explain the axiom that has guided mainstream economic thought since the Enlightenment; namely, that economics comes down to rational choices made by individuals. "Economists focus on a particular view of human behavior—that of *homo economicus*" (Ekelund & Tollison 2000: 9). Homo economicus is said to be guided by rational self-interest when deciding how to allocate limited resources to satisfy wants (Figure 1.1). Sellers always attempt to maximize profit, while buyers try to obtain goods at minimal cost. Indeed, modern mainstream economic theory postulates that individuals perform a cost-versus-benefit analysis on every economic decision they make, whether in purchasing a home, selling a musical instrument, buying groceries, "networking" for career opportunities, perhaps even in choosing a life partner. Today's economists call homo economicus rational choice theory. Wherever one begins to study economics at the university level, one is taught this neoclassical paradigm: that rational choice and cost benefit analysis are the bases of individual economic decision-making.

Homo economicus may be traced to the Enlightenment, and found in the writings of Adam Smith, who famously claimed that in a market economy, human beings have a "natural propensity" to "truck, barter, and exchange," and that "it is not from the benevolence of the butcher, the brewer, or the baker that

Figure 1.1 Homo economicus. Courtesy Wikimedia Commons.

we expect our dinner, but with regard to their self-interest" (Smith 1776, Bk. I, chaps. 2 and 3). John Stuart Mill wrote that economics was that subject concerned with man "solely as a being who desires to possess wealth, and who is capable of judging the comparative efficacy of means for obtaining that end" (Mill 1844 IV:321). The growth of trade; the increasing need for money, banking, and credit; the accumulation of capital and the growth of business organizations— these, fueled by the growing conviction that material wealth was a sign of divine favor, combined in what Max Weber called the "spirit of capitalism," responsible for the development of the Western economy from the Reformation to today's consumption-oriented society (Figure 1.2; Weber 1930). Weber's contemporary Werner Sombart claimed that this new spirit "was dominated by the principle of pursuit of gain or acquisition, which formed the central core of economic rationalism"[11] (Baldwin 1959: 6).

Economics emerged as a separate entity when moral philosophers began to wonder how the public good could possibly be served by a nation of self-interested individuals. Adam Smith argued that homo economicus does not intend to promote the public interest, but that he is "led by an invisible hand" to do so—in Smith's words, "to promote an end which was no part of his intention. By

Figure 1.2 Cartesian consumers and rational choice. Shopping mall interior, Montevideo. Courtesy Wikimedia Commons.

pursuing his own interest he frequently promotes that of the society more effectually than when he really intends to promote it. I have never known much good done by those who affected to trade for the public good" (Smith 1776 Bk. IV, chap. 2, sec. 9). Smith asserted that in a market economy individual actions taken on the basis of self-interest harmonized for the greater good.

Needless to say, homo economicus has had, over the years, its share of critics. Feminist economists claim that economic "man" is characteristic of male gender behavior, ruthless and competitive. Self-interest, they claim, is just another word for acquisitiveness, and there is more to the public good, or public wealth, than the accumulation of material capital in a society. Another line of critique points out that individual economic behavior is not always the result of rational, cost-benefit analyses; otherwise, why do most contemporary advertisers target consumer desire, not rational choice (Figure 1.2)? The field of behavioral economics arose to consider psychological and other factors in individual economic decision-making (Diamond & Vartiainen 2007). While some regard it as an alternative to rational choice theory, behavioral economists nonetheless take for granted that economic actions are driven by self-interest. Third, while individuals often do make rational choices to maximize personal benefit and minimize cost, self-interest is also served by direct aim at public benefit, as occurs when people choose to recycle waste, bicycle to work, or volunteer time for charities or civic organizations. Self-sacrifice for the greater good of the family or community or a cause one believes in may not maximize material wealth. Finally, ecological economists point out that neoclassical economics neglects environmental constraints and impacts on economic activity (Daly & Farley 2010).

It is not a universal truth that human beings desire to grow wealthy. The economist Jeffrey Sachs claimed to know how to relieve poverty in Africa: development agencies should give farmers fertilizer and machinery so they could grow a surplus, and then they would reinvest money thus obtained to enlarge their farms. In that way African farmers would grow their economies. Do the same for all industries and poverty would subside (Sachs 2005). Sachs's well-funded Millennium Villages Project tried this idea out, but it largely failed. Generalizing broadly, when an African farmer grows a surplus, instead of reinvesting the money he gives it to his cousin who needs it (Munk 2013). Compared with modern, Western societies, the values in traditional, African ones were and to some degree remain communal, not individualistic. I do not mean to overlook the complexities of social behavior, motive, and values in all communities and societies. Yet precisely because of those complexities homo economicus plainly is cultural, not natural. Some persons understand that health, balance, and well-being are what they truly want; and that beyond basic food, clothing, and shelter these derive from a combination of satisfying work, a loving community, physical and mental health, and rewarding social networks, among other things.

A sound economy starts from the premise of the soundly connected community rather than the atomized individual. Instead of presuming a society of individuals always behaving selfishly, as Adam Smith famously did, assume that individuals usually behave according to the cultural principles of their social groups. Where the culture directs people to behave as selfish individuals, they will behave in that fashion; but when the culture directs otherwise, they will behave otherwise. Rational behavior in one society only seems irrational in another. It is rational for an African farmer to benefit a cousin first, farms second. This behavior is not selfish, yet it is self-rewarding insofar as personal relations are strengthened and the entire community, including the individual, benefits. Any settled community will exhibit both participatory and presentational group behavior, of course, while individuals will find themselves in both participatory and presentational situations. Nonetheless, the sound and intersubjective connection among co-present beings that underlies participatory behavior establishes the horizontal personal relationships that characterize egalitarian exchanges, whereas the unsound, subject-object connection that underlies presentational behavior establishes the impersonal, contractual, and asymmetrical power relationships that characterize unjust ones.

What if, instead of assuming that by nature homo economicus employs economic rationality to manage the allocation of scarce resources, one considers the types of social groups in which economic exchanges take place, and tries to understand how and why these exchanges are made? Participatory groups communities are integrated because of personal relationships. Presentational communities are individuated and governed by contracts and law. Homo economicus is constrained by the former and facilitated by the latter. In other words, a minimally regulated market economic system based in competition and economic rationality functions within societies that value individualism and free choice, unencumbered by other considerations such as obtain in close-knit, integrated communities. Free or minimally regulated market economic systems function most efficiently when goods are regarded as commodities, bought and sold in the marketplace, wherein each music has its price, or economic value; and where trade is protected by a rule of law, not custom or tradition. In a sound economy, on the contrary, exchanges will be based in the principle of commonwealth. In its original usage, "commonwealth" is a translation of the Latin *res publicae*, or public things. The *Oxford English Dictionary* dates its first use to ca. 1470, when it meant the public welfare or common good. In this formulation, public good, or res publicae, will increase not in proportion to the rise in the GDP but in proportion to the rise in public well-being, or happiness, which resists quantification.

A sound economy rests in interdependence, both embodied and represented in sound vibration, presence, co-presence, communication, and community. In contrast with homo economicus, therefore, we may posit a different model, *homo reciprocans*, in which cooperation or reciprocal behavior among community members is paramount. Here the common good is not the sum of private goods, but rather the emergent good of the social group and its environment as a whole, which requires balancing individual wants with group goods and at times requires that individuals refrain from maximizing personal wealth in order that the common wealth may increase (Figure 1.3). Homo reciprocans is the characteristic economic expression of participatory social groups, while homo economicus aligns better with presentational groups. Homo reciprocans economic activity is characteristic of gift economies such as music-making groups in which a commons of musical resources is shared; but it also applies to commodity exchanges when, for example, the participatory group is a cooperative unit, as in a food co-op.

Within Western history, the idea of a cooperative economic commonwealth surfaces from time to time, usually in the form of a social group that bands together for common economic ends. A cooperative economic commonwealth is an expression of a sound community, modeled by social democracy (Titon 2001: 10). One of the early formations of a cooperative economic commonwealth was an English group known as the Rochdale Pioneers, who in 1844 envisioned

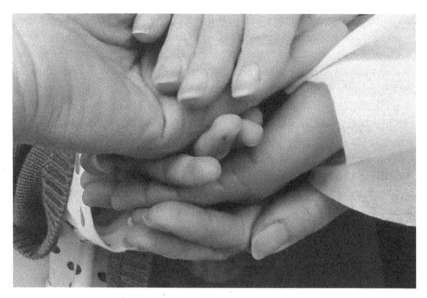

Figure 1.3 Homo reciprocans. Courtesy Wikimedia Commons.

a consumer co-op, housing co-ops and a manufacturing co-op. In the nine-teenth and early twentieth centuries, progressive political thinkers in Europe, the UK, and the United States called for worker and buying co-ops; several were established. Labor unions were an outgrowth of this movement. The Common Market and European Union embody many cooperative economic principles. In many parts of Europe and North America today are community-supported agricultural units (CSAs), and food and consumer co-ops, usually associated with locally sourced, organic food and other products. In some, members share the work involved in production, transportation, and distribution. Market price does not result from freedom among buyers and sellers to bargain; rather it is a fixed, "just price" that reflects the actual cost of the materials, including envi-ronmental costs, as well as a reasonable wage to maintain the worker.[12] Fueled by the internet, the sharing economy, in which people participate in collabora-tive consumption, is increasingly popular among millennials (Hamari, Sjöklint & Ukkonen 2015). In a recent essay on "Participatory Economics and the Commons," the economist Robin Hahnel sums up the ideas of a cooperative ec-onomic commonwealth: "Whatever is needed to support a people's way of life should be the common property of all, managed by all, for the benefit of all." The author further defines economic justice as "compensation commensurate with sacrifice and need, to be achieved while fostering human solidarity, protecting the environment, and ensuring efficiency" (Hahnel 2015: 35, 37). Hahnel calls this "participatory economics." Based in a sound, cooperative connection among co-present beings, participatory economics is an expression of a sound economy.

A sound economy is a just economy. Today, economic justice for musical communities plays out in the arena of cultural policy. I turn now to economic justice issues in the sustainability of traditional cultural expression and knowledge, what UNESCO terms intangible cultural heritage (ICH), within a modernizing and developing world. ICH "includes traditions or living expressions inherited from our ancestors and passed on to our descendants, such as oral traditions, performing arts, social practices, rituals, festive events, knowledge and practices concerning nature and the universe or [sic] the knowledge and skills to produce traditional crafts" (UNESCO 2016). In many community cultural contexts, exchanges of ICH remain largely participatory while personal relations still govern these social and economic exchanges, even when the communities that observe them are part of greater social structures. Traditional medicinal practices in the rural Americas and Asia; the traditional foodways, rituals, and ceremonies of immigrant and ethnic groups; and musical and craft traditions that can be traced to earlier centuries are examples of ICH. Modernization can help: an herbalist on the Cumberland Plateau in Kentucky and Tennessee keeps track of her clients and appointments on her cell phone.

Several reasons are advanced for conserving traditional, folk, and Indigenous cultures. One is fairness: cultural equity, an application to human societies of the Enlightenment natural rights doctrine for individuals. Just as all human beings have the right to life, so all human societies have the right to just treatment, which includes the right to a continued existence that maintains cultural integrity (Lomax 1972). Another reason is pragmatic: diversity, for the sake of maintaining a stock of traditional knowledges, practices, and adaptations to the changing conditions of life on planet Earth (UNESCO 2001). For example, adaptations to climate change may be observed among populations that have inhabited the same areas of the globe for millennia. A third reason is aesthetic: the cultural productions of diverse societies—their music, their visual arts, their crafts—make unique contributions to the history and heritage of human creativity. A fourth reason, which I will shortly examine in detail, is economic: traditional cultural knowledge and expression may be viewed as resource assets that, made into commercial products, can generate income for its practitioners that will enable them to maintain their practices.

Culture workers, Indigenous and non-native, along with agencies and policymakers, have devised various conservation and protection strategies. One is resistance. For example, in *Penobscot Nation vs. Mills*, Penobscot Native Americans in the state of Maine utilized the judicial system to maintain their traditional rights to waterways on the grounds that US law recognizes them as a sovereign nation (Lewey 2016). A second strategy adds value to traditional knowledge and expression by terming it cultural heritage. With this added value, practitioners and the public at large may be less likely to abandon or discard it in the face of modernization and change. A third strategy considers ICH to be intellectual property, and therefore eligible for protection under copyright law, a strategy to be discussed shortly. A fourth conservation strategy is documentation and preservation in archives. A fifth strategy encourages ICH's ongoing expression through public exhibition.

Exhibitions have become a favorite means of celebrating and preserving traditional cultural expressions. UNESCO Conventions (in effect treaties) have proclaimed as ICH masterpieces hundreds of rare and endangered language, music, dance, and theatrical traditions throughout the world, while national and regional governments have singled out hundreds more (UNESCO 2015). Significantly, the majority of UNESCO's ICH inscriptions according to the 2003 Convention are in music. Members of the cultures that carry them find employment in demonstrating their ICH by singing, dancing, storytelling, craft-making, and so forth, offering the general public a representation of authenticity. China, for example, claims to have spent $10.5 billion on cultural undertakings in 2015, of which more than $300 million went to heritage tourism (ChinaCulture 2016). $300 million is more than the combined total budgets of the US National Endowments for the Humanities and for the Arts. Although the United States has not signed onto the UNESCO ICH Convention, the United States has long supported ICH exhibitions. Some are funded by the US government, as, for example, the National and the Smithsonian Folk Festivals. Some are supported by state government—nearly every state in the United States has at least one official state folklorist, whose job is to locate, document, present and celebrate folk arts. Heritage tourism is the favored vehicle. The Folk and Traditional Arts Division of the National Endowment for the Arts is devoted entirely to promoting ICH. Private funding for exhibitions in the form of donations, tax breaks, alliances with chambers of commerce, business interests, and the like adds to ICH support in the United States. Americans for the Arts, a Washington, DC-based nonprofit NGO devoted to advancing the arts in the United States, stimates that all the arts (including ICH, a small part of the whole) generate $135.2 billion of economic activity in the United States annually (Americans for the Arts 2013). Based on figures for 2015, the National Endowment for the Arts calculated that the arts added $764 billion to the American economy, or 4.2% of the US Gross Domestic Product (Cascone 2018). Estimating the economic contribution of the arts clearly is not an exact science.

When it was developed in the United States in the 1970s, federal- and state-sponsored ICH preservationists called what they were doing cultural conservation. In the new millennium, the operative term is "cultural sustainability," a vanilla concept that few public folklorists or applied ethnomusicologists could disagree with. Yet regarding ICH as both a cultural and an economic asset places it into the realm of economic rationality. Does putting it to use in this way safeguard ICH and the social groups that carry it? Might it contribute to sustainable development? UNESCO believes that it will (UNESCO 2013). Or does ICH tourism, by means of commodifying traditions, distort and undermine them?[13] Under a regime of neoliberal economic rationality, exemplified in sustainable development, can intangible heritage conservation be characteristic of a sound economy?

David Throsby is today's foremost theorist advocating for the economic benefits of ICH (Throsby 2010). He argues that the arts are best viewed not as an alternative to or a respite from a base and commercial world of money-making but, rather, as an engine of economic competition and growth. The arts have significant economic consequences, local and global. Throsby devotes an entire chapter to cultural heritage as an economic engine. His argument offers a seductive line of reasoning because it makes the arts (and their advocates) more powerful players in public policy debates. However, his argument that the arts are economically valuable cultural assets rests on a problematic elision of value and values.

When Throsby writes that cultural heritage has economic value he refers to its commodity exchange-value. As long as heritage requires funding, as long as cultural tourists buy it for a price, as long as the money supports the heritage industry, heritage has an economic value.[14] But Throsby also claims that music and the arts have a use-value that he calls cultural value. He lists several kinds of cultural value: aesthetic, spiritual, social, historical, symbolic, and authenticity value, among others. Cultural value is realized by a social group; it consists of collective benefits that, he claims, cannot be factored out solely to individuals. Cultural value is present in those aspects of a group's lifeways that members of the group have strong feelings about, either positive or negative. That is, they have aesthetic feelings, spiritual feelings, feelings concerning social solidarity or solitude, and so forth. Cultural values are impossible to quantify. Cultural value exists outside of, or in addition to, the realm of commodity exchange. Cultural value, according to Throsby, is "beyond price" (Throsby & Hutter 2008).

Although art's economic value is priced at its commodity exchange-value, cultural values are not priced; they are principles and standards that guide individual and group behavior. In short, cultural value is invaluable. Yet in advocating for the economic use of cultural heritage Throsby paradoxically turns cultural values, which a community shares in a cultural commons, into assets of measurable financial worth that can enter a calculus for a cultural policy operating within the framework of a neoliberal economic rationality based in property rights, market competition, efficiency, and growth. Then, instead of operating as a critique of the social structure, or as providing an alternative social structure as a cultural commons, Throsby enlists heritage to serve a very different end, namely economic growth. In the name of sustainability, heritage is co-opted into the very same economic rationality that has made neoliberal culture unsustainable in the first place. The root problem, I believe, lies in exhibiting cultural values rather than embodying them. ICH marketing warps the dynamic and organic textures of cultural ecosystems, distorting what they need in order to thrive and sustain themselves.

Insistence that art is a cultural asset objectifies and propertizes it; that is, it turns commons into property. Whether private property or public, it remains property, something that can be owned. Roman law, from which much Euro-American law is derived, had a named category for publicly owned property: res publicae—public things, or property that the state owns on behalf of the people. In the United States, the idea that intangible cultural heritage could be property owned by individuals, or owned by the state, seems absurd. Quite the contrary in China, where heritage is property owned and regulated by the state on behalf of the people. But what if heritage were regarded as the property not of the state but as a possession of the community that carries it? What good might it do to claim that communities own their heritage collectively, as property, by virtue of something that we might call cultural rights? Would it be possible to safeguard and thereby conserve it under international copyright law?

This very argument has been advanced in the 2007 UN Declaration on the Rights of Indigenous Peoples in order to help protect the heritage of Indigenous communities from exploitation (United Nations 2007). The UN Declaration is a proclamation, however, not an instrument with the force of law. It would not have prevented instances in which European and American performers have profited enormously from copying Indigenous music. From Africa alone, examples include Paul Simon's album *Graceland*, Herbie Hancock's "Watermelon Man" (from his *Headhunters* album), and the music of the French duo Deep Forest. Simon later did help the black South African musicians whom he drew upon, but neither Hancock nor Deep Forest shared their wealth with the African pygmies whose music they copied. Indeed, when ethnomusicologist Steven Feld asked Hancock if he felt any obligation to compensate the pygmies, he replied that this kind of borrowing was normal in African and Afro-American culture: "It's a brothers thing," he rationalized, as his bank account swelled while the pygmies way of life deteriorated (Feld 2000: 257).

Such musical exploitation pales in comparison to the profits pharmaceutical corporations derived from exploiting Indigenous medical knowledge, and to the profits from textiles imprinted with native art. For example, an Australian Aboriginal artist named Johnny Bulun Bulun, along with the head of his tribal clan, sued an Australian textile company for putting a design from one of his paintings on fabric. The textile company claimed these images were folkloric, in the public domain, and therefore everyone's property. The textile company prevailed in the Australian courts (Brown 2004). But if the artist's community had been able to maintain a collective copyright to the traditional design, would the artist have been protected?

International copyright law at present results from the negotiations among sovereign nation-states; an overarching international copyright law currently does not exist. When and if it did, it would appear in the form of a United Nations Convention, to which various sovereign nations would (or would not) agree. Today, proposals for international copyright law are in the domain of the UN's World International Copyright Organization (WIPO). Its international anti-piracy efforts are directed chiefly at protecting individuals and corporations (legally, considered as individuals) in one nation against illegal copying and marketing in other nations. Protecting the rights of Indigenous cultures to their creations would require extending the copyright concept from individuals to collectivities, perhaps considering them as corporate bodies. When UNESCO began its efforts to safeguard masterpieces of intangible cultural heritage, they tasked WIPO with writing copyright law that would offer ICH legal protection. As Regina Bendix explains, WIPO seeks "to delineate a 'legal life' for cultural knowledge and traditional expressions, firming up implicit values and owner-ship" (Bendix 2013: 23). WIPO therefore regards cultural heritage as community property assets needing protection: "Intellectual property . . . can be developed, owned, managed and commercialized to generate an economic return . . . as ec-onomic assets, the value of which can be optimized by proactive policies and strategies" (WIPO 2006: 2). They state that "WIPO [is undertaking] negotiations with the objective of reaching agreement on a text of an international legal in-strument (or instruments) which will ensure the effective protection" of ICH (WIPO 2016: 1).

WIPO's cultural asset-think envisions an economic marketplace with com-modity exchanges of intellectual property. "The IP [intellectual property] system provides a way for these intangible assets to be owned, disseminated and traded, thus enabling creators or owners of intellectual property rights to reap some ben-efit from their own work or from their investment in a creation" (WIPO 2011: 3). This protection is justified not only by asserting proprietary rights, but also by proposing that copyright stimulates creativity and invention. "By providing a stable environment for marketing products protected by intellectual property [law, WIPO] also oils the wheels of international trade," the agency maintains (WIPO 2004: 22). Finally, WIPO claims that "Indigenous and local communi-ties seek appropriate and practical ways of preserving, promoting and protecting their cultural and intellectual heritage as a means of sustaining their cultural in-tegrity and promoting their own sustainable economic development consistent with their collective values" (WIPO 2011: 20). Here, WIPO couples cultural heritage to sustainable economic development, with the caveat that this be consistent with the Indigenous peoples' collective values. But what if those values are not oriented toward economic development? The Indigenous culture that refuses to protect heritage by copyright risks exploitation in the international marketplace. If their cultural values are not commodity-oriented, if traditionally they view heritage as social exchanges that adjust and maintain personal relationships, copyrighting culture would pressure them to think of culture as an economic asset instead. For WIPO, the IMF, and others whose goal is to lift Indigenous societies out of material poverty through sustainable economic development, this change in Indigenous worldview could be a positive good. But if sound economics is a viable alternative to cultural asset-think, it would be a disaster. As I write this (2017), WIPO has not issued a final recommendation for a legal instrument that would protect intangible cultural heritage worldwide. It has, however, published a booklet aimed at traditional and Indigenous communities, which aims to "encourage and empower Indigenous peoples and local communities to use intellectual property strategically, in line with your specific business, cultural and/or developmental needs," taking into account the ways property laws differ according to region and nation (WIPO 2017).

Andrew Weintraub argues persuasively that intellectual property rights were designed to protect individuals, and that therefore they are a poor instrument for protecting community rights. He writes that "intellectual property rights laws were created for Western music made for (potential) profit, with specific characteristics (namely, an original work by an author that is fixed in a tangible form of expression). These conditions are antithetical to the collective nature of traditional music" (Weintraub 2009: 7). That is, traditional music often (though not always) does not have a known individual author. Complicating matters further, in some Indigenous societies the author may be a known, but other-than-human, individual: a plant or animal. In short, intellectual property rights law was crafted to protect something of a very different nature than intangible cultural heritage. To assert that ICH is the possession of a community is to distort its meaning as some social groups understand it, and in so doing to put it at risk of becoming something else, namely property in the commercial international marketplace, when it is not conceived as property at all.

How effective has heritage been as a means of conserving traditional culture? The results are at best mixed. To mark a tradition as ICH, UNESCO requires that a nation must first nominate it and then agree to document and safeguard it. Nominations are reviewed by an international panel, including folklorists, anthropologists, and ethnomusicologists. By now, hundreds of examples of ICH have been so marked, often with cultural tourism resulting.

Sometimes these efforts result in a revitalization of traditions, even when cultural tourism fails (Hawes 1992: 339–341). But heritage has sometimes fallen victim to unintended negative consequences. For example, Western music historians and sinologists portrayed the Chinese *guqin* as the meditative instrument of ancient scholars (van Gulik 1969). Confucius was said to have been a renowned guqin player and its ancient repertoire, written on scrolls in Chinese characters, is among the oldest extant musical notation. Ancient Chinese paintings depict the tiny figures of the scholar, followed by his servant carrying his guqin, as they walk on narrow mountain paths. The rarefied guqin tradition supposedly fell very gradually into decay, enjoyed a small revival among the cognoscenti in the nineteenth and early twentieth centuries, and then almost disappeared during the Cultural Revolution. In marking it as an ICH masterpiece, UNESCO hoped that guqin would be revitalized. However, the music historians overlooked that alongside this meditative scholarly style there existed a loud, aggressive, vernacular guqin style, oriented to popular performance, military rather than meditative in expression. When guqin was marked as ICH, this vernacular style was in much better condition than the nearly moribund meditative one. The wrong music became UNESCO's unintended major beneficiary (Yung 2009).

Other troubling consequences have arisen from the politics of heritage: interference from promoters, bickering among artists, and distortions of historical fact in the interpretive presentations (Noyes 2014: 16–17). Elder artists whose skills have deteriorated may, for political reasons, be enlisted to perform, with unfortunate results for the tradition and psychological harm to the artists because their failing bodies can no longer perform up to expectations (Hanson 2014). Moreover, traditional cultural expression does not obey national boundaries. The same musical tradition occurs among related populations in certain neighboring nations, as in the Andes, for example, or in China and Mongolia. In such cases, sovereign nations have presented rival claims to UNESCO. Cultural politics determines the outcome, with the loser much disadvantaged. Internal politics is involved when a nation decides among which traditions to nominate, while UNESCO politics mixes into the final decisions. Another unfortunate consequence is that most economic benefit has gone to the documentarians, promoters, and local businesses that support the tourist economy, rather than into the communities and the artists that carry the heritage itself. A further problem is that marking a tradition for ICH tends to freeze it in its reconstituted form, working against the cultural dynamics of change that keep traditions alive in the first place.

Negative consequences such as these have made some public folklorists and applied ethnomusicologists, at least in Europe and the United States, think that rather than marking ICH as a cultural asset and exhibiting it for economic development, forging partnerships with traditional musical communities interested in developing resilience is a better means toward sustaining the integrity of their expressive cultures. Although this is not a new strategy—some applied anthropologists, ethnomusicologists, and public folklorists have for decades collaborated with and advocated for these communities—today many more endorse participatory action research, community self-documentation projects, and efforts to improve the cultural soil, as it were, rather than to target particular genres and traditions. We believe these interventions, when socially responsible and done for the benefit of the communities, will prove more sustaining than heritage conservation. Old Regular Baptists, for example, have been able to conserve the oldest, English-language sacred music in continuous oral tradition in the United States in this way (Titon 1999). They do not wish to become the objects of cultural tourism, however, nor to propertize and monetize heritage.[15] Robert Baron reviews many public folklore interventions of this type, pointing out that the European critical heritage studies movement has overlooked US attempts at strategic alternatives (Baron 2016). Heritage (if we must continue to use the term) in sum should be considered a commons, shared but not owned, and not as an engine of a tourist economy. Heritage is best regarded as held as a trust for present and future generations. It is best managed by means of collaborative efforts among stakeholders.

Sound economies are built from the bottom up, on the model of the shared commonwealth, the commons, and cooperative ventures. These center not upon individual self-interest and economic rationalism, but rather upon a balance in the personal relations among individuals in the social group, on the one hand, and the economic interests of the group as a whole, on the other. This expansion to a larger, more inclusive frame of reference—that is, from the individual to the group—is typical of ecological science, wherein individuals are considered within the larger group of populations or species, populations or species are framed within the larger grouping of communities, and a community is considered together with its abiotic environment to make up an ecosystem. Two movements within economics that manifest an expansion of scope and frame are worth considering briefly in the context of a sound ecology: environmental economics and ecological economics. The field of environmental economics arose in the late twentieth century to solve developmental problems in Third World countries. Modernization depended in part on convincing Indigenous populations to think of the environment as a resource for economic growth, as Westerners have thought about the environment for many centuries. But environmental economics, conceived as a branch of developmental economics, aligns with the UNESCO paradigm of sustainable development. In so doing it would, in theory at least, support heritage as an engine of economic growth and modernization. The end result, as for example in China, would be marginalization of heritage as a relic of the past, something for the contemporary tourist gaze.

Ecological economists (Figure 1.4) accept many of the claims concerning market efficiency made by neoclassical economics, but they reject the idea of unlimited economic growth, pointing out that in a world of finite resources, even technology cannot continue to grow the economy indefinitely (Costanza et al. 2015). Once this is recognized, sustainable development may take place, but with the understanding that development means change not growth. Ecological economists call for redistribution of wealth so that everyone has at the least an income floor above the poverty level, access to adequate health care, and so on. Yet ecological economists do not as a rule challenge the fundamental assumptions of economic rationality and individual self-interest. For them, economic justice is redistributive, not reciprocal; and this requires a highly centralized government to tax and redistribute, as well as the consent of the governed. A sound economy, on the contrary, is built locally, from the bottom up.

No economic exchange is made in isolation. It cannot occur outside of a group, even if it is only a group of two. A sound connection by means of co-presence asks what is in the economic interest of the community as well as the individuals within it. Cooperative communities offer a better chance for individuals, social

Image credit: University of Vermont Gund Institute for Ecological Economics.
Used with permission.

Figure 1.4 Ecological economics. Courtesy of the Gund Institute for Environment, University of Vermont.

groups, and our planet. Although a sound connection (in the sonic sense) does not necessarily lead to well-being—sounds have been used by states and other powerful entities to control crowds and torture prisoners (e.g., Ross 2016)—the fact is that sound reminds us that we are connected: our personal stake is simultaneously everyone else's. Our sound ontologies and epistemologies are relational; our commonwealth is a universal kinship. Recognizing that interdependence is primary, a sound ecology envelops a sound community that will enact a sound—and just—economy.

Notes

1. The present essay, written in 2017, originated in my 2015 plenary address to the joint ICTM-SEM Forum in Limerick, Ireland. I elaborated these ideas in my third Basler Lecture, "An Economy of Sound," at East Tennessee State University on April 12, 2016. In both the plenary and the Lecture I critiqued the unsound economic rationality that regards the cultural heritage of traditional music as an economic asset. I am grateful to Beverley Diamond and Salwa El-Shawan Castelo-Branco for inviting me to present at the Forum, and to Ted Olson, Keith Green, and Lee Bidgood, my hosts at ETSU. My epigraph is from Booth (1996: 2).
2. = economic man (Latin). See discussion later in this section.
3. Applied ethnomusicology "is best regarded as a music-centered intervention in a particular community, whose purpose is to benefit that community. . . . [It is] guided by ethical principles of social responsibility, human rights, and cultural and musical equity" (Titon 2015a: 4). See also Seeger in Volume I of this compendium for comparison with applied anthropology; and Pettan, also in Volume I, for a discussion of applied ethnomusicology in the International Council for Traditional Music (ICTM).
4. In the Justinian sense of the term, justice renders every person and group what they are due (i.e., what they deserve). Distributive justice considers the way goods and benefits in a society are distributed. As employed by applied ethnomusicologists and public folklorists, justice (often termed social justice) is guided by principles of fairness and informed by Rawls's "difference principle": namely, that social, cultural, environmental, and economic inequalities should be arranged for the greater benefit of the lesser advantaged. In this essay I am considering justice chiefly in relation to humans, but elsewhere I have considered ecojustice (the application of justice within a broader ecological context including the interrelations among animals, plants, landforms, forces of nature, etc.) in more detail (Titon 2019). See also Hamill, this volume, for a study of ecojustice among the Spokane.
5. An initial presentation of the project as a whole may be found in Titon (2015c). The project was the basis for my four Basler Chair Lectures in the spring of 2016 at East Tennessee State University, on Sound Experience, Sound Community, Sound Economy, and Sound Ecology respectively. Its eco-philosophical roots are forthcoming in the *Oxford Handbook of Ecomusicology*, edited by Sabine Feisst. Its latest iteration may be found in Titon 2020.

6. The separation of the thinking and knowing subject from the external object is often termed Cartesian dualism.

7. See Wong, Volume I, for a discussion of sonic experience as witnessing.

8. This has long been thought to characterize traditional folklore: songs and ballads, folktales, customs, Indigenous knowledge, all passed down from one generation to the next, authors long forgotten, and presently a community possession and resource. For a modern application of this idea to Irish traditional music, see McCann (2001). See also Titon 2016.

9. I am not concerned here with the technical aspects of economic theory, and their application to supply, demand, the market economy, wages, investments, GDP, and so on. Rather, the axioms underlying neoclassical economic analysis—what it takes for granted about economic behavior—are my focus.

10. Economics was a branch of moral philosophy before it became a separate science. Adam Smith was considered a philosopher in his own day, not an economist; his first book was *The Theory of Moral Sentiments* (1759). Five centuries earlier, Thomas Aquinas wrote about economics as moral philosophy, particularly in his consideration of "just price," that it was immoral to take a profit without having added value to a good.

11. The descriptor "economic rationalism" was embedded in the critique of economic rationality as long as 100 years ago.

12. "Just price" revives a medieval European concept; for more on just price see Baldwin (1959).

13. Almost as soon as UNESCO's Conventions were put into effect, a lively debate ensued over the politics of choosing ICH masterpieces, whether the ICH designations were accomplishing UNESCO's intentions, and over UNESCO's intentions themselves. See, for example, McCann (2003), Titon (2009), Weintraub & Yung (2009).

14. In the United States, although most folk festivals charge no admission, ICH practitioners sell their products there.

15. For example, although they have been a subject of attention from journalists and scholars, they have refused to cooperate with documentary filmmakers and with for-profit organizations interested in bringing their music to the attention of the wider world. In this they are similar to Amish and to some Indigenous communities. As Elwood Cornett, Moderator (elected leader) of the Indian Bottom Association of Old Regular Baptists told me, "I would not be willing, and I am not willing, for it to be commercialized in any kind of way. . . . Over the years, many years, a lot of people have flown in and looked at us and flown out and wrote, and it's been, I hope, a bigger embarrassment to them than it was to us" (Cornett 1990).

2

Music for Global Human Development

Michael Frishkopf

"Big Problems" and the Rending of the Social Fabric

Poverty, extreme inequality. The top 1 percent own 50 percent of global assets; the bottom 50 percent own less than 1 percent; nearly half the world's population lives on less than $2 per day (Shorrocks, Davies & Lluberas 2015: 99; "Global Issues" 2016). *Disease, substandard health care.* 2.5 billion people lack access to proper sanitation (WHO 2016). The deadly Ebola virus killed over 4,800 people in Liberia (Data Team 2016), where there is only one physician per 100,000 people, compared to 245 in the United States ("Physician Density" 2016). *War, violence, forced migration, refugees.* The Liberian civil war caused over 800,000 to evacuate the country (UNHCR 2006); over 800,000 were killed in Rwanda in just 100 days (Dallaire & Beardsley 2005); around 11 million Syrians have fled their homes since March 2011, and 13.5 million require humanitarian assistance within the country ("Syrian Refugees" 2016). *Slavery.* There are an estimated 20 million slaves in the world today, more than a quarter of them children ("Slavery Today" 2016). *Illiteracy, gender inequality.* Nearly 17 percent of the world's adult population is illiterate, two-thirds of them women ("UNESCO Statistics" 2016). *Lack of freedom.* Some 36 percent of the world lives under dictatorships; another 24 percent is only partly free ("Freedom House" 2016). *Hunger.* Worldwide, one in nine people is chronically undernourished. "Nearly half of all child deaths under age five are due to malnutrition, which claims the lives of about 3.1 million children per year" ("IFPRI" 2016). *Sexism.* A senior UN official reports Britain to be among the most sexist countries in the world (Sanghani 2014). *Racism.* "Black Americans are 2.5 times as likely as white Americans to be shot and killed by police officers" (Lowery 2011). *Xenophobia.* In a 2014 poll, 66 percent of French think there are too many foreigners in France (France 24 2016). *Division. Apathy. Hopelessness. Despair.*

The modern world is afflicted with "big problems"—massive violations of human rights, flagrant injustice, prejudice, inequality, social disintegration— too large to be conceived except through numbers that mask their underlying human dimensions. Looming far larger than the individual tragedies providing

Michael Frishkopf, *Music for Global Human Development* In: *Transforming Ethnomusicology.* Edited by: Beverley Diamond and Salwa El-Shawan Castelo-Branco, Oxford University Press (2021). © Oxford University Press.
DOI: 10.1093/oso/9780197517550.003.0003

anecdotal fodder for the press, they often trigger far less compassion for their anonymous victims.

Ironically, for those not directly affected, smaller problems are more moving than large ones, because they present victims as human, individual, sui generis, not gathered in quantitative masses; thus humanized, they more readily trigger empathy, even action. Mother Teresa is supposed to have said, "If I look at the mass, I will never act. If I look at one, I will." At the other end of the human-itarian spectrum, Stalin told Churchill, "When one man dies it is a tragedy. When thousands die it's statistics" (McCullough 1992: 505). A well-known ex-perimental result shows that compassion collapses in cases of large numbers (Slovic 2007).

Big problems lack a human face; they dehumanize because they are of transhuman scale. In fact, they are not human problems directly of the lifeworld; rather they are problems of the system, that emergent social structure regulating the lifeworld through institutions—governments and corporations—appearing beyond the control of individuals (though this is an illusion: the system depends on the lifeworld, and its strategic actions are ultimately subject to our control).

. Big problems are only crudely grasped through statistics, too multidimen-sional to be fully understood through numbers; such representations are not conducive to generating affective connections that might trigger action. They divide the afflicted from each other, and separate them from the rest. They also afflict the "unafflicted": threatening the moral self-image (Jordan, Leliveld & Tenbrunsel 2015) of those who live in comfort and yet fail to act to help their fellow humans (beyond token, conscience-assuaging charitable contributions), splitting ideals and realities of the ethical self. These divisions constitute a vast obstacle to empathetic understanding in the world today, catalyzing social dis-integration and anomie. Reflecting and promoting global dehumanization, they are tearing the social fabric apart.

What can music do to reverse this trend? How can musical discourses and practices support social reintegration and rehumanization of social relationships? How can music help create a new "global human," a world citizen whose empathetic horizons extend far beyond the usual boundaries of family, ethnicity, class, community, or nation?

M4GHD

Music for Global Human Development (M4GHD) is a model for grassroots, collaborative, project-based participatory action research in ethnomusicology, toward social integration and rehumanization, addressing big problems in a sustainable and empowering manner. Each such project assumes the form of a diverse, far-flung Participatory Action Research (PAR) network (Kemmis & McTaggart 2005: 580), promoting music-centered communication (cognitive and affective) effecting socio-cultural transformations for human well-being.

M4GHD seeks to improve human life through positive, sustainable social change: abstractly, toward peace, justice, equality, freedom, social cohesion, cultural continuity, and civil society, as well as more quantifiably, toward reduced poverty and unemployment; improved education, health, and literacy; reduced crime, violence, and addiction; and cleaner, more sustainable environments, ultimately supporting the ability of each person to reach her or his full human potential in a rapidly globalizing world.

As has been evidenced in "edutainment" programs (UNESCO 2015, Singhal 2004, Sabido 2004), under the broader rubric "communications for development" (C4D) (Servaes 1996), song lyrics can effectively disseminate explicit public service messages supporting such goals. M4GHD can do the same, perhaps more effectively through collaborative participatory methods.

But successful M4GHD also strengthens and extends the global *social fabric*, the lifeworld's essential intersubjective network within which mutual humanity is recognized, and upon which real social progress depends. Embedded within that fabric is the PAR network at M4GHD's methodological core, serving at once as the *means* of effecting positive social change, and as an *instance* of that change.

These PAR networks, open and collaborative, are far-flung, criss-crossing the world's primary social fissures, local and global—what peace theorist Galtung (1996: 38) called "fault lines," boundaries of nation, ethnicity, race, gender, wealth, education, and profession—including musicians and producers, academics and students, community leaders, and others. They invite full participation, collectively determining, executing, evaluating, and revising action plans. Most important, the network links developed and underdeveloped worlds. Through music, such networks induce empathetic relationships challenging system-induced dehumanization, reflected and reinforced by big problems, across differences in culture, language, and religion, gaps in education, and standards of living.

The right kind of participatory, flexible music—and the term "music" is here broadly construed to include all *active* "musicking" (Small 1998), including applied ethnomusicology itself—operating within a communicatively connected social network enables what I call "socio-sonic resonance": cognitive-affective buildups resulting from feedback loops of "thought-feeling," affectively charged interactions by which communicative parameters are tuned, and empathetic understanding amplified, as participants are drawn together in intensive shared experience. Resonance thereby transmutes social *network* into social *fabric*. Beyond any intrinsic value, such music serves as a humanizing *social technology*.

Such "music" also lies at the core of M4GHD, causing the social network of the collaborative team to resonate, transforming it into social fabric, and to expand as participation broadens. Resonant PAR networks become engines of social change through sustainable interventions, not by *acting upon* the "other" as an object, like ordinary technology, but by *incorporating* the "other" as a subject, an active network participant, giving voice to people in difficult situations, connecting participants through empathy, turning despair to hope in the developing world, and apathy to compassion in the developed world, and stirring both to action.[1]

PAR networks, centered on locally rooted musics, "popular" or "traditional," sometimes featuring development issues in lyrics, thus simultaneously support a larger goal: the broader rehumanization of social relationships, particularly those straddling dehumanizing gaps and rifts in the social fabric, both locally and globally. By including participants from all walks of life and regions qua persons (not as representatives of institutional positions), the PAR network instantiates a personal rather than positional social structure (cf. Frishkopf 1999: 186ff), rooted in the lifeworld, distanced from an increasingly destructive system.

Besides formulating sustainable musical interventions, M4GHD projects also include research seeking to evaluate project impact, providing guidance in the PAR cycle from planning to action to observation to reflection (Kemmis & McTaggart 2005: 276). M4GHD thus combines activism with a research agenda seeking to understand its own effectiveness, in the action research tradition of social psychology (Lewin 1946) and anthropology (Tax 1975: 515).

In the final analysis, M4GHD is a human method—collaborative, participatory action research—applied toward a human aim, a global "human development," as well as the development of the "global human" who views the world in a more humanly interconnected way. In the spirit of PAR, aims and methods fuse into a continuously unfolding process, each round of research ideally enhancing the efficacy of subsequent action, as its network expands to encompass and transform more and more people and relationships within its scope.

Lifeworld and System

Jürgen Habermas offers a productive framework for the diagnosis and treatment of big problems as arising from a decoupling of system and lifeworld.[2] The lifeworld comprises ordinary, lived, intersubjective reality, locus of shared meaning, connection, and affective solidarity. Relationships within the lifeworld—conceptualized as a social network (Scott 2000)—exist between real people, not the positions they occupy, sometimes attaining the status of empathetic relation, resembling what Buber, in a mystical vein, called "I—Thou" (1958), and related (see Grinnell 1983) to the reciprocal intersubjective relation Schütz (following Husserl) termed a "living social relationship" or a "pure We" (Schütz 1967b: 32,

74–77; Schütz 1967c, 156–157, 163–165; Schütz 1967a: 23, 30, 37) involving direct, mutual recognition of humanity. The aggregate of such relationships— what I am calling the "social fabric"—provides the lifeworld with its core, social solidarity.

Network structures of the lifeworld are evanescent because they comprise people in direct relation with one another. Each individual is unique and irre- placeable; social continuity is assured only through cultural continuity: the transmission, largely informal and oral even in literate societies, of knowledge from one generation to the next. This process is at once highly robust, because massively parallel, and precarious—lost after a single generational gap. Culture is malleable and adaptive; change is expected, indeed necessary. Brittle culture, rigidly locked down as "tradition," will snap. The danger to the lifeworld comes not from change but from system-induced discontinuities, unraveling the social fabric to serve its interests.

The system, by contrast, is emergent, rooted in the lifeworld. Providing a networked set of positions mediating human interactions, and exhibiting struc- tural "flow through" rendering it durable independent of position occupants, the system is characterized by instrumental action, guided by the "steering media" of two subsystems—economy and polity—toward accumulation of power. Thus, the corporation acts toward accumulation of money (financial power), while the state acts toward accumulation of political power (Habermas 1984: 165); both do so through the accumulation of technological power.

The system, contingent on the lifeworld, has no independent existence, re- maining abstract and invisible except insofar as it is partially "incarnated" in or- ganizations (e.g., political parties, state bureaucracies, corporations). The system does not create meaning (a feature of the lifeworld) but exploits it as disguise, or incentive. Thus consumerism appeals to human-level drives (e.g., family, food, sex) in order to accumulate money, while political parties appeal to social identi- ties in order to accumulate support; both do so through system agents disguised as lifeworld actors.

Thus described, the system may appear antithetical to humanity, but it was not always so. With the rise of large, complex societies came social differentiation, including what Durkheim termed the division of labor (1964); at this juncture the system arose as a regulator, necessary for integration beyond the lifeworld's face to face interactions. Durkheim called this function "organic solidarity," arguing that it replaced the "mechanical solidarity" of smaller-scale societies; Weber called relationships of this type "associative," in contrast to "communal" relationships of the lifeworld (Weber 1978: 40–41). In such an arrangement, system-lifeworld interactions were mutualistic.

But with gradual percolation of system logic (the inexorable pursuit of money and power) overriding the cultural continuities of "morality" or "tradition" that formerly kept it at bay, along with an increase in technological power (deriving from the system-induced accumulation of scientific knowledge and capital), the system was vastly empowered, ultimately becoming a single global entity. Bureaucratization began to follow its own independent rationale, as noted by nineteenth-century theorists such as Ferdinand Tönnies and Max Weber: the rise of Gesellschaft ("society," comprising roles and indirect relations) at the expense of Gemeinschaft ("community") (Tönnies, in Adair-Toteff 1995: 61–62); "disenchantment" draining meaning from the world (Weber in Koshul 2005), or distorting meaning to serve its ends.

At this juncture, system and lifeworld began to "decouple," their relationship turning from mutualism to parasitism, what Habermas terms "the colonization of the lifeworld" (Edgar 2006: 17–21), risking wholesale destruction through pathologies: social disintegration, a collapse in mutual understanding, and general anomie.[3]

In complex societies, civil society, and its discursive counterpart, the public sphere, provide crucial lifeworld checks on this colonization. They thrive within public spaces between the economy (private sector) and the state (public sector), and depend heavily on cultural continuity. But the system invades these spaces and threatens these continuities, seeking maximal control, though masked by faux organizations and discourses (e.g., apparently "free" press and broadcast media controlled by corporate interests).

The system's socio-cultural incursions distort the lifeworld, introducing pathologies, undermining civil society and the public sphere. Mapped into the system via occupation of its structural positions, individual actors function instrumentally, dehumanizing others as means toward goals that serve the system as a whole. The system itself develops unevenly; possessing neither intelligence, foresight, nor empathy, it cannot avert internal conflict. Violence between subsystems, through war, repression, or ecological destruction, damages the lifeworld, but also impairs the system's ability to function. Responding blindly to its environment, the system induces internal as well as external lifeworld threats (e.g., civil war or climate change). But the system—arising through instrumental rather than communicative action, and valuing only quantitative accumulation—lacks the communicative capacity to avert disaster. Without the intelligence and humanism of the lifeworld, the system is unsustainable. The irony is that death of the lifeworld host implies death of the system—as for any parasite.

Implicitly, and sometimes explicitly, system actions foster dehumanization, because the system comprises a network of "I-it" relationships imposed upon those inhabiting its positions, whose relations to each other are always system-mediated, though this objectification is often hidden behind lifeworld values.

The food industry offers a ready example; an advertising executive ("I") seeks sales to a consumer ("it"), masked by humanistic images (a happily dining family) without regard for nutritional value, worker exploitation, or agricultural sustainability, dehumanizing the consumer, the worker, and future generations (for an exposé of the economic subsystem see *The Corporation* 2016). The system thus exploits human meaning and desire (for love, pleasure, food, comfort, security) in order to coerce people into objectified relations.

How to defend the lifeworld against such system depredations? In Habermas's view, the lifeworld is sustained by "communicative action," rational communication seeking understanding and consensus, not instrumental control.

I argue, however, that such rational consensus is never sufficient to maintain the lifeworld, because solidarity and consensus are affective, and therefore a combination of socialized thought and feeling is required to achieve them. Indeed, responding to Tönnies, Weber noted that "communal" social relationships typifying Gemeinschaft are "based on a subjective *feeling* of the parties, whether affectual or traditional, that they belong together" (Weber 1978: 40). Likewise, Durkheim stressed the importance of "collective effervescence" in maintaining solidarity (Durkheim 1995). Music provides the means of creating and maintaining such sentiments, by weaving (or reweaving) the *social fabric*.

Reweaving the Social Fabric

For each individual there exists an intersubjective "ego network" (Wasserman & Faust 1994: 42) of lifeworld connections, representing what Alfred Schütz called "consociates": those individuals with whom she or he interacts directly (for Schütz this meant face to face interaction (1970: 170), though given the prevalence of electronic communications today we may add various forms of mediated interaction as well), and who may (or may not) interact with each other; the ego network includes all such connections. Multiple networks of such "consociates" overlap to cover the entire lifeworld. But this social network of the lifeworld may be weakly connected in general, and limited to experiential connections.

The social fabric is defined not by objective connections between subjects in the realm of experience and sensation—what Buber termed "I-it" relations (a type applying equally to instrumental relations mediated by the system)—but by a qualitatively different sort of connection transcending sensory experience and centering instead on affective, intersubjective relationships, what he called "I-Thou," similar to Schütz's notion of a "living relationship" or the "pure We," as described earlier. I term the resulting intersubjective connection a "thread." It seems clear that such threads must form the lifeworld's crucial support; what is essential then is to spin and maintain them, and to weave them into ever-larger swatches.

I classify threads of the social fabric according to generational differences, sorted into two classes. The social weft connects individuals within a generation, while the social warp comprises threads connecting individuals whose age difference exceeds a generation. Using this nomenclature, we may classify a social fabric as being more horizontal (primary links are intragenerational; the weft is stronger) or more vertical (primary links are intergenerational; the warp is stronger). Ideally, the fabric will be strong in both directions.

The modern system frays the social fabric through destruction (violence, poverty, ecodisasters) wrought by blindness, but also strategically, replacing lifeworld threads with synthetic connections to serve its ends: the artificial warp of ethno-nationalism toward political exclusion, and the artificial weft of generations, toward economic consumption.

M4GHD aims to oppose such tendencies by developing PAR networks as microfabrics, personally (not positionally) connecting far-flung project participants occupying a range of social groups, and open to wider participation. The result is local reconnection, while weaving an unprecedented global fabric, providing a renewed basis for cultural continuity and civil society, and a thriving public sphere. Simultaneously, such music can propagate explicit development messages aiming to transform attitudes and behavior. By reweaving the social fabric, M4GHD helps protect the lifeworld against system depredations.

M4GHD projects fall into two types, though there are overlaps (see Figure 2.1). Some center primarily on (re)weaving the weft, riven by system-induced vertical divisions—ethnic, racial, class, gender—that have led to major social problems, about which there is widespread consensus. Such projects, known collectively as

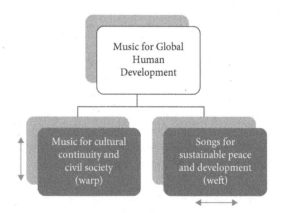

Figure 2.1 Music for Global Human Development, and its two primary subdivisions.

"Songs for Sustainable Peace and Development" (SSPD) frequently deploy lo-cally rooted popular music styles, freighted with messages designed to change attitudes and behavior. Digital music media and local stars are used to extend range, and ensure sustainability through replication and rebroadcast.

An instance of this approach is "Sanitation" (Frishkopf 2017, Frishkopf & Morgan 2013b, Frishkopf & Morgan 2013a), involving a PAR network con-necting local Liberian celebrity artists, producers, and media specialists; Canadian faculty in music and global health; a founder of a small NGO devoted to post-conflict Liberia; and a music producer in Canada. Together we produced a song, music video, and music-based documentary about sanitation in Liberia, unifying Liberians around a crucial postwar development issue, while raising awareness globally. The films—including interviews with the artists—were screened at a number of conferences, as well as on Liberian television, and the song also became popular on Liberian radio.

Other projects center more on (re)weaving the warp, riven by system-induced horizontal divisions—the separation of "generations" and consequent break-down in cultural continuity; such projects may depend more on encouraging "traditional" music, fostering connections across generations through face-to-face participation. Here what is important is not rigid preservation of "tradi-tional music," but rather its intergenerational transmission, serving to maintain social connections and continuous cultural identity.

For these projects, known as "Music for Cultural Continuity and Civil Society" (MCCCS), stars and lyrics are less crucial; cultural continuity is implicit in the very act of performance. Sustainability is promoted through establish-ment or encouragement of local performing groups, usually comprising youth (but with consultation from their elders) who maintain practices through oral transmission.

An instance of this approach is "Kinka" (Frishkopf 2007, Norvor 2007), for-ging intergenerational continuity through revival of a traditional Ghanaian music style among youth, many of whom had drifted away from traditional music toward more passive consumption of popular styles, resulting in a gener-ational gap. The project included a traditional Ghanaian composer, a Ghanaian producer, an American recordist resident in Ghana, and a performing group, with collaboration from local radio. By producing a cassette we managed to rein-vigorate the music through regional radio stations; youth responded by returning to rejoin the Kinka group. A CD version with extensive booklet followed, produ-cing greater awareness among non-Ghanaians; this "documentary CD" has been used in educating students about music and culture of Ghana ever since, and revenues flow back to support Ghanaian artists.

Ideally, both SSPD and MCCCS projects aim to be "double sided," criss-crossing boundaries between developed and developing worlds, and (differently) addressing both, so as to create awareness, shift attitudes and behavior, inspire empathy and hope, and extend the PAR network in both directions. Some projects evince features of both SSPD and MCCCS (e.g., Frishkopf, Abu, et al. 2016; Frishkopf, Hamze, et al. 2016).

On Development and "Human Development"

Most privileged residents of the "developed world" learn of problems afflicting hundreds of thousands, or millions, as passive consumers of the system-dominated infotainment industry. Feeling powerless and apathetic, they mostly tune out. The media stages of such big problems exist, ironically, within very small boxes (television, radio, iPad), dwarfed by a larger context (the kitchen needs cleaning!); the "news" follows big problems with "human interest stories," warm, amusing, and distracting, all amid endless advertising for luxury goods. So long as big problems do not affect them directly the privileged do not respond, except with an occasional donation.

While not always aware of the fact, the privileged are shielded by a system blocking the underprivileged from view, especially dispassionate immigration policies establishing whole countries as gated communities, designed to maximize wealth and control. The privileged cannot empathize with inhabitants of a contrasting lifeworld so long as they only experience the "other" in aggregate, mediated by a dehumanizing system, precluding intersubjective connection. But in ignoring those who suffer they risk self-injury, because they do not accept themselves as uncaring.

In the developed world, the media system regularly replaces real people with ersatz substitutes, like unseen body snatchers of science fiction (Finney 1955), typically celebrities with one-way relationships to ordinary people. But the privileged of the developed world may experience the system as benign, if alienating, blissfully unaware of its unsustainability. By contrast, in the underdeveloped world the system appears overtly unjust, brutal, violent; the frayed social fabric cannot protect the impoverished from the big problems that afflict them.

Development programs were supposed to address such dire conditions. Yet most of these programs were determined by the system, adjusted to support its accumulation of money and power, while excluding ordinary people from active participation. The system did not attribute the root of big problems to human (in)action and a frayed social fabric, but rather to more immediate material causes, requiring remedial resources (food, medicines, teachers), the industry to produce them, and the money to pay for them.

The concept of "development" emerged after World War II, encapsulated in the so-called Truman Doctrine (1949), calling for developed world technology to enhance productivity and alleviate poverty in the developing world of newly decolonized nations. During this period, "development" was tantamount to economic growth via technology. For decades, two development metrics prevailed: economic output and industrialization.

Both support the system: greater productivity implies bigger markets, and industrialization requires developed world technology. Further, such metrics do not reflect equality and social justice. Thus the aims, methods, and actors of such development projects were all very far from the human beings they were putatively intended to serve. On the contrary, by relying on non-human metrics summarized in aggregate statistics, such development was entirely dehumanized! Over subsequent decades these programs largely failed, even according to their own metrics (Escobar 1995). The problem of dehumanization was exacerbated by the inheritance of a mechanistic frame: treating people as objects, as statistics, as nonhumans.

In the early 1990s, a few economists began to question the relevance of such metrics to the actual quality of human life, introducing the concept of "human development" (Sen 1999, Haq 1995) along with a new "human development index," HDI ("Human Development Index" 2015, UNDP 2014). But HDI didn't necessarily change anything on the ground, however good the intentions. For one thing, given the near perfect correlation between the two sorts of metrics (Figure 2.2), how different could their resulting policies be?

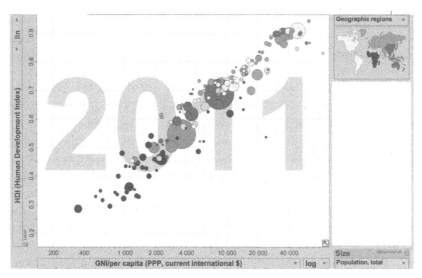

Figure 2.2 Gross National Income (GNI) per capita and the Human Development Index (HDI) are well correlated across countries. Here, circle area represents population. (Free vizualization from gapminder.org, CC- BY license).

For another, both kinds of metrics aggregated people as dehumanizing statistics that, even when calling attention to regions of need, do not directly address the underlying root cause of most big problems: the fraying of the social fabric. Indeed they exacerbate it. Certainly they don't contribute to humanizing global relationships or fostering the global human. While the concept behind the new index may have been sound, the aims, methods, and actors of this new approach were the same system-level structures already in place.

Thus the immediate response to problems of poverty, sickness, and hunger from the international development system has been limited, objectifying, and superficial, addressing short-term cause and effect. Such solutions tend to draw upon what the system does best: providing technologies that control materiality. What is urgently required is a more humanistic, far-sighted approach operating in parallel, addressing long-term needs and the underlying cause: a damaged social fabric. Nearly all big problems stem from self-inflicted wounds whose solution inheres in reweaving our global social fabric, unraveled by dehumanization, in a vicious circle as both cause and result of big problems. If technology were the solution, how could such problems persist in a world of technological riches? Furthermore, why don't we all try harder to ameliorate them?

Dehumanization, Rehumanization, and Empathy

As full recognition of the "other" as subject (human being) precludes inaction, inaction implies (as both cause and consequence) misrecognition of the "other" as object (dehumanization).

When a well-dressed businesswoman happens upon a well-dressed businessman collapsed on the sidewalk she rushes to call 911; she has encountered a recognizable human being in urgent need of help. But a hungry child far away, a homeless person collapsed nearby, or (a fortiori) a large number of them, are dehumanized. Consequently, observers are not propelled to action. System institutions (governments, NGOs, IGOs, corporations) may act, but only according to an instrumental logic that is always dehumanizing. But the logic also goes the other way: having failed to act, the privileged seek rationalization in dehumanization; "those people were not worth saving, they earned their fate, they are uncivilized, they are not like us." Inaction reinforces the dehumanization that allowed it, the rationale of rationalization.

Some may feel that the word "dehumanization" is too strong except in exceptional cases (e.g., European dehumanization of African slaves, Nazi dehumanization of Jews, Hutu dehumanization of Tutsis); some writers advocate a spectrum of objectification, from "casual indifference" at one end to full-fledged "dehumanization" at the other (Rector 2014: 9–10). Feminist critiques focus on "objectification" of the female body (Nussbaum 1995). But Volpato and Andrighetto provide a suitably broad definition: "Dehumanization is the act of denying humanness to other human beings" (2015). Indifference and objectification are merely subtypes.

Investigative journalist Gitta Sereny interviewed Franz Stangl, Kommandant of Sobibor and Treblinka Nazi extermination camps, as he was brought to trial in 1970. She writes: " 'Why,' I asked Stangl, 'if they were going to kill them anyway, what was the point of all the humiliation, why the cruelty?' 'To condition those who actually had to carry out the policies,' he said. 'To make it possible for them to do what they did' " (Sereny 1974: 178).

Psychologist Nick Haslam investigated implications of denying "uniquely human" attributes versus denying "human nature" attributes, producing two models: the former "animalistic dehumanization," and the latter "mechanistic dehumanization." Haslam draws attention to the contrastive affective dimensions of each model; animalistic models produce disgust and contempt, whereas mechanistic dehumanization produces indifference. The former creates sub-humans, the latter nonhumans. (Haslam 2006: 258). But while extreme dehumanization—for example, as manifested in genocide—rely on the former type, it is the latter which accounts for most dehumanization in the world today: not to justify the elimination of others, but simply as a means of living with their suffering, in the shadow of big problems, treating afflicted others as aggregated "nonhuman humans."

The episodic evils of genocide or ethnic cleansing are historical exceptions to a far more mundane, ongoing, pervasive dehumanization: that some are consistently treated as less human than others, and this fact is all the more disturbing for being nearly unremarkable. For the system, the privileged, individual life of the developed world carries far greater value than the aggregated remainder, the human corollary to the economic-political "1 percent." The system's colonization of the lifeworld is both cause and effect of this situation, since dehumanization implies acceptance of substandard rights and freedoms, and extreme inequality, both between "developed" and "underdeveloped" countries, and between center and margin even in the former, and system mediation is facilitated by a thinly woven social fabric. Both types are attributable to, and reproduce, what Durkheim, in his analysis first of the division of labor, and then of suicide, called *anomy* (anomie): an excess of individuation, fraying social bonds of organic solidarity, producing moral breakdown (1964, 1933, 368).

The social fabric, constituting subjective bonds of subjective recognition, is damaged when we fail to see each other as fully human, and we have ceased to see each other as fully human because the social fabric has been rent by a global system—dehumanized, and dehumanizing—that colonizes the lifeworld, in inexorable pursuit of money and power, co-opting people to use each other instrumentally, as objects. The two conditions exist in a vicious cycle.

Instead of the "I-you" relations of a lifeworld in which I communicate with my fellow human being, even the idealized "I-thou" advanced by Buber, Dewey, and others, we are propagating a paradigm of "I-it" or even "it-it," the only relation known within a system that does not recognize human beings at all, except in order to exploit them.

As Marcuse remarked: "in the technological reality, the object world (including the subjects) is experienced as a world of instrumentalities" (2002: 223). With the rise of technology, the system and lifeworld, formerly mutualistic, are locked in a destructively vicious circle, in which the system, hungry for money and power, is forced to exploit the lifeworld ever more vigorously the more it is weakened. Dehumanization is a self-fulfilling condition, as we have seen: the more I dehumanize others, adjusting my ethical standards to match, the more I am forced to do so, in order to rationalize them.

Dehumanization has existed throughout human history; what is new is the tipping point in the system-lifeworld balance. How to break the cycle? If insularity and social distance reinforce dehumanization, then perhaps connection and empathy can reverse it, producing a more "human" development.

What is required is the introduction of a non-technological mediating agent, and a different sort of method, one focused less on technological interventions and statistical assessments, and more on grassroots, collaborative, human and humanizing connections, restoring the social fabric protecting the lifeworld. For Durkheim, extrapolating from Australian societies, social solidarity is to be sought in affective empathy (Meštrović 1992: 146), produced through the mediation of transformative, participatory, interactive performance, often centered on sound, from political oratory to religious ritual (Durkheim 1995: 212, 218).

In M4GHD the mediating agent is music, the method is Participatory Action Research, and the aim is "global human development." With deliberate irony, I call M4GHD "social technology," not because it is technology in the system sense, but in order to validate it from the system perspective, while also calling sharp attention to the limitations of this concept.

Global (Human Development), (Global Human) Development, and Participatory Action Research

The solutions to big problems appear out of reach. Yet inasmuch as the problems are human-made, they admit human solutions, through concerted human effort and coordinated action. The primary obstacles are not technological, but attitudinal, repairing disconnections in the social fabric.

What is required is a change in attitude and practice, producing a new level of engagement, social connectivity across boundaries, empowerment and action, transforming I-it system mediated relations into I-thou relations of the social fabric, locally and globally.

The humanization in "global human development" differs sharply from that of the HDI, measuring well-being without proposing new solutions. Furthermore, alongside global "human development," "global human development" also implies emergence of the "global human," whose lifeworld is defined by inter-subjective threads extending beyond the local. Such a human development is entirely centered on human connection, rooted in the lifeworld. Here the mod-ifier "human" applies not only to objectives—for example, health, education, connection—but also to methods and participation. It implies, in particular, ac-tive collaboration with those who are in greatest need of assistance, those whose lifeworld has been most thoroughly decimated, invited to join the project as full-fledged participants, never as disempowered, anonymous objects to be uplifted or researched.

Participatory action research (PAR; see Kemmis & McTaggart 2005, Rahman 2005, Fals Borda 2005, Kemmis, McTaggart & Nixon 2014: ch. 1, Loewenson et al. 2014, ICPHR 2013), offering a powerfully interconnective model for col-laborative applied ethnomusicology, is central to this task, for its networks can link formerly disconnected social spaces. The PAR model centers on a radical rethinking of the relationship between "researcher" and "researched," combining committed, egalitarian *participation*, transformative *action*, and applied *research* aimed at positive, sustainable social change, recognizing empathetic connection as the basis for action and understanding.

This kind of "human development" contrasts sharply with the usual implications of techno-economic advancement, typically propelled by "experts" from without, and reducing whole populations to numbers. It is at once more ethical, for its humanized relationships, and more pragmatic, for those whose lifeworld is endangered are best positioned to understand what they need in order to sustainably maintain it.

Through PAR, the marginalized are empowered and given voice within an ac-tion research network founded on an inclusive "We," including defining object-ives and devising methods in concert. Development strategies that disempower in order to empower are tautologically doomed, their ethnocentrism far more dangerous for being unleashed outside the "ivory tower," all too easily becoming yet another form of domination (Escobar 1991). PAR takes the opposite ap-proach, centered on a dynamic network of interconnected collaboration, shifting and expanding as the project spirals through its multiple phases: planning—action—observation—reflection (Figure 2.3).

PAR pairs action with research in the "action research" tradition (Lewin 1946, Tax 1975): projects seeking positive change are observed, using both qualitative and quantitative methodologies (including ethnography), in order

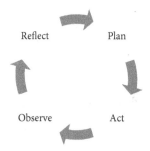

Figure 2.3 Participatory Action Research: a collaborative research cycle for positive social change. Ideally, the cycle becomes a spiral, with upward movement representing social progress (after Kemmis & McTaggart 2005: 276).

to assess impact and provide guidance aimed at improving results in the following round.

Ideally, this PAR network comes to exemplify the sought-after social transformation, helping repair violence wrought by social distance. *As the PAR network expands, gathering more and more participants into its fold, it becomes the change it seeks.*

Music for Global Human Development

M4GHD comprises music-centric projects, each enacted by a dynamic PAR network deploying music as a social technology for positive humanistic change. As we have seen, the essence of that change is the reweaving of the social fabric, beginning with the ever-expanding PAR network itself, toward restoring the lifeworld and repelling the system. I have argued that the solidarity required to weave the social fabric is affective as well as cognitive, depending on both shared thought and feeling. Why should music be important to the formation of such PAR networks? How does music weave the social fabric?

Music's Key Attributes

A number of key attributes enable music to fulfill this role. In this section I consider these attributes within a series of concentric rings: acoustics, psychoacoustics, communication, socioacoustics, and resonance.

Acoustics and psychoacoustics. Music's capacity to maintain the social fabric stems from three sonic properties: temporality, superposition, and diffraction. The first means that as music exists in time, it aligns us in time, thereby effecting social coordination, a "mutual tuning-in" (Schütz 1951: 92). The second means that multiple sound sources add, implying that louder sources eclipse softer ones, and that acoustically complementary sounds can harmonize. The third means that sound diffuses around obstacles. Due to its diffractive nature and linguistic centrality we are constantly attuned to sound; as Schafer wrote, "there are no earlids" (1994). Taken together these acoustic and psychoacoustic properties indicate the power of participatory music to gather, focus, express, coordinate, organize, align, and galvanize group solidarity, while blocking competing signals.

Communication. If language is the quintessential human attribute then so is its primordial verbal expression in sound. Music carries speech with an array of paralinguistic devices, expressively manipulating time, timbre, and pitch, thus amplifying affective connection. The same devices enable collective textual performance, without jeopardizing comprehension. Thus song contributes both collective feeling and thought toward group solidarity.

Socioacoustics. At the center of music's social role is voice, metaphorically and literally as the actor's sonic-social extrusion into the lifeworld.[4] Voice doubly presents the self within the lifeworld; it is the central disembodied individual attribute ("my voice"), a sonic aura capable of indefinite extension beyond bodily limits into the intersubjective domain, and a "hook" by which we interact— through both thought and feeling—with others. Carrying language modulated through paralinguistic expression, voice enables empathetic exchange of thought-feeling, the primary basis for "I-thou" relationships. But voice can also detach from the agentive individual, when it comes to represent the collective, becoming quasi-autonomous.

Considering the centrality of voice, and its quasi-autonomous status, one begins to understand how and why music offers the most powerful social expression of our humanity. Music moves us and music moves us together, building collective experiences, and extending the social fabric through the weaving of new I-thou relationships.

In view of this fact, I claim for music the status of human being—the "human nonhuman," a counterweight to the "nonhuman human" of systemic dehumanization. Music is not a signal from sender to receiver, as communications theorists would have it, but an "affecting presence," a "presentation of being" (Armstrong 1975: 19–20), a person-like intermediary whose relationships to both sender and receiver are immediate and personal—"I-thou"—thus drawing them together, grounded in expression and empathy. If solo music establishes a connection from individual to "music" to group, collective music-making develops connections among co-performers also. Music is qualitatively different from communications—speech, text, email—because as the "human nonhuman," music occupies nodes of the social network, catalyzing formation of the social fabric. Rather than "mediation" we should see in music a kind of "immediation" (Armstrong 1975: 19). In this way, music weaves the social fabric, in its weft and—over time—its warp, between participants.

Besides its networked position, music also catalyzes collective action that weaves the social fabric by establishing a shared substrate. Analyzing the basis for coordinating collective action, Chwe (2001: 19) has called attention to "common knowledge," recursively definable as that which everyone knows, and which everyone knows is common knowledge. Music's power to carry "thought" while mobilizing and addressing large numbers of people generates common knowledge. But music also generates "common feeling," providing the basis for a Durkheimian "collective effervescence" (Frishkopf 2010: 22–23). Through common knowledge and common feeling, music catalyzes the "We," weaving the social weft and warp through performance and transmission. Through group participation, music generates shared experiences, and sediments collective affective memories, bestowing upon itself the power to subsequently retrieve them as well (Jäncke 2008). Music thereby evokes and underscores the continuity of collective identity both cognitively and affectively.

Music for M4GHD

So far I have outlined musical attributes that support the (re)weaving of the social fabric. But the music that is the lifeblood of M4GHD is a *particular kind* of music.

First, music is never an unequivocal good. Not all music is conducive to weaving the global social fabric or supporting M4GHD. Some lyrics may oppose connection, or weave exclusionary social fabrics that work *against* human development. Music as thought-feeling can be peaceful, or it can be hateful, exacerbating social divisions, for example, nationalistic music glorifying one nation at the expense of another, or ethnic music that stirs prejudice.[5] M4GHD must not strengthen the fabric of a particular group at the expense of another. Its music must avoid colonization by the system. M4GHD must resist the system, remaining rooted in the lifeworld. Its PAR network must guard vigilantly against these dangers.

Second, toward connectivity, the concept "music" must broaden to Small's "musicking" (Small 1998), except that members of M4GHD's PAR network must *actively participate* to enable resonance. Thus a PAR network may involve one person singing, another clapping, a third recording, a fourth dancing, others promoting, composing, mixing, or fundraising, planning, interviewing, or critiquing . . . all actively involved and connected through such activity.

Third, such "music" must be adaptive: flexible in form and content, and enabling sonic, behavioral, and discursive interactivity, feedback loops by which it adapts to environment and participants. Through this cybernetic system, social impact is maximized. The social fabric tightens as such "music"—gradually "tuned" through feedback—draws participants together, producing socio-sonic resonance.

Resonance entails expressive feedback loops of thought-feeling, enabling local adaptation and power, creating network solidarity through powerful, connected, shared experience, thus (re)weaving the social fabric. Such resonance may arise quickly in face-to-face performance, or more slowly when "music" is mediated; impact of the former upon participants is stronger, while the latter is broader in scope. Such resonance helps inoculate the lifeworld against systemic colonization via integrating flows of thought-feeling, encouraging mutual recognition of participants' humanity, using the human nonhuman (music) to guard against systemic dehumanizations (the nonhuman human).

Through resonance, a social network is transformed into social fabric. That fabric may endure beyond performance when other factors hold the network together, as is the case for a village periodically performing a public ritual for its "collective effervescence." In such cases resonance leads to the emergence of fabric as a durable social structure, but entirely rooted in the lifeworld.

The PAR network is of this more durable type. Connected through musical interactions of various sorts—including but not limited to performance—and definitionally open to collaborative participation, it may resonate through adaptive feedback, through interactions of participants, and in the cycling of its four phases (see Figure 2.3). *Through such resonance, the PAR network itself becomes social fabric, a microcosm of its aim: social integration, social solidarity, cultural continuity, and civil society, restoring humanity to a damaged world order.* All that must happen to address big problems is a gradual expansion of that network to become larger and more diverse, connecting more people from different groups and walks of life, rehumanizing relationships toward human development, through the advent of the "global human."

Coda

M4GHD's aim and method thus converge: social integration and rehumanization, a restoration of the lifeworld's intersubjective fabric through resonant, personal, humanized connections erasing boundaries and bridging chasms separating human beings by citizenship, ethnicity, education, language, and gender, countering the unprecedented level of disconnection wrought by an increasingly brutal, colonizing system. Through musical resonance, M4GHD forges humanized connections and disseminates development messages on a human scale, not only within the developing world or developed worlds but between worlds. Each project begins with an open, egalitarian PAR network demanding humanized relationships rooted in the lifeworld; this network becomes a microfabric, a model for replication and a starting point for unbounded expansion, toward global "human development," and the development of the "global human," the empathetic affirmation of the "Pure We" of humanity. Music is a social technology—humanized and humanizing—capable of catalyzing such changes (Figure 2.4).[6]

Figure 2.4 Music for Global Human Development: Participatory Action Research cycling toward a stronger social fabric through resonance (see m4ghd.org).

Notes

1. It is important to underscore that these "worlds" cannot be geographically demarcated on a map; they interpenetrate even in the most "developed" regions. But always the system hides inequalities of the developing world through masking, objectification, and dehumanization.
2. The following account of system and lifeworld is inspired by Habermas, drawing also on the phenomenology of Husserl, Schütz, and Buber. I do not claim to provide a faithful representation of anyone's thought.
3. When exactly system and lifeworld shifted out of balance is debatable. Perhaps—as in so many historical trends—there was no moment of shift, only of recognition. Certainly humanity never lacked for cruelty in the name of politics or economy.
4. Arabic recognizes the connection between sound and voice in a single word: *sawt*.
5. For more examples of various types, in relation to peace studies, see Urbain (2007: 2).
6. For more information about M4GHD in theory and practice, please visit http://m4ghd.org.

3

Reengaging Sound Praxis in the Real World

Politico-Epistemological Dimensions of Dialogue and Participation in Knowledge Production

Samuel Araújo

A steady and recently expanding stream of literature in ethnomusicology and related fields—e.g., the anthropology of music and sound—has brought to the fore issues such as the consistently asymmetrical social relations between scholars and the peoples with whom they work, and the different implications and sometimes antagonistic interests of people taking part in a given research initiative. In such contexts, the challenges of balancing or merging the proactive political stances oftentimes taken by scholars with those of their interlocutors who envisage many forms of activism, thus open debates on interpretive protocols (e.g., distancing, non-interventionism, neutrality, objectivity) or procedures (e.g., participant observation, interviews, separation between fieldwork and analysis—still worth conceptualizing as "academic").[1] A crucial part of the effort of working through divergent and asymmetrical social relations are attempts at producing comprehensive overviews of the relevant literature, through mapping, sorting out, and critically assessing major trends, their foundations and approaches, as well as their corresponding qualifiers, most if not all of which derived from the social sciences where work has been characterized as applied, collaborative, advocacy, public, engaged, participatory, or otherwise (Pettan 2008, Harrison & Pettan 2010, Harrison 2012, Dirksen, 2012, Harrison 2014, Rice 2014, Titon 2015, Pettan 2015), allowing the debate to proceed on more solid grounds.

A pioneering collection of articles meant to address changing conceptualizations and approaches in the field of ethnomusicology (Pettan 2008) emerged from contributions to a double panel "The Politics of Applied Ethnomusicology; New Perspectives" during the 39th International Council for Traditional Music (ICTM) World Congress in Vienna (2007), which consequently led to the creation of a Study Group on Applied Ethnomusicology at the same event. Svanibor Pettan's article in that volume provides an overview

Samuel Araújo, *Reengaging Sound Praxis in the Real World* In: *Transforming Ethnomusicology*. Edited by: Beverley Diamond and Salwa El-Shawan Castelo-Branco, Oxford University Press (2021). © Oxford University Press. DOI: 10.1093/oso/9780197517550.003.0004 of events leading up to the panel presentations and examines taxonomical issues in relation to specific approaches in applied research. He then presents a number of themes (diasporas, migration, refugees, ethnic minorities) on which applied research approaches might focus as a way of empowering communities and individuals whose voices might not be considered in broader political arenas. Presenting examples of his own work that demonstrate how applied research is able to empower oppressed or even silenced voices in such contexts, Pettan stresses the value of such work and emphasizes how it should be seen as complementing more conventional forms of academic scrutiny. The article solidly legitimizes different kinds of academic approach (which do not stand in opposition to but complement standard research), but it does not engage further the implicit epistemological questions of whether applied approaches, in themselves, might be considered research—what would qualify them as such and what standing would they have vis-à-vis other kinds of research.

A similar position in another significant attempt toward a comprehensive assessment of applied approaches in ethnomusicology and their eventual interrelationships appeared in an essay collection (Harrison, Mackinley & Pettan 2010) stemming from the first meeting of the ICTM Study Group for Applied Ethnomusicology, which took place in Ljubljana in 2008. In its Introduction, Klisala Harrison and Svanibor Pettan provide an overview of how such approaches were configuring new directions in the field, relating them to broader debates on the social responsibility of scholars to the people with whom they work.

All of the above contributions are careful in stressing non-opposition of applied ethnomusicology to academic standards, extending and complementing the latter's essentially reflexive aims. Nonetheless, an article by Ana Hofman (2010) raises a concern about whether and how standardized forms of academic knowledge production might be used as an ultimate form of subjugation of the Other. More precisely, she points out as still problematic some of the politically correct procedures in applied ethnomusicology, such as feeding back scholarly work to communities or undertaking scholarly informed advocacy, both of which tend to maintain the privilege of academic discourses that interpret exploitation, while presuming or implying that their interlocutors are unreflexive. She also presents a question that might seem, to some readers, a rather discomforting one: where might one (or why might one not) fit into this discussion other models such as the Yugoslav socialist tradition of cultural production based on self-management and joint work among scholars, cultural workers, policymakers, and community members, a tradition that challenges oversimplified dichotomies between "pure" and "applied"? In other words, have retrospective overviews of applied ethnomusicology been simply considering applied research an extension of conventional epistemologies or are we in fact challenging the "purity" of those epistemologies by exposing their vested interests and related agendas? (I shall return to this point when examining some

Latin American perspectives on both dialogic and participatory research forged in the 1960s and 1970s). More recently, in her oral presentation during the SEM-ICTM Forum, Hofman has also called into question an additional dimension of the assimilation and naturalization of applied research within a neoliberal academic context, the overexploitation of scholars, and mainly of women, required to meet never-ending quantitative measurements of impact in order to legitimize their scholarship: the size of the target audience, examples of practical applications of the research, and so on, regardless of the increasingly precarious labor conditions in academia.

Three more general overviews, respectively by Harrison (2012, 2014) and Rebecca Dirksen (2012), provide detailed critical assessments of the diversified field of applied ethnomusicology, its potentials and challenges, questioning the epistemological grounds on which it might be conceptualized as research in itself beyond complementary relationships with conventional forms of academic knowledge production. The first article by Harrison (2012) pursues the important task of sorting out epistemologies behind the various strands of applied ethnomusicology examining what might bind them together as an epistemic community,[2] a concept she borrows from Peter M. Haas. In a later publication, Harrison (2014) analyzes Applied Ethnomusicology as an expanding field, which by then seems relatively legitimized in major academic societies such as SEM and ICTM, and comprises different focuses, theoretical guideposts, and approaches, as well as debates on its definition, as it enters what she terms a second generation. One might argue that her analysis of the increasing interest in Applied Ethnomusicology is limited to context-specific cases (e.g., a significant reduction of academic jobs involving teaching and more standardized forms of research, which might be true in the US context but not necessarily the same elsewhere) or that it does not address in depth the sociohistorical conditions imposing, for instance, given agendas on research financing institutions, notably requiring assessments of quantitative impact (quite often but not exclusively practical) as an evaluation criterion of scholarly work, but Harrison's thorough effort in systematizing the relevant literature is an undoubtedly a key contribution to the central debate in this compendium.

Another in-depth overview is the one presented by Dirksen (2012), who initially recalls earlier arguments by authors such as Jeff Titon and Gage Averill on how the history of applied dimensions in the ethnomusicology practiced in the United States is not duly accounted for in influential published recollections of the field that seem reluctant to deal with an aspect that might compromise its scholarly character (this resembles similar issues raised in other humanistic fields such as anthropology, discussed later in this article). This argument is of interest here since, in itself, it would imply that the often-alleged emergence of applied disciplines in the humanities during the second half of the twentieth century is much more a matter of recognition and exposure rather than actual innovation or paradigm shift. By carefully scrutinizing several trends in applied work derived from the literature in English, Dirksen offers an interesting panorama of the motivations behind and approaches to, as well as the pros and cons of, an intensified commitment of scholars to their interlocutors' struggles and self-defined goals. She also recalls earlier discussions by folklorists on how application may also stem from ethnographic research conducted under apparently neutral and objectifying academic standards, by no means thought of or claimed as applied, relativizing the often naturalized neutrality and objectivity of "pure research," a point also sustained by this author in a previous publication (Araújo 2008). Dirksen also formulates a compelling question to which this paper's title seeks to react:

> Today, applied ethnomusicology stands in firm response to "does it even matter?" and "what does it mean for the 'real world'?" in an era when intellectual occupations are frequently dismissed as irrelevant and elitist, and the arts and humanities are too often written off as fluff or luxury. (Dirksen 2012: np)

The most comprehensive presentation to date of the literature in question is the *Oxford Handbook of Applied Ethnomusicology* (Titon & Pettan 2015). Jeff Titon's opening article reaffirms his view that "[a]pplied ethnomusicology puts ethnomusicology to practical use . . . guided by ethical principles of social responsibility, human reciprocity and cultural and musical equity" (2015: 4). Titon stresses its relative separation from standard research models or goals as well as its foundations on ethical ideals. Ethical motivations have been undoubtedly a driving force behind the growing commitment of younger generations of ethnomusicologists to applied research. However, one might still argue that such a stance in itself still places a great deal of power in the hand of scholars, since all of the three ethical aspects that Titon names, which may be applied to contrasting and even antagonistic perspectives, still depend on how, in each specific research initiative, the objectives, protocols, and products are negotiated and validated by interlocutors who may hold different interests and perspectives on the outcomes.[3] In the same reference source, Pettan (2015) restates and expands his previous remarks in the 2008 volume of *Musicological Annual* but now also accounts for the consolidation of applied research in ethnomusicology (see also Harrison 2012, 2014; Dirksen 2012; Rice 2014), while acknowledging that the initiatives he considers as applied may comprise, in fact, significant internal differences and eventual divergences.

A still more recently published special edition of *The World of Music*, aimed at presenting an overview of Brazilian ethnomusicology, suggests that the Brazilian field as a whole is firmly established on similar commitments to those identified above as specific to applied ethnomusicology (Luhning & De Tugny 2016), although there is very little or no reference to the English language publications mentioned in my previous paragraphs. Besides raising questions about how universal is the perceived singularity and relative devaluing of applied research in the world's distinct academic traditions, this specially themed volume also exposes the issue of language barriers that may obfuscate other narratives that contrast with the ones available in English-language sources.

In any case, these overall assessments of the literature have all stressed how these perceived trends have impacted the academic field of ethnomusicology in terms of concepts and practices of training, researching, and publicizing results. They also make similar calls for changes in the institutional workings of universities and other research institutions, opening up a renewed debate on the dichotomy between "pure" and "applied" research in ethnomusicology (Harrison 2014) at a time when many are asking what the humanities still have to say to the "real world" (Dirksen 2012).

Acknowledging the plurality of intellectual principles, research focuses and approaches, as well as the institutional conditionings and practices, critical assessments have usually defined the broad field with which they aim to engage as applied ethnomusicology—or, as phrased by Pettan (2015), ethnomusicologies. Only exceptionally (see Hofman 2010) have these assessments paid close attention to how these perceivable changes may be but symptoms of larger determinants worth investigating further. These broad factors that shape applied work include social welfare–insensitive, market-ridden world politics, a reality made increasingly clear since the disintegration of the so-called Soviet bloc, and the concomitantly triumphant announcement of influential truisms such as "the end of history" and the like, by spokesmen of a new, or neoliberal, world order. Soon afterward, after the 2008 global economic crisis, the evident fragility of nation-states or other forms of resistance as mediatory instances to any sustainable notion of social life raises concern about the reality of generalized disorder and even worse prospects than those of neoliberalism, imposing more clearly the necessity of any research to position itself even more clearly with regard to its macropolitical stances.

This chapter is concerned with grounding and problematizing a new ethnomusicological praxis based on the assumption that we openly engage with our interlocutors' existential and political struggles, while highlighting the potentials of and challenges to notions of dialogue and participation in the course of such initiatives. I focus on the praxis of influential Latin American scholars engaged in processes of broadly defined social change. I argue for a simultaneously political and epistemological approach, integrating horizontal modes of knowledge production, individual or collective action, and public policy making and implementation revolving around sound praxis, conceptualized as:

Articulation between verbal and non-verbal discourses, actions and policies concerning sound, presenting themselves, oftentimes in subtle or imperceptible ways, in the daily life of individuals (amateur or professional musicians, non-musicians, cultural agents, entrepreneurs, legislators), collectives (collectives of musicians, fans, professionally related social positions) and institutions (enterprises, unions, governmental agencies or NGOs, community councils, schools). (Grupo Musicultura 2010)

Politico-Epistemological Shifts in the Humanities; General Perspectives

In either individual or collective publications (e.g., Araujo 2008, 2009; Araujo and members of Grupo Musicultura 2006), I have attempted to clarify my own stances on the relationships between academics and the public at large in knowledge producing processes, by emphasizing conceptual, theoretical, and methodological aspects of relevance to a critical examination of dialogical and participatory research on music and sound. Following particularly the publication of texts such as *Writing Culture* (Clifford & Marcus 1986) and *Anthropology as Cultural Critique* (Marcus & Fischer 1986), to name just two widely known titles in English,[4] a growing literature has stressed the necessity of self-criticism and remodeling in anthropology, and later in ethnomusicology (e.g., Rice 1987, Barz & Cooley 2008) in the face of a wider global awareness of the political conditionings and power of academic representations, as well as of the great political and economic imbalance between interpreting and interpreted individuals and collectives around the world. Furthermore, this literature has taken up the task of rethinking modes of producing knowledge through politically self-conscious intercultural dialogue, requiring not only new theoretical frameworks and new context-sensitive writing strategies but also concomitant methodological innovations, especially ones aiming at developing more horizontal relationships among research subjects. One such methodology came to prominence when reconsidering the different modes of participation in the research and recognizing the textual (co)authorship of people otherwise classified as informants or non-academic interlocutors. Luke Lassiter, one of the more thoroughly engaged US-based anthropologists in this self-critical strand, has argued (Lassiter 2005) that collaborative work in the sense of work that is applied to the interlocutors' self-voiced interests became no longer a matter of choice but a necessity for any ethnographic work nowadays, due to the growing political awareness of academic interlocutors in the field. Neutrality can no longer be (if it ever was) imagined or taken for granted in exchanges within and beyond the academic field.

According to Lassiter (2005), what he terms collaborative work in mainstream anthropology has a long-standing, though unrecognized, history traceable to the deep involvement of Lewis Morgan in the political struggles of the Iroquois by the mid-nineteenth century. Adding a perspective on how such work influenced a praxis for social change in other contexts, Brazilian anthropologists Jean Tible (2011) and Mauro Almeida (2004), among others, have also highlighted the impact Morgan's work had on both Karl Marx and Friedrich Engels, two other "applied scholars" (see also Rosenberry 2005), so to speak. Marx was led to change his thinking about "primitive accumulation" societies, and to reconsider New World Indigenous conceptual references and modes of life no longer as simply past evolutionary stages but as cultures of interest to a socialist reinvention of social and economic relations.

However, even such an impressively comprehensive account as Lassiter's reference work leaves out a few other important collaborative, and indeed more radical, theoretical and methodological currents in social studies. Influential ones were, for instance, developed in the turbulent Latin American political context of the 1960s and 1970s, pioneered by the world-acknowledged Brazilian educator Paulo Freire and his *Pedagogy of the Oppressed*, and by Colombian sociologist Orlando Fals Borda, a groundbreaking proponent of so-called Participatory Action Research (PAR or, in his native Spanish, IAP). It is very difficult, no doubt, to synthesize the complex theoretical guideposts and contextual underpinnings of the respective work of these engaged Latin American scholars of the 1960s and 1970s, in many ways convergent although strikingly developed in ignorance of one another. Nonetheless, there is a highly significant difference between, on one hand, Freire's and Fals Borda's efforts and, on the other, what Lassiter offers us as examples and potentials of collaborative ethnography in the United States. Both Freire and Fals Borda, like many of their contemporaries, were deeply committed to palpable sociopolitical change not only in what I would term defensive, micropolitical tactics, such as longer-term collaboration or co-elaboration of texts, something which is indeed part of their respective knowledge producing strategies, but also in broader status quo-challenging macropolitical struggles such as opposing unjust control of the State or even contesting altogether the oppression perceived in European-derived notions of a nation-state. Resounding in their work is an awareness of central notions of socially naturalized oppression, violence, and exploitation, inscribed in broader worldviews supportive of the status quo. To reiterate this point, I might note the similarity to Marx's well-known formulation in his Theses on Feuerbach: beyond interpreting the world for knowledge's sake, the knowledge that actually matters is the one that changes the world. While Lassiter seems to consider deeply intersubjective and more horizontal dialogue between academics and non-academics as a significant change in the United States as well as in other contexts of advanced capitalism, and indeed it is, Freire and Fals Borda point at radically changing the status quo itself in emerging nation-state economies as their ultimate point of inflection. For them the stakes are higher.

The following section will contextualize and explain further this point, attempting to highlight how such stakes may expose how naturalized may be both the presumed purity of "pure" research and the presumed practical essence of "applied" scholarship. Incidentally, it aims to problematize what is usually assumed as an epistemological guidepost for applied academic work: that it is a problem-solving initiative based on shared interests of scholars and their interlocutors.

Inequality, Pedagogy, and Social Change in Post–World War II Latin America

The Cold War and the strong politico-ideological tension between capitalist and socialist, the Second Vatican Ecumenical Council (II VEC) and its emphasis on inter-religious dialogue, and the Cuban Revolution of 1959 all played an unequivocal role in opening up new political scenarios in Latin America through the 1960s and 1970s. From insurgent anti–status quo movements to nationalistic trends opposed to the control of continental politics by US interests, allied with local elites, came the production and diffusion of alternative theories of social change in several fields, from political economy to arts and culture. In distinct ways, this simultaneous intellectual and political praxis became a crucial weapon in the fight against the fast-paced transformation of raw material feeding the economies and patriarchal societies. Latin American nations became industrialized satellites of world imperialism, and this concomitantly produced tension through accelerating urbanization and the formation of new bottom-up social movements, while the patterns of inequality and social injustice forged historically throughout Latin America increased even more. Among such examples of praxis for social change, two distinct but in many ways intersecting trends are worth highlighting here, both of which had close ties with the second Vatican Ecumenical Council and its self-proclaimed openness to dialogue: namely the ones known as Popular Education and Liberation Theology. The former had as pioneers two pedagogues with Catholic academic backgrounds, Paulo Freire (Brazil), creator of a dialogical literacy teaching method, and Ivan Illitch (born in Austria, and working from the mid-1950s through the 1960s in Puerto Rico and Mexico), a theologian trained in Rome. Liberation Theology obtained public exposure in the early 1970s through the writings of Catholic theologians such as Gustavo Gutiérrez (Peru) and Leonardo Boff (Brazil), as well as by Rubem Alves, a Brazilian Presbyterian theologian who also became strongly associated later with Freire. According to Leonardo and Clodovis Boff:

At a meeting of Latin American theologians held in Petrópolis (Rio de Janeiro) in March, 1964, Gustavo Gutiérrez described theology as critical reflection on praxis. This line of thought was further developed at meetings in Havana, Bogotá, and Cuernavaca in June and July, 1965. Many other meetings were held as part of the preparatory work for the Medellin conference of 1968; these acted as laboratories for a theology worked out on the basis of pastoral concerns and committed Christian action. (Boff & Boff 1987: 69)

In many ways, Popular Education has its origins in sources similar to those of Liberation Theology. The work of Freire on critical (or, as he put it initially, liberation) pedagogy, in particular, has been a crucial reference worldwide not only for the field of pedagogy in general but also for other academic and cultural fields in general, such as theater, as in Augusto Boal's "theater of the oppressed." Freire's work also had an impact on the ethnomusicological experiments undertaken since the year 2000 by successive generations of researchers and different research groups associated with the Ethnomusicology Laboratory at the Federal University of Rio de Janeiro and in an interesting combination of Boal's proposals with engaged forms of ethnomusicology, and in the work of Tan Sooi Beng in Penang, Malaysia, where her work merges traditional theater, music, and dance in the service of migrant communities' self-defined goals, amid their struggles for recognition.

Freire's major work, *Pedagogy of the Oppressed* (1970), sets forth a foundational opposition between what he termed a liberation and a banking model of knowledge acquisition. In his formulation, the former was based on horizontal dialogues dissolving hierarchically oppressive relationships between educators and students. The latter, on the contrary, reinforced such hierarchies and fostered among students a culture of silence, aimed at naturalizing a social world pervaded by conflicting interests and relations of violence and dominance. Previously published texts by members of Grupo Musicultura have attempted to highlight the singularities and challenges of working under the premises of liberation pedagogy:

In Freire's work conflict and violence are already inscribed in all sorts of oppressive social relations which make knowledge not only hostage to dominant groups, including the dominants among their own kind, but also unviable a priori once any truly theoretical treatment of conflict as a socially produced fact renders impossible the perpetuation of dominance itself. If we dare to summarize Freire's postulates in a single sentence, we perhaps should say that without a radical reconfiguration of the community of knowledge producers in a veritable horizontal fashion one can only hope that conflict and hostility may not stomp onto one's own front yard at any minute—a reality which has grown in people's awareness throughout the globe due to the recent disturbances in Europe's "third world" neighborhoods. (Araújo and members of Grupo Musicultura 2006: 290)

Since then this reference to the changing context of European migrant communities around 2006 proved to be just a pale prediction.

Participatory Research Frameworks in the Social Sciences

With a doctoral degree in sociology from the University of Florida (1955), Orlando Fals Borda, himself of Presbyterian background, became acquainted with action-research methods after World War II, when community-sensitive principles and problem-solving goals were integrated into development policies in Europe and other parts of the world. These methods contributed to sociology a practical, if oftentimes highly contested,[5] dimension. After returning to Colombia and while decisively contributing to the foundation of the country's first sociology department in 1959,[6] at the Universidad Nacional, Bogotá, he became involved in the dramatic political events and debates of the day. Through his thoroughly documented empirical work, he had already aimed to inform policy making on highly sensitive issues such as agrarian reform. This effervescence enabled him to maintain close ties with the progressive ecumenical movement, mainly through a fellow sociology colleague, Father Camilo Torres, a priest with a degree in sociology from the University of Louvain, a reputed Catholic institution in Belgium, whose work aligned with the II VEC currents and echoed its "option for the poor" in Colombia. The death of Camilo Torres in an armed confrontation with government forces in 1966 was one of the driving factors leading Fals Borda to think and write about the shortcomings of revolutionary movements in Latin America. This represented a new turn in his theoretical and methodological perspectives, getting closer to Marxian postulates of non-neutrality in social scientific thought and embracing ideals of fusing theory and practice as praxis. As an effect of a curricular reform in 1968 and under a new directorship, the Sociology Department virtually banned empirical research in favor of regular bibliographic studies of classical sociological literature, that is, authors from Europe and the United States. Fals Borda left the Universidad Nacional and, in 1972, co-founded La Rosca, a foundation for research and action that started to work closely with peasant organizations in land disputes with landowners and struggles to effect the disappropriation of private rural estates for collective use. La Rosca's basic approach consisted of forming research groups with the participation of

professional researchers and activists, including local artists and, very significantly, musicians (Rojas Guerra 2010).[7]

By the early 1970s, Participatory Action Research (PAR) is for Fals Borda the
means of tying knowledge-producing academic engagement organically with
the production of what he called popular science with the aim of changing the
status quo. PAR, he argues, entails, first of all, working on problems and issues
defined by interlocutors, with decision-making processes defined by a given collective, ideally on an equal-vote basis, although this may take a different turn in
contexts subject to other consuetudinary norms. From his experience, as well
as my own, in many if not all situations, horizontal decision-making processes
recognize each individual opinion as equal in principle to any other, but not
that all of them are qualitatively equal. For example, certain individuals, for one
reason or the other, may feel unable to formulate an issue or problem. Others
may not feel well enough informed to prioritize a proposed focus over another
one, while others will fear their stances may collide with those held by other
participants perceived, for one reason or the other, to have a more knowledgeable stance either on particular issues or in general. This complex and endless
process demands a constantly self-critical and ever-evolving method, adjustable
to newer circumstances and newly grasped complexities. In one of Fals Borda's
retrospective accounts, significantly titled "The Problem of Investigating Reality
in Order to Transform It," he assesses the issue in the following manner:

> The most adequate solution came from the dialectical method as applied in
> complementary steps and alternating steps, thus: (1) initiating an exchange be-
> tween known or preconceived ideas and facts (or perceptions of the same) with
> adequate observation of the social milieu; (2) continuing with action at a local
> level so as to confirm in the milieu that which was to be conceptualized; (3) re-
> turning to reflect upon the experimental role in order to detect more adequate
> ideas or shed light on old concepts or theories so as to adapt them to the real
> context; and (4) returning to the beginning of the research action so as to con-
> cretize it in the climax action. These steps came to be carried out in an endless
> manner." (Fals Borda 1979: 39)

As later noted by another Colombian scholar, anthropologist Luis Guillermo
Vasco Uribe, in Fals Borda's work, methodologies should be developed simultaneously out of participatory strategies with this reciprocal and endless feedback
between thinking and action. This fact problematizes general characterizations
of applied research as based on any kind of problem-solving goals, since in many
cases the actual solutions will lay beyond the scope of isolated and time-confined
research experiences. What Fals Borda points at here is how this dialectic should
aim at more complex and locally ingrained enunciations of problems, assessed

systematically on the basis of action results and constantly feeding back new processes as if in a spiral movement. However, argues Vasco Uribe, no matter how more democratic and praxis-based was the intention of Fals Borda and his associates, the subsequent conceptualization of PAR models has been primarily undertaken by academics and school-educated interlocutors whose main task was feeding back such models to the communities they work with.[8] This conceptual work was left then to be carried out systematically by the academics in sessions parallel to the decision-making assemblies, thus maintaining the separation between subject and object. In this manner, criticizes Vasco Uribe, Fals Borda and his associates in PAR initiatives in Colombia fell back into the same dead ends that their, no doubt, more democratic research frameworks aimed to surpass. As part of a newer generation of Colombian researchers also working on participatory, praxis-based frameworks, Vasco Uribe argues that this separation between conceptual and empirical work not only hindered the presumed goals of developing self-determinacy and autonomy among oppressed or subaltern communities but missed the more crucial epistemic difference: the materiality or in-process character of the interlocutors' concepts that the scholars attempted to account for. This in-process character, according to Uribe, exposed the conventional field-and-lab protocols of anthropology as a way of depotentializing self-determinacy and autonomy, and also of pre-empting concepts significant in thought systems other than the rational, objectifying Western model, the only one really counting in academic discourse.[9] Writing in 2002, Vasco Uribe accounted for the merging observed in Colombia in the 1970s between Indigenous struggles and the radical politico-epistemological struggles of local anthropologists, which he saw as quite distinct from those of post-modern anthropologists in the United States: "For us [Colombians], the key question was: How can we achieve a complete transformation of the anthropologist's craft?"(Vasco Uribe 2011: 19).

He did not fail to reassert, however, the most fundamental aspects of Fals Borda's and his associates' formulation of praxis as the central tenet of a renewed discipline:

> For many others . . . practice is still understood simply as a set of material activities, conceived to some degree in isolation from theory. Alternatively, practice is viewed as a collection of purely individual actions, the transformative potential of which is almost nil. These notions are quite distinct from that of transformative practice in the Marxist sense—from what some call "praxis." Based on an erroneous notion of practice, the problem of space is frequently hidden, inexplicit, and peculiarly managed. A specific form of territoriality is created for the purposes of ethnographic research, in which there is a space reserved for practice and a different one for theory." (Vasco Uribe 2002: 21)

But such thoughts are just a prelude to his final urge to move academic research beyond the standards of PAR toward a more radical politico-epistemological change:

> In my opinion, to break with this state of affairs, which impedes the possibility of making room for the knowledge and ways of knowing of popular sectors, we must build upon the act of confrontation (which can also be called dialogue) in the creation of new research techniques and methodologies. The development of these methods must be nourished by the forms of knowledge and theorizing of popular sectors. It is in confrontation with people that both our knowledge and theirs will be validated, refined, and combined to produce concepts, methods, and procedures for activist research (*investigación-acción*), ways of knowing and doing that are novel, creative, and, above all, transformative of reality. In the face of this, the authority and power of the ethnographer are only broken when certain central assumptions are accepted and acted upon in the field:
> - local participants assert control over the research;
> - the ethnographer's opinion is but one of many;
> - the ethnographer's opinion must be discussed with the local participants;
> - local participants formulate their own research proposals;
> - oral narratives are accepted as truth, and not mere discourses." (Vasco Uribe 2002: 28–29)

Not having space enough to pursue much further this commentary here, I will just briefly add that critiques elsewhere in Latin America raised similar issues to Vasco Uribe's stance on fundamental differences between legitimized conceptual work in Euroamerican-centered academia and equivalent, but not the same, intellectual traditions in countries of the Global South. One significant example is the influential theoretical work of a contemporary of his, Brazilian anthropologist Eduardo Viveiros de Castro, based primarily on his research among Indigenous societies. One of his most provoking articles, significantly titled "The Relative Native" (Viveiros de Castro, 2013 [2002]), asks this fundamental and only elusively simple question: what if we take the native seriously?[10]

To Viveiros de Castro, taking other people seriously should mean, as also postulated in a different way by Vasco Uribe, to avoid reducing the terms under which each society and its members pose their problems, in ways that may be irreconcilably different from the way that the culture of anthropologists, and by extension ethnomusicologists, poses its own problems. It may also entail, as asserted by Paulo Freire among others, many other things: developing reciprocity, not charity; being transparent about one's social position and political stances; exercising the difficult art of maintaining a critical distance while strengthening commitment; understanding "field" and "lab" as being reciprocally implicated, that is, inseparable, in a perpetual dialectical relationship rather than as static, objectified spaces or places where one undertakes different tasks; and a permanent, thorough and critical linguistic investigation including both unfamiliar and familiar language usage as a way to "read/listen to the real world."

Conclusion

Having worked intensively with research collectives on issues conceptualized as sound praxis, developing context-sensitive, horizontal approaches that dialogue critically but not exclusively with the ones very briefly summarized in the preceding sections, my particular views on the "pure" vs. "applied" dimensions of research, also asserted in previous publications (Araujo 2008) point simultaneously at their epistemic vagueness, on one hand, and, on the other, their potentially illusionary, manipulatory foundations, privileging an only imagined objectivity at the expense of encumbering concrete subject positions that range from the most laudable to the most despicable.

The presumably self-evident meaning and political correctness implied in terms such as advocacy, engagement, application, collaboration, and others often blur the politically deplorable anti-social, classist, racist, sexist, LGBTphobic, colonialist, and exploitative ends to which such terms may be put, a point made several times in the social sciences (Hale 2007) and by a few of us in the field of ethnomusicology (e.g., Seeger 2008, Araujo 2008, Dirksen 2012). What is one aiming at when invoking such terms to characterize one's research? Strong theoretical and methodological grounds to provoke a sustainable and evolving reversal of social conditions that currently are leading to harsh or even bloody exploitation, disputes, and wars? Or just a vague declaration of good intentions based on an illusory enactment of peace and conciliation at the surface of prolonged and sometimes enhanced injustices, inequalities, and conflict?

If calling research applied—or characterizing it as some sort of advocacy, public, or engaged work—is not in itself a diacritic sign of intrinsically positive outcomes, where do we stand and what should we aim for as an academic field that is in search of, not only studying the world in abstract, but concretely changing it toward better, horizontally negotiated standards of social equality and justice, ecological balance, and relatively peaceful coexistence? Is there a role, and which role might that be, for a field of knowledge production such as ethnomusicology, particularly when institutionally maintained by public funding? Isn't the fetishized use of presumably politically correct terminology obscuring rather than clarifying what ideally any ethnomusicology should in principle be: a committed, critical engagement with human difference that goes beyond false dichotomies between theory and practice and demands from all scholars of music and sound deep thinking about the reciprocal implications of both theory and practice as praxis?

The stance taken here argues that no adjectives (applied, advocacy, engaged, public, etc.) are needed to properly qualify politically engaged scholarship in ethnomusicology, if one takes as the field's mission, as Vincenzo Cambria (2008) has argued, the study of difference through conceptualizations of music and sound, in many if not most circumstances framed by inequality, exploitation, and injustice. As we have seen, a similar point has been made by anthropologist Eduardo Viveiros de Castro, urging his field to take difference seriously, by taking seriously, and not condescendingly, as also remarked by Paulo Freire, its interlocutors' conceptual frameworks, and refusing to domesticate them under the scholar's own conceptual references or to confound the latter with the former, as in many attempts at translating "the native mind." In this sense, to acknowledge the political dimensions of knowledge production is to work in the midst of a permanent relational tension among subjects, acknowledging the distinct conceptual apparatuses and action tools everyone uses to make sense of their lived, real-world experience.

Notes

1. This text is an extended version of a shorter paper presented in the plenary session Power and Real World Intervention, held during the Forum "Transforming Ethnomusicological Praxis Through Activism and Community Engagement," the first academic event ever co-organized by the Society for Ethnomusicology (SEM) and the International Council for Traditional Music (ICTM). The presentation was shared with other two, given respectively by colleagues Tan Sooi Beng and Ana Hofman, in a session mediated by Deborah Wong. To the three of them, my deepest appreciation for the rich discussions generated by the panel. The contents of the article mainly result from an ongoing participatory action-research initiative in Brazil, jointly conducted by the author, students at the Federal University of Rio de Janeiro, and residents of one of Rio's largest favela areas under a grant (PQ1) awarded by the National Council for Scientific Research and Development (CNPq), 2014–2018. Additional perspectives on the ways Participatory Action Research strategies may work in other contexts have been made possible by a CAPES-FCT grant, 2014–2016, for a project jointly carried out with a research collective led by Professor Susana Sardo at the University of Aveiro, Portugal, and integrated with research by, among others, Dr. Ana Flavia Miguel, Rui Oliveira, Celso Lopes, Fred Cabral, and Ricardo Cabral, focusing on the Cova da Moura neighborhood in Lisbon.
2. "The term 'epistemic community' refers to a collective of people—including, for instance, ethnomusicologists, musicians, community members, or people from other disciplines—who work together toward solving and analyzing a particular problem or issue-area whose terms are epistemologically defined." (Harrison 2012: 506).

3. See also Shelemay (2013) for a thorough discussion of how complex ethical concerns in humanistic research may be.

4. These are two influential narratives on a self-perceived crisis of representation produced in the 1980s North American anthropological milieu but their theses were not necessarily endorsed nor, when partially acknowledged, as much impacting in other regional and national contexts, in a few cases having antecedents ignored in so-called mainstream scholarship, as we shall see later in this text.

5. Seen as a potential disguise for CIA spying and US propaganda.

6. Today's Faculty of Social Sciences of Universidad Nacional de Colombia is named after Orlando Fals Borda.

7. Worth noticing here is Fals Borda's own training and practice as a choral conductor in the Presbyterian context he was raised in. Such capacity apparently allowed him to make his own transcriptions and analyses of local musical repertoires, supporting some of his writings about histories of given peasant communities.

8. In an influential article on applied/public ethnomusicology, Dan Sheehy (1992) stresses feeding back communities with models they can put into use as one of the main goals of the field.

9. It should be noticed, nonetheless, that Fals Borda's already mentioned article (Fals Borda 1997) devotes its first section to show how the rationalistic, objectifying Western sciences and philosophies have always maintained links with the empirical conditionings of their existence in time and space.

10. Viveiros de Castro's formulation may be, of course, contrasted to and even contested by the expanding body of Indigenous theory being produced worldwide. On the other hand, one might argue his question still holds validity if one starts to wonder about on what level and to what extent has this reality actually changed the political economy of the academic milieu, beyond what some scholar have labeled "tokenism."

4

Silenced Registers of Ethnomusicological Academic Labor under Neoliberalism

Ana Hofman

We are gathered around the computer on the first floor of the municipal building in Maré, the second biggest favela in Rio de Janeiro. A group of people is dedicated to the same goal: to complete the revision of the latest version of a collectively written piece by Musicultura group about music and violence in pacified Maré, already accepted for publication.[1] While carefully following the process and occasionally participating in a lively debate, one thought constantly nags me: in the current criteria for academic excellence as it is set down in Slovenia, where I come from, this collective endeavor would be considered "invisible" academic labor. That does not mean that we do not practice collaborative research or are not dedicated to community work, but in the current radical reshaping of the practices of academic labor, such an engagement, although ostensibly present, is gradually pushed away from the horizon of our professional landscape. The allocation of public funds is based on quantitative criteria, which include, apart from the assessment of external funding acquired by scholars, points collected from publications and citations in the last five years. In my professional setting, one of the most important aspects of collaborative research—co-authorship with our research partners (see Araújo 2006)—is increasingly being replaced by an emphasis on co-authorship among academics to raise the metrics of productivity. That means that I could hardly afford to participate in a collectively written piece by Musicultura since it would not bring me any points.[2] In such an academic setting, only producing research that is goal-oriented, measurable, and assessed by peers enables my survival in the academic market.

I deeply believe that the conditions just described here are not merely national or Europe-specific, but reflect global tendencies in reshaping the academic field. Such tendencies relate to the precarization of the academic labor force; less governmental funding, especially in the arts and humanities; competitiveness due to the lack of funding; the accelerating pace of work; and scientific production[3] governed by funding structures and consequently the loss of researchers' autonomy. All these tendencies are deeply involved in the construction of the neoliberal academic subjectivity, which is a result of the process of the

Ana Hofman, *Silenced Registers of Ethnomusicological Academic Labor under Neoliberalism*
In: *Transforming Ethnomusicology*. Edited by: Beverley Diamond and Salwa El-Shawan Castelo-Branco, Oxford University Press (2021). © Oxford University Press. DOI: 10.1093/oso/9780197517550.003.0005

commodification of academia through profit-oriented policies (Barry, Chandler & Clark 2001).[4] Strongly influenced by my experience with the Musicultura group, I started rethinking my own position as an academic in the current transformation of patterns of academic labor, commodification, and precarization, each of which is a subject in every subsection of this article. Specifically, I aim to demonstrate how the current process of the neoliberalization of academia made it necessary to direct our attention toward the role of ethnomusicology as *knowledge-production labor*. I believe that in current discussions about new modes of academic professionalism led by public interest groups (see McIntosh 2013), and a need for a new knowledge economy in ethnomusicology (see, e.g., Harrison, Mackinlay & Pettan 2010), it is important to shift the focus from the constant emphasis on the collaborative relationships with our social partners. Instead, I argue that the claims for alternative knowledge production cannot be made without challenging the relations of power at the very site of knowledge production and the material conditions of our ethnomusicological labor. Inspired by Michel Foucault's lecture on how philosophers rarely deal with their own *actualité*,[5] in this article, I would like to address the *actualité* of ethnomusicologists' living reality as academic laborers. I pose the following questions, which I believe can contribute to critical debates about twenty-first-century ethnomusicologies and their potential futures: How can we discuss a more diverse, critical, and impactful future for ethnomusicology in the sense of the "self-transformation" and "self-emancipation" of the discipline as institutional practice and academic labor? How do current transformations of labor for scholars ubiquitously reshape the very notion and practice of public-oriented scholarship and the praxis of "applied ethnomusicology"?

Knowledge Application: A View from the Neoliberal Periphery

Discussing ethnomusicology's (self-)positioning as a discipline, Maureen Mahon and other participants at the SEM President's Roundtable 2012 in New Orleans expressed anxiety about the visibility and audibility of ethnomusicology, the relevance of its subject matter, and reasons other scholars do not engage with our ideas or cite our writings as much as we might wish. They said it was important to reflect on how we choose our academic topics and which subjects are "worth" addressing in academia (see Mahon 2014: 329). Apart from this example, scholarly accounts rather rarely discuss the organizational structure and the institutional and funding politics that constitute the production of knowledge.[6] The global economic crisis that started in 2008 accelerated changes in many aspects of the academic landscape, exacerbating the already existing precarity of academic labor, and the reduction of education to vocational training. As a result of the decline in direct government funding, many European public higher education and research institutions have been compelled to seek new sources of income. This increases the emphasis on the commodification of academic inquiry and makes the university simultaneously a site of capital accumulation and dispossession. Such "austerity management" has also produced more visible symbolic and financial gaps between market-useful disciplines (particularly in the field of STEM—science, technology, engineering, and mathematics) and less market-relevant disciplines (such as the arts and humanities). In the context of what can be called accelerating academic capitalism (see Slaughter & Larry 1997, Slaughter & Rhoades 2004), the economic role of universities has become focal and universities are increasingly evaluated from an economic perspective (Ylijoki 2010: 367).[7] As a result of that stance, some authors insist on using the term "neoliberalization" rather than neoliberalism (see Peck & Tickell 2002: 463). Following that, I approach the neoliberalization of academia as a multifaceted and continually changing set of processes—both ideological and structural—that take different forms in different environments.

The post-socialist context of Slovenia shows a number of the paradoxical (dis)continuities, challenges, and consequences of present tendencies with some locally or nationally specific features that influence the daily work and lives of students and academic and administrative staff in different ways. A comparative study we completed within the GARCIA project[8] shows that the economic crisis caused more radical cuts in public funding and that the academic field is from 2011 onward under the greatest pressure of economic constrains (Černič Istenič et al. 2014). Since higher education and research were exclusively state-funded during socialism and rare private institutions started emerging only from 2000 on, the currently increasing trend is to adjust to a corporate model in which research is increasingly treated as a business (Kolšek & Gregorc 2011). Existing public research institutes[9] (like the one in which I am currently employed) depend almost entirely on short-term "project financing," since the small amount of more stable program funding (for up to six years) cannot cover the salaries of all the employed researchers. In practice, this means that the main source of funding is external, usually through EU programs or the market. Researchers are forced to "take care" of their own salaries like any other entrepreneurs, which does not leave scope for a more devoted kind of academic engagement or, especially, for societal commitment that is critical or that runs counter to mainstream research practices. Rhetoric of "opening" the arts and humanities to transnational and transdisciplinary frameworks often masks requirements for third-party fundraising, and processes of rigid evaluation, and assessment of academic excellence based on a criterion of hyper-productivity (publications, mobility, and both international and local network memberships).[10]

Although interpreted differently in different disciplinary communities and institutional contexts, these structural transformations have serious implications for researchers' subjectivities, particularly those in their early careers who face growing and often conflicting expectations, pressures, and demands (Acker & Armenti 2004, Deem 2003). Epistemic autonomy and producing reflective knowledge become increasingly difficult, as there is less time for it in an increasingly competitive and profit-driven social-economic system. This leads to what Robert Hassan calls "abbreviated thinking" and instrumental knowledge focused on the here-and-now (2003: 237). Such trends are in opposition with main postulates of the humanities (and ethnomusicology) as a self-reflective praxis (Araújo 2009), which points out that we should understand ethnomusicology as a form of political work or intervention in which failures and obstacles are equally or even more important than successful projects or research outcomes (see Seeger 2008, Araújo 2009). Conditions for practicing such forms of knowledge intervention in the Slovenian academic environment are challenging as they are not credited in any way that would aid survival in the academic market.[11] Ethnomusicology, which has received institutional recognition in a majority of North American and European universities,[12] still struggles for its place in higher education and research structures in Slovenia as it is not formally recognized as a discipline by the national research agency and is under the pressure of further marginalization. This is particularly the case when ethnomusicology is an elective or represented by just one faculty member or precarious researchers with short-term contracts, which increases the discipline's institutional fragility.[13]

The Precarity of the Academic Labor Force and Applied Work

Recently, several studies focused on the precarious status of professional musicians, the reality of their working conditions, and the stratification between the successful ones who incur all the privileges of the music market, on the one hand, and the ones who suffer because of their lower profile/status, on the other (see, e.g., Stokes 2002, Stahl 2012, Sakakeeny 2013, 2015, *MUSICultures* special issue "Music and Labour," 41, no. 1 [2014]). Many scholarly accounts also address the role of musicians' professional associations in struggles against their precarious position and examine their tendencies toward unionization (Williamson & Cloonan 2016, Vidmar 2017), their everyday life, working practices and economic status, as well as their position as immaterial laborers (Hofman 2015), also in the post-recording, digitalized music market (see Hesmondhalgh & Baker 2011). However, while theorizing musicians as laborers and analyzing their precarious labor conditions, scholars rarely discuss their position as a part of the global struggles of precarious immaterial laborers, which would include reflexive accounts of the economic situation of the researchers themselves. In the European context in many cases, ethnomusicologists, particularly at the early-career stage, share the fate of professional musicians and other precarious workers, unable to stand up for themselves because of the lack of union support or political representation.[14]

In the last two decades, European universities have witnessed radical growth in the number of academics working on short-term employment contracts. As highlighted by the *Draft Report on Atypical Contracts, Secured Professional Paths, Flexicurity and New Forms of Social Dialogue* (European Parliament 2010) we ascertain: a general decline of wages, the casualization of work, the deregulation of workers' benefits and social programs, and a stagnating rate of unionization. In Slovenia, the number of temporary contracts increased after the introduction of the Act to Restore Public Finances in 2012. According to this Act, universities and research organizations cannot replace retired academic staff with new employees.[15] Therefore, temporary contracts become the prevailing form of employment for academics in early career stages. The statistical data from 2012 show that in Slovenia, for those aged less than forty-four, 86 percent of male PhDs and 88.5 percent of female PhDs are employed temporarily (Černič Istenič 2017: 63), which also proves a gendered aspect of precarity. One of the factors that led to the precarization of academic staff was the "Bologna system," which resulted in massive access to PhD degrees. Research institutions try to obtain a maximum number of doctoral students, while the number of permanent academic posts and permanent higher education positions are not in proportion to the rising number of PhDs and postdocs. This is the case especially in the humanities, where employability in non-academic sectors (such as industry for the STEM graduates) is less likely (for a cross-European comparison including Slovenia, see Dubois-Shaik & Fusulier 2015: 214). Doctoral and postdoctoral students thus increasingly grasp at temporary job opportunities and become a cheap source of teaching staff and are not given any institutional permanence or affiliation; they are sometimes even classified as administrative and technical staff, as in Italy or Switzerland (Dubois-Shaik & Fusulier 2016: 13).

Yet in line with neoliberal logic, career instability in academia entails a singular paradox. On the one hand, the instability of work is countered by greater flexibility and autonomy in the management of working hours. Flexibility makes this profession attractive, despite associated difficulties for those who have extra-professional care duties. On the other hand, salaries for researchers are often much lower and their unstable working conditions may continue for long periods before eventual (but not certain) professional stabilization. Paradoxically, the post-doctoral position that should be a transitional period is prolonged for an unlimited period and early-career scholars continue to perform "invisible" labor.

The idea of nomadic subjects, which has been often romanticized through the narrative of "independent professionals," is a buzzword for constant instability, part-time contracts, and professional identity that is adaptive, flexible, open, and opportunistic, as pointed out by Sennett (1998). New graduates entering the job market are advised to be flexible, able to adapt to shifting conditions, and to cultivate business skills and entrepreneurial thinking as they enter the dynamic sector. As Ana-María Alarcón-Jaménez writes in the issue of the SEM Student News dedicated to the job market: "Hiring conditions in temporary job contracts make it quite hard for people my age to start up a new chapter in life, and after almost fifteen years of traveling around [...] to live in the same place for a long period of time seems like a sweet but unattainable dream" (Alarcón-Jaménez 2016).

The case of Slovenian research institutes shows that the neoliberalization of working conditions and academic culture has led researchers to become "traders with knowledge" (Rizman 2014: 457). The economic, social, and cultural relevance of research is organized around two axes: the legitimation of inequality as the natural effect of competition and a shift toward the notion of human capital and entrepreneurship. As mentioned, researchers are expected to be responsible for their own existence and to adjust to the enterprising spirit of the "new, dynamic economy." This illustrates a more general neoliberal setting in which, as Lazzarato asserts, workers are not even any longer workers—manufacturers of value—but competitive, individualized human capital (2009). The increasing competition between institutions and departments as well as the reduction of cooperation and solidarity in the struggle for limited funding unveils the complex issue of growing inequality in the academic environment. An overall emphasis on "competition" over collaboration secures privilege for higher-positioned scholars, top universities, and scientific fields with good services that are able to access funding. Researchers who enjoy the "privilege" of stable employment often lack understanding for the ones employed in a short-term position, who are considered "low-class" academics (Nikolaidis & Maroudas 2013: 137). Due to the growing inequality among academic staff, a relatively homogenous group of a small number of professors (often still white and male) enjoys the "privilege" of tenure and is often unaware of the situations of colleagues in unstable and short-term positions who are not able to advocate for themselves. In Deborah Wong's words, this derives from "the political economies of uneven access to resources and the intervention of education (and performance) into those economies" (2006: 263). Inequalities further weaken the coherence of the academic community and the possibility of collective resistance to new policies. Instead of resistance to these ideologies, values, and policies, academics are pressured to choose compromise and cooptation.

In other words, an emphasis on productivity and competitiveness makes it nearly impossible to navigate between building an academic career and simultaneously confronting the hegemonic structures of academic labor. As a consequence of instability, the work of precarious academics is often fragmented and externally scheduled with few opportunities for profound and long-term research. What is considered desirable behavior for researchers is shaped by the dominant norms of academic excellence as well as by standards of scholarly productivity, the publish-or-perish culture, and the marginalization of non-commodified research. The imperative of continuously proving one's merit for the potential renewal of contracts makes early career academics struggle with overwork and hyper-productivity. The conditions often result in burnout, anxiety, isolation, and trouble managing family life and work load at the same time (particularly an issue for female academics). Constant struggles for survival in the academic market undoubtedly prevents the development of critical thought and diminishes the possibility of socially engaged academic work.

Moreover, the precarization of academic labor reshapes knowledge production and erodes academic freedom. Tenure or a stable position are factors that provide economic stability that also guarantees a certain level of academic freedom (Stergiou & Somarakis 2016). As many scholars have confessed, undertaking socially and politically engaged research prior to tenure proves to be extremely difficult. Working on politically sensitive topics or confronting governments, political parties, corporations, or administrative bodies is far less possible before obtaining tenure or a professorship, since political commitment and open activism can greatly impact successful career development. Neoliberalization of academia requires exclusive and undivided loyalty from researchers, and this is why any attempt by the precarious academic subject to be involved in socially engaged work involves ethical, methodological, and strategic dilemmas and challenges. And if we understand "applied" as a social activist agenda, as Dan Bendrups proposed (2015: 74) or, as Anthony Seeger has asserted, if more ethnomusicologists see their future in becoming public activists and intellectuals (2008: 272), we should face the consequences of the increasing precarization of the academic labor force and reconsider the role of academia as a catalyst of social intervention.

Applied vs. "Applied": Ethnomusicology under the Pressure of Applicability

As mentioned in the previous sections, public research institutions in Slovenia (particularly in the arts and humanities) are faced with limited national research funds, which forces them to look for other funding possibilities, mainly for short-term projects. This makes researchers to be transformed into what can be called a "projectariat" (evoking both "precariat" and "proletariat"). The most important source of funding is "applicative projects" (e.g., INTERREG or HORIZON EU programms), whose goals are to produce fast and superficial applicative knowledge that can be used in solving already recognized "concrete societal problems" (see Fakin Bajec & Sitar 2017). Project durations are usually up to three years, in which one year is dedicated to problem identification and knowledge providing, while other phases are reserved for implementation. The main motivation behind the trend to shift research development policies toward applied research is that knowledge produced within academia is not adequately or profitably exploited (Economakis, Maroudas& Kyriakidou, in Nikolaidis & Maroudas 2013: 139).[16] Consortiums of project partners must include local municipalities, start-up firms, local community representatives, NGOs, and so forth, shifting understanding of researchers as knowledge producers to the position of consultant, described in the term "knowledge providers." Research activities within these types of "applied projects" do not include long-term research or in-depth scholarly publications. In relation to this problem as she faces it in her own work, Naila Ceribašić writes: "The primacy of the former scientific presentation of researched communities and music in the form of scientific studies increasingly displaces various types of professional accounts on this and that—from writing proposals of scientific projects, through self-analysis, strategic and action plans and related documents in the system of science and higher education, to the elaboration and expertise for various clients in the culture and economy" (2015: 198–199).

The fact that "the application of academic knowledge" or producing a "socially responsible knowledge" are the goals most emphasized in national and European research programs reveals a complex rearticulation of how we understand and practice applied scholarship. Moreover, I would argue that processes of neoliberalization in academia fundamentally reshape the core of what applied scholarship should mean. I would like to claim that we face what Jacques Rancière defines as "a critical dissensus" (Rancière 1999) about what applicative knowledge is. Critical dissensus is the term he uses to mark a difference within what is the same and a sameness of opposites (Bowman & Stamp 2011: 2), which in this case is not a conflict between two opposite meanings of applied scholarship, but the conflict about what "applied" *is*. Instead of the dichotomies between "pure/impure," "practical/theoretical," "inside/outside academia" that are usually in question when considering the new public profile of ethnomusicology, I believe that there is a deeper dynamic at work, one related to changing working environments and ethnomusicological professional identities, visible in:

1) A lack of agency of academic laborers to frame the dominant concepts and categories, when constructions of research come from "outside" (funders and legislators).

2) As a result of the first, dwindling scope for critical thinking because the role of professional academics is shifting from knowledge producers to knowledge providers who do not question power structures. Such a shift also diminishes existing diversity and the potential pluralism of research done within the institutionalized framework.

Both claims reflect the structural flaw that does not enable alternative knowledge production, which can provide ethnomusicology with a way out of the conceptualizations of "applied scholarship" that go hand in hand with neoliberal politics. As a result, applied ethnomusicology, in order to consolidate its place within the "purist" academy has to go in line with the profit-oriented demands of industry. This view has been posited by Williams, who argues that profit-driven motivations are not antithetical to "either performing musicians *or* the research academic" (Williams 2015: 798) and argues for the role of applied scholars as facilitators between various parties, such as communities, performers, promoters, corporations, and cultural policy makers.

What I think we should be careful about is that this kind of societal need for an "applied" knowledge economy leaves little room for critical thinking or research that proposes in-depth and sustained socio-political engagement as knowledge-producing praxis. On the surface, in terms of the institutional academic environment the distinction between academic and applied work seems to be less sharp than it once was, diminishing the existing diversity and pluralism of knowledge application. On the one hand, we can hardly say that there is something wrong with producing applicative knowledge to develop solutions to concrete problems; and many such projects have concrete outcomes and can be socially beneficial. Yet on the other hand, this tendency promotes one specific conceptualization of application and particular modes of knowledge production, without critical consideration of the very condition under which knowledge is produced, the relation with the funders or sponsors, the possibility of failure or critical analysis of the social benefits of the "results." Such a neoliberal goal-oriented understanding and valuing of knowledge application corrupts academia as a space of collaborative and autonomous critical knowledge production. Moreover, it further pushes applied scholarship under the influence of employability that is dictated and restricted to profit-driven goals. Ceribašić asserts that the quest for applied knowledge did not come simply as a result of humanism, but as a sustainability strategy under the conditions of market pressure in the humanities from the 1990s on. She discusses the ambiguity of knowledge application when presented as the prospective goal of academic activity (Ceribašić 2015: 187) and as the requirement in the current neoliberalization of academia, which, to a large extent, is silenced in most ethnomusicological writings.[17] Taking into account current global changes in academic labor,[18] we can go further and say that both "typical" (academic) and "alternative" (applied work in the public or private sector) are both increasingly structured by the commercialization of the discipline.

Therefore, although the general trend of applicability tended to be presented as a multifaceted and dynamic praxis of producing socially engaged knowledge, it has turned out that one particular type of knowledge is the most valued: the profit-led one. It also proves fundamental to address a condition in which we can be "applied," yet politically disempowered. This means a danger that applied scholarship might close the very field it wants to open: social engagement is also a concept on the neoliberal horizon, where insistence on applied knowledge prevails. Because of that, the field of "applied" knowledge could easily be neutralized as merely a "place" from which you can say, act, and behave "against," but without any serious consequences to the power structures (Gržinić & Tatlić 2014: xi).

Toward a Politics of Vulnerability and Self-Organizing Ethnomusicology

At the end of the 1990s and the beginning of the 2000s, a strong movement toward socially engaged scholarship and activism started in US academia. As Radder points out, scholars opened a debate about forms and formations of research, pedagogy, praxis, and activism (2010). Ethnomusicology was a part of that emergent movement, predominantly by promoting multiculturalism in curricula and public policy as practice-oriented action (Titon 1992: 315). Scholars discussed how ethnomusicology should be included in the mission to critically reconfigure academic praxis toward a socially engaged university (see Usner 2010). A gradual shift from the university as a nonprofit entity to a corporate one thus brought the need to think in the framework of what John Brewer articulated as the "new public social science" or "public interest science" (see Brewer 2013 and Krimsky 2003).

However, in the last decade, many critical voices have warned that academia as a center of criticism is increasingly enlisted in the service of the status quo and that "autonomous science" is not an empirical reality. Studies of corporate and neoliberal academia (see Etzkowitz 1998, 2004, Ziman 2000, Bok 2003, Slaughter & Rhoades 2004, Resnik 2007, Hessels & van Lente 2008, Montgomery & Oliver 2009) assert that major decisions that affect the organization and nature of the university and research are based primarily on economic criteria. We know that funding policies have always shaped the methodological procedures, appraisals, and questions of scientific inquiry. In the neoliberal periphery of post-Yugoslav societies that I come from, however, we often hear that the current model of public higher education and research is unsustainable, which is used by elites in power as an excuse for privatization. The privatization of higher education is not simply an economic matter, but an ideological, representational, and symbolic undertaking, which opens new relations between knowledge production and power. As Titon writes about the US academia, the core of the false separation between academic versus applied ethnomusicology has to do with the isolation of private universities from public life in the United States, while public institutions are constantly threatened by budget cuts that also keep them from engaging further with the existing society (2014). And if one of the goals of ethnomusicological praxis is a path toward the transformation of the ivory tower, with professional ethnomusicologists as gatekeepers, we should critically examine the material practices of academic labor, particularly in the light of increasing privatization of higher education and research in Southeastern Europe.

This article does not offer a solution but rather calls scholars to encounter and rethink the global transformations that radically reshape what applied ethnomusicology is and should be. Drawing on Wong's inspiring deliberation of usually unspoken dimensions of ethnomusicologists' lives in music departments when she also reveals the powerful conceptual distinction between anger and frustration, in which the former has a strong potential for being used as a "politicized response" (2006: 273), I believe that we should openly express our anger about the material condition of academic labor as an important part of our "applied" work.[19] I argue for the importance of taking an active stance on the challenges we face as academic laborers: a kind of exposing/displaying of our vulnerability.[20] Sharing personal struggles, feelings, and strategies can help us to mobilize our vulnerability in shaping collective strategies to question the current conditions, concepts, and practices of knowledge production. To practice critical and emancipatory ethnomusicology, we have to take a position of shared responsibility and extend debates about the conditions of academic labor. And these debates should include not only the unstable and dangerous environments when it comes to research and fieldwork (Rice 2014: 192), but also our basic working conditions—as exhausted academics with temporal and underpaid contracts. This requires that we make alliances across disparate and fragmented voices within academia, since "runaway contingency has left all of us vulnerable" (Nelson 2015: 17). Sharing this vulnerability can be a step toward what Polanyi defines as a "self-governing science" (1962) or even as ethnomusicology as self-organized praxis and non-neutral, "self-interested science" (Pels 2003).

This contribution is constrained by the various conditions it describes. The time management of my own early-career precarious position in the institutional framework where ethnomusicology is unrecognized as a discipline and has an institutionally marginalized status, a working migrant and the mother of a seven-year-old daughter, my everyday experience of academic labor and growing time pressure when it comes to the gendered practices of work, all greatly influence the quality of this contribution. I am also obliged to note that this chapter is published as a result of two EU-funded projects, R&I PEERS and ACT. I tendentiously do not put these words in the acknowledgment section. They close this text in order to contribute to more open reflection on our vulnerabilities as academic laborers, but also to rethink our possibilities of action.

Notes

1. See the Vortex Music Journal of the University of Paraná, *Revista Vórtex* 3, no. 2, edited by Laize Guazina. Thanks to Samuel Araújo and all the other members of Musicultura and the Laboratory for Ethnomusicology for our intensive and fruitful exchange during my three-month research visit at the School of Music of the Federal University of Rio de Janeiro as a fellow of the State Research Agency of Rio de Janeiro (FAPERJ).

2. In the current criteria for measuring academic excellence in Slovenia, writing an article or book chapter with more than three people gives the researcher approximately the same number of points as one conference paper presentation.

3. I do not use the term science exclusively in relation to physical or natural sciences, but as a synonym for the academic field or academia, as it is used in this way in the European context.

4. The claim that commodification of academia has particularly increased in the past decade does not imply that academia as "pure" and unaffected by economic forces ever existed at all, as Hans Radder asserts (2010: 9–10).

5. See: Michel Foucault—The Culture of the Self, First Lecture, https://www.youtube.com/watch?v=CaXb8c6jw0k.

6. With the exception of Deborah Wong's (2006) and Jeff Todd Titon's contributions on his Sustainablemusic blog (see: http://sustainablemusic.blogspot.si).

7. While speaking of the neoliberal academy, I do not intend to essentialize as it is necessary to differentiate between different academic institutions and national higher education and research systems. The authors of the special issue of the journal *Anuac* 5, no. 1 (2016) titled "Anthropologists in/of the Neoliberal Academy" assert that we should go beyond a general understanding of neoliberalism as a generic trend and focus on "various ways in which policy changes are introduced and managed, at times accommodated but sometimes resisted, subverted, or challenged by different subjects according to their visions of the university's purpose" (Heatherington & Zerilli 2016: 42).

8. GARCIA (Gendering Academy and Research: Combating Career Instability and Asymmetries, http://garciaproject.eu) is the EU-funded project in which I was involved as a leader of the Slovenian research team. In the course of the project (2014-2017), quantitative and qualitative analysis provided a comprehensive overview of the gendered aspects of labor conditions (particularly of early-career academics) in the seven European countries involved in the project (Austria, Belgium, Iceland, Italy, the Netherlands, Slovenia, Switzerland). The qualitative analysis was based on more than two hundred interviews (with men and women in the social sciences and

humanities, excluding the arts) conducted among two target sub-groups: postdocs and newly tenured researchers/academics (both those who are still employed in higher education and research organizations and those who have left), who expressed their current experience of academic labor conditions.

9. Predominantly research-oriented institutions.

10. For a recent debate about inter- and intradisciplinarity, and decoloniality, see Ceribašić (2019).

11. Anthony Seeger already warned us that applied projects by academics are dwindling, since it is difficult to have them endorsed in accordance with established scholarly criteria (Seeger 2006).

12. For institutional conflicts that ethnomusicologists experienced and the struggles for the place of ethnomusicology in higher education during the 1990s, see Wong (2006).

13. About the status of ethnomusicology in Slovenia, see Hofman (2019).

14. For more general discussion on precarity of early career academic laborers, see Teeuwen and Hantke (2007), Armano and Murgia (2013).

15. On recruitment and promotion policies in Slovenia, see Knežević-Hočevar, Petrović, and Hofman (2015).

16. In the volume of *Ethnomusicology* dedicated to public policy, Jeff Todd Titon argued already in 1992 against this claim, calling it misleading (Titon 1992: 316).

17. Although I do not completely agree with her critique of issues of authoritative voice and the expected goals of applied research.

18. Further impact caused by Covid-19 pandemic is yet to be seen.

19. The editors of the column "The State of the Field" in the 2016 volume of *SEM Student News* acknowledged that, although they usually receive numerous submissions, for the issue dedicated to finding paths in the job market, students hesitated to discuss their stances on ethnomusicological training for fear that that would jeopardize their career once they enter the job market (Hunter 2016: 5).

20. I do not see vulnerability as something that should be overcome, but draw on Judith Butler's approach to the politics of vulnerability (see Butler 2014).

5

Sonic Mapping and Critical Citizenship

Reflections on LimerickSoundscapes

Aileen Dillane and Tony Langlois

Ethnomusicology has long been concerned with how and why people make music and, in more recent times, with sound environments, moving beyond traditional definitions of what constitutes music in/as culture or as "humanly organized sound" (Blacking 1973). For some time, ethnomusicology has been moving away from generating data and ethnographies solely for knowledge consolidation within the archive and exchange within the academy. The discipline now also embraces research that is applied outside of academic contexts in very tangible ways, through working with communities who determine how best such knowledge can serve those at the center of a project. In this chapter, we push at the borders of what it is that ethnomusicologists study, moving decisively toward sound, and, by extension, seek to expand what counts as applied ethnomusicology (Pettan & Titon 2015). We do so by championing an interdisciplinary approach to better understand and harness the sonic environments of people living in a multi-ethnic, post-industrial city in order to create a framework for a critical, participatory citizenship that has social awareness at its core. Such research is timely, given the unprecedented movement of people, particularly economic migrants and refugees, as we strive for new ways to shape public and political discourses about migration (Haynes et al. 2016) in order to counter discrimination. With the rise of neoliberal agendas, often with concomitant policies of austerity, the resilience and rights of less privileged classes are being severely tested, with social, political, and economic disenfranchisement on the rise. Through creative, enabling collaborations that give people an opportunity to come to know and appreciate the Other and to find ways to actively engage with their locality in order to channel their positive transformative agency, Applied Ethnomusicology has the capacity both to intervene and contribute to community building, a reflexive social awareness, and vibrant citizenship. These are lofty aspirations for "mere" ethnomusicologists, perhaps, but as Jeff Todd Titon has pointed out, "we are meddlers" and "experimenters" and are "committed to putting ethnomusicological knowledge and insight to practical use . . . guided by values" (Titon 2015: 158).

Aileen Dillane and Tony Langlois, *Sonic Mapping and Critical Citizenship* In: *Transforming Ethnomusicology.*
Edited by: Beverley Diamond and Salwa El-Shawan Castelo-Branco, Oxford University Press (2021). © Oxford University
Press. DOI: 10.1093/oso/9780197517550.003.0006

This chapter reflects upon an ongoing project conceived in the socioeconomic and political context of Limerick City in the southwest of Ireland, which has undergone considerable social, economic, and demographic upheaval in the past twenty years. LimerickSoundscapes is, in the simplest of terms, a sound-mapping project generated *by* and *for* the citizens of Limerick, which takes form, at least in one iteration, as an online interactive website.[1] It is also a project, we believe, that is capable of being modeled elsewhere in terms of its aspiration to mobilize citizen sound recordists in order that they might creatively engage with their urban environment in a shared project of "doing," while concurrently generating a wealth of sound data for a variety of potential usages as determined by these collectors, now and into the future.[2]

Here, we outline the origins and underlying principles of this interdisciplinary project, first, by placing it in its local context, considering the importance of sounds for people living in the city. We then discuss our intellectual scaffolding, clarifying the ways in which LimerickSoundscapes draws inspiration from urban ethnomusicology, urban studies, and sound studies, and compare and contrast the project's approach with other soundscape initiatives. We then describe the 2013 pilot project in detail, from recruitment process to the generation of the first sound files. This pilot project culminated in the drafting of a model for further application in Limerick and potentially elsewhere. Here, we underscore not only the importance of the sound data collected but also, in particular, the notion of an active and participatory citizenship to which the project aspires, undergirded by critical, pedagogical concerns. We conclude with a reflection on the project to date, emphasizing the importance of the "doing" and of the applied dimension of such work; on our openness to seeing the project evolve with partners; and on our hopes for its resilience into the future.

Origins and Premise of LimerickSoundscapes

In the summer of 2013, members of the recently formed LimerickSoundscapes research cluster, an interdisciplinary, university-based team involving ethnomusicologists, sociologists, media and information technology specialists, and soundscape composers, initiated a small soundscapes pilot project in the city of Limerick.[3] A small, multi-cultural and post-industrial city with a heritage extending back to Viking settlements in 812, Limerick has had a tumultuous social, political, and economic history. The city is currently undergoing a (stalled) process of government-sponsored, urban regeneration following decades of social challenges, including high unemployment rates, rapid demographic shifts brought about by global migration, social disenfranchisement in marginalized neighborhoods, gangland criminality, and considerable stigmatization by national media (Devereux et al. 2011). Limerick's largest university, the University of Limerick, is located in a relatively affluent suburban neighborhood. Viewed primarily as a science and technology university with partnerships oriented more toward industry, research, and development, the university has consciously sought to engage with the city and its citizens in more meaningful ways.[4] It is from this crucible and socio-historical context that the LimerickSoundscapes project gradually emerged, bringing together researchers with different skill sets, disciplinary backgrounds, and varying interests in sounds and/or people.

The basic premise of the research perspective of the project was and remains quite simple, informed by those disciplines involved in its conception, as we outline shortly. Sound is cultural (Bull & Back 2003, Erlmann 2004), so the sonic realm is therefore an ideal medium for exploring various productions, interpretations, and creative imaginings of place as sensuous, geographic space, and place as social order and social relations (Cohen 1995). Such factors as ethnic background and social class are likely to influence not only the sounds of a place, but also the ways in which various listeners hear them. Sounds/noise are a fundamental part of the life of the city and its citizens. The experiences of individuals (at home, at work, socializing, passing through, or simply being in the city) are shaped and mediated by sounds of all kinds, and sounds (including music) are deeply implicated in the production of place itself. It is a core assumption of the project that individuals and communities do not inhabit the same sonic place. Physiologically, older people do not hear the same range of frequencies as they did in their youth and very frequently we *choose* to hear, ignore, or technologically drown out sounds, depending on our social background or personal preferences. In addition, it is assumed that one part of a city will not sound the same as another, that each will have a particular sonic ambience at a certain times of day or season and that these sounds will change over time depending upon the use of space, among other factors. Positioning community groups as recordists, selectors, editors, and moderators of material allows the project to access those sounds that are signifiers of place to the people who inhabit them, rather than from a researcher's perspective.

The LimerickSoundscapes project began by seeking to include people from all walks of life who were interested in becoming "citizen collectors" and generating materials that "sound out" their city (Cohen 1995; 2012). This approach is different from the norm in Soundscapes Studies, where a relatively small group of recordists "collect" sounds they consider to be representative of a particular location. Collections of this kind are often put into the service of other creative activities, such as soundscape compositions (Truax 1999, Schafer 1977). Effectively "top-down" in structure, many soundscapes projects have tended to be less concerned with the experience of the citizen in the understanding, and even capturing, of those soundscapes. Instead, the issue of sonic, environmental degradation and its impact for humanity in general has been central to the field of acoustic ecology. There are examples of soundscapes models emanating from ethnomusicology, including Sonor-Cities in Greece[5] and SoundscapesRostock in Denmark,[6] neither of which uses citizen collector models but both of which provide strong frameworks for engaging in historical and current ethnographically based music and sound research. This approach to sound collection, which privileges expert recordists, has most probably arisen because of the historical cost and complexity of high-quality equipment. Considerably cheaper digital recording technology enables wider participation in the project, and alongside this comes the recognition that the sonic environment of individuals and families are unique and considerably more complex than the designers of earlier projects might have realized.[7]

With its focus on the city, and deriving much of its theoretical scaffolding from sociology, urban ethnomusicology is a discipline that puts human creativity, activity, and agency at the center of its applied research agenda. That said, urban ethnomusicology, because it draws upon a tradition of working with small communities, has been primarily concerned with the music practices of ethnic minorities and migrants (Hemetek & Reyes 2007, Shelemay 2006, Toynbee & Dueck 2011) rather than a city as a whole. Studies of music performances staged in the city, along with the consumption practices of urban dwellers, have also come to the fore. Cities have, more and more, been understood through their musical soundscape (Jurkova 2012, Bohlman et al. 2007), but in general, urban ethnomusicologists have been less concerned with the broader sound experiences of people in the city. It is for this reason that we have also turned to other disciplines in order to shore up the model of engagement for LimerickSoundscapes. It could reasonably be argued that a "sonic turn" has taken place in the humanities and social sciences over the last decade, with increasing attention paid to the sonic environment in a number of disciplines, including urban studies (see Dillane et al. 2015). There have been a number of reasons for this, aside from the gold-rush spirit of academia, hurriedly mining a previously neglected field. We would suggest that these reasons fall into aesthetic, environmental, and, above all, technological camps.

To consider the first of these, cultural attitudes toward nonmusical sound have broadened into mainstream aesthetic appreciation, in part due to creative developments in film sound design, the appropriation of found sonic objects in music-making, and the combination of both in gaming soundscapes. Groundbreaking composers from Pierre Schaeffer, through John Cage to Brian Eno, have challenged the boundaries between planned and accidental, music and ambience, and whether or not listeners are conscious of their provenance, such originally avant-garde approaches have gradually become a part of everyday musical media.

Other pioneers like R. Murray Schafer (1977) and Hildegarde Westerkamp (1974) have been more concerned with the uniqueness and fragility of sonic environments. Soundscape studies, in which the sounds of locations are recorded, mapped, and analyzed, have been established in numerous cities, mobilized in no small part by the World Forum for Acoustic Ecology (WFAE). In order to hear afresh, they tell us, we need to practice attending to details that we habitually tune out but which are revealing of the worlds we inhabit. Of course, ethnomusicologists have always been interested in music in context. Steven Feld (1982), for instance, encourages us to take this approach further, to hear the environment as an inherent aspect of music, as it is for the Kaluli with whom he has worked. Similarly, anthropologist Tim Ingold (2000) has drawn attention to the sensory experience of place and its role in culture. In recent years, architects too (Treasure 2012, Blesser & Salter 2007) have begun to develop an appreciation of place that is not primarily visual.[8]

The third, and probably the most important, factor in this relatively sudden attention to sound is the emergence of high-quality, lightweight, and affordable digital recording equipment, alongside the potential to share material online. Just as in the 1960s cheap portable cameras radically changed the ways in which people saw themselves and could look back on events in their lives (Sontag 1977), so sound recorders offer similar reflective possibilities in the sonic field. The sound recording capabilities of "smartphones" have been utilized in a number of online recording projects because their ease of use allows spontaneity and instant sharing on free platforms such as Soundcloud and the Soundmap app. Unlike earlier soundscape projects, which were carried out by a small number of individuals with cumbersome equipment, contemporary initiatives recognize that ubiquitous technologies allow a multitude of personal sonic experiences to be collected and disseminated, democratizing recording in the way that the Kodak Instamatic made "snapshots" a popular and intimate medium distinct from the privileged realm of the professional photographer.

This democratizing capacity has a second and equally important dimension. We are also interested in how sound collection might serve as a means of mobilizing civic engagement, in order to create a participatory and creative citizenship for the diverse array of people living in cities (a point which we explore in greater depth later in this chapter). In taking this practical, applied approach, the LimerickSoundscapes project proposes that *sound* is also a democratic tool for activating critical citizenship in dense, urban spaces shared by citizens from a diverse range of backgrounds.

In sum, bringing these Soundscape Studies together with (Urban) Ethnomusicology, further informed by Urban Sociology as well as Acoustic Ecology, LimerickSoundscapes constructs its intellectual and applied approach from the following themes and ideas:

Sound, Music, Representation and (re)Generation: Fieldwork and sustained engagement with music/culture and sonic environments is the hallmark of ethnomusicology, manifesting in various modes of ethnographic representation, including sonic and visual. Within this approach, giving voice to the Other is a matter for constant reflection and reflexive practice. Agency is central so we must always ask who is representing whom/what and on whose authority (Barz & Cooley 1997). Music and sonic environments are tied intrinsically to expressions of identity (Stokes 1997, Tuan 2004) and sound is, in many contexts, social, cultural, as well as ideological (Turino 2008).

Theorizing the City: The city is geographical, spatial, and ideological, a nexus of real and imagined relations (Krims 2007). As such, the city has a sonic topography and its citizens negotiate urban spaces in particular ways (Bohlman et al. 2007). Lives are made more meaningful through interactions with the environment but also especially with each other (Hannerz 1980). With its dense population of diverse peoples, the city, in particular, becomes a theater of social action and citizens, dwellers of the city, occupy various roles. Their experiences are framed in particular ways (Goffman 1959). In turn, we each hear, perform and navigate the city differently (Finnegan 1989), and the resultant experiences can be mapped in creative ways (Cohen 2012). The city also sounds noises, unintentionally or without a performance frame, and such sounds shape and mediate everyday experiences of place (Truax 1999). The urban soundscape is typically dominated by the anthrophony, the sounds generated directly and indirectly by human activity; however, other categories of sound also exist and warrant attention. These include the biophony (the sounds of animals other than human) and geophony (the sound of wind, rain), which are frequently drowned out, or merely not noticed (Krause 2012).[9]

Locating the Perceiving and Critical Body: Phenomenologists and cultural geographers assert that to live is to live locally and this experience is mediated through the body, the senses, and memory (Feld & Basso 1996). We may live in a globalized, interconnected world but we experience it locally, intimately, and somatically. The performing individual, as part of an urban collective and as a practitioner of everyday activity, is therefore at the heart of the research question (De Certeau 1984). The degree to which his or her experiences are underpinned by particular pathways to understanding, optimally leading to social justice and equality, by being seen and heard and given opportunities, is crucial (Harvey 1973).

The Citizen Collector Model for Urban Soundscapes

From the outset, the research project has established two, clear objectives. First is the production of an interactive website, a tangible and very visible product of the research that is the public face of a soundscapes project (available at www. limericksoundscapes.ie; see also Figure 5.1). This prototype database structure has been carefully designed to ensure optimal data-mining capabilities as well as a high-quality user experience (see Dillane & Langlois 2015). Since 2013, samples of the sonic environments and experiences of members of Limerick's diverse population have been placed on an interactive map, a resource that will be added to over time. The idea is that the site will offer a detailed, geo-tagged acoustic representation of the city as it exists in the present and how, in time, these will become representations of the past and present. The second objective, which comes first in the actual research process, is concerned with the generation and modeling of a collaborative, reflexive methodology, involving the research team, individuals and groups in the city, who have complementary stakes in developing a textured, sonic narrative about the place in which they live/play/ work/research. The website and the collaborative methodology are part of an iterative and recursive model. In other words, the website becomes an ongoing *process* of reflection, representation, and action, while the collaborative *methodological process* itself becomes a type of output, dealing with the dynamics of negotiating and sharing/shaping a research project.

Welcome to the Limerick Soundscapes portal. We want to make this a permanent institution with layer upon layer of sounds available to you. This will allow you the listener to explore the sounds of the city wherever you are. If you have sounds to add please contact us with the details.

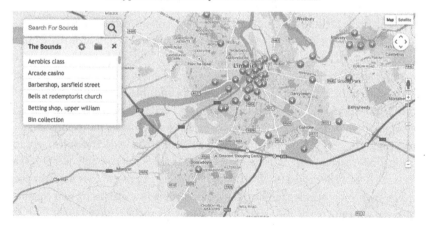

Figure 5.1 LimerickSoundscape Portal. Screen grab from the Interactive Limerick Soundscape Website.

In sum, if the overarching aim of LimerickSoundscapes is to engage in a local partnership between people in and of Limerick City and the research team, the materials generated are already being put into service in the following ways. The project is creating a tangible resource over which the people of Limerick can feel ownership. Their sounds and creative interpretations are reflected back, representing familiar and new facets of the city to them. This in turn is helping to create pathways for education, promoting a sense of participation and belonging for any citizen, regardless of background, ethnicity, class, or creed. For example, a group of participants from the National Learning Network—young adults with mild intellectual disabilities—engaged with the LimerickSoundscapes project in order to learn new skills and complete a community-based educational program. In 2016 this group was awarded the AONTAS Star award and a National Award, for the best adult learner's project in the province of Munster for their work with LimerickSoundscapes. The competences they have acquired are transferable to other members of their own group and to others who seek to take part in the project as learners become trainers. This is but one example of the multiple ways in which the project might generate other forms of knowledge building and exchange and, in time, other tangible outputs may include downloadable MP3 walking tours, city-centered interactive spaces, compositions, and geo-locative apps that would allow visitors to hear the place they are in from the perspective of other listeners, in other seasons. As a reflexive and reflective methodology that has *partnership* and *agency* at its core, the project endeavors to promote new ways of engaging in research that merges best practice from ethnographic fieldwork and action research in unique and innovative ways that have multiple applications across a variety of disciplines, including ethnomusicology, sociology, and urban planning.

Before outlining the pilot project, from recruitment process to initial sounds gathered, it is worth summarizing the three key, interrelated reasons why the research team decided to test and put in place this idea of a *citizen collector* model. First, the LimerickSoundscapes cluster members agreed that any project of this nature ideally ought to be owned by the people of Limerick, in part to be sustainable into the future, but also because the question of ownership is crucial in any collaborative project, from the point of view of trust, partnership, and democratic, civic engagement.[10] In this way, LimerickSoundscapes has many objectives in common with projects elsewhere. One example is the "Citizen Scientist" sound-mapping project in Salford in the UK, where people with smartphones were invited to upload sounds directly to the project website (Mydlarz 2013). However, a key difference between that project and the LimerickSoundscapes approach is the lack of direct human interaction and ongoing dialogue with people in the former. Also, the Salford team has critically reflected on the potential limitations on attracting participants from different demographics because not everyone has access to smart technology.

Second, the LimerickSoundscapes team is aware that it is important from a research perspective to explore the degree to which the choice of actual sounds recorded differs from person to person, not just in terms of the significance a recorded sound has for an individual but also in terms of its inherent sonic qualities and technical features. As Tony Langlois has stated, "cities are people, and in order to capture their collective sound worlds it is crucial to involve as many "ears" and experiences as possible" (2013: 4). Third, the adoption of a pragmatic, crowd-sourcing model of data collection means a large pool of individuals has the potential to access many more sonic environments, particular in the various private spheres, than any team of researchers would. For example, the sounds of domestic life are personal and therefore often only accessible to the individuals who inhabit them. Similarly, there may also be certain sounds (including musics) that emanate from cultural practices or environments within a city that are not open to community outsiders. These include religious practices, ethnic celebrations, and the like (Gaver et al. 1999).

From Pilot to Model

In 2013, the pilot project was undertaken with small groups from a range of community-based organizations. These organizations included Active Retired Citizens, Headway Ireland (for people with brain injuries), local community and parish groups, and Doras Luimní (Irish for "Door to Limerick," an organization that supports new migrants and asylum seekers). The rationale behind approaching such groups directly, as opposed to sending out general invitations, was simple. These groups were already well established, allowing the research to begin quickly, and they reflected some of the communal diversity existing within the city. It also allowed the researchers to discover how various communities, age groups, and ethnicities were disposed toward such a project.[11]

The next step was to provide the technological infrastructure. With some financial support from Mary Immaculate College, the Bestsoft company based in Dublin designed a web interface. This combined a simple database linked to a cartographic API (Application Programming Interface) and a basic Wordpress editing system. Using this interface, sound files could easily be linked to subject matter, time of recording, and location.

The small number of digital recorders made available to the project served their purpose very well. Recordists felt comfortable with the equipment, which was easy to use and resilient. From the project's perspective, it was important that the devices themselves, though capable of high recording quality, were not so expensive or delicate that they couldn't be left with recordists who had received only introductory training. Originally, separate handheld stereo microphones were tested with the equipment, but were found to be less robust and with poorer recording quality than the inbuilt microphones. As a result, the project invested in a number of high-quality windjammers, which were essential for recording in the open air, something that many of the recordists wanted to do. The addition of these windjammers to the devices improved recording quality substantially without adding potentially breakable electronic equipment. Inexpensive headphones were also acquired, as otherwise it was hard for participants to hear their own material with any clarity. More to the point, collectors came to the realization that the best way to record the sounds was to listen through the focused headphones, which heightened their sonic experiences of the public and private spaces they entered in order to capture sounds of their city. Recordings made during this period included sounds of fountains, recycling activities on the docks, people emerging from nightclubs, hair being cut at a barber's, religious services spilling out onto the main street, buskers, car horns, bells, street-cleaning vehicles, aerobics classes, birds in a garden, and many more (all available on the website). The editing of the pilot recordings was carried out by the research team using Pro-Tools or Logic software. These programs are too complex for non-specialist use but the freely downloadable Audacity program is quite adequate for the purpose at hand, with Sound Studio being recommended for ease of use and high quality at a low cost.

The pilot research stage lasted two months over a summer period, and from this study a structure and approach were devised for engagement with subsequent groups. Ground rules were also developed in order to protect the rights of recordists over collected materials and to protect the identity of individuals whose voices are heard in recordings. Regarding the latter, it was agreed that although it was important to record voices (as a core element of a "lived-in" soundscape), efforts should be made to remove names or other indicators that would identify an individual to those who didn't already know them. Logging recordings under the names of recordists allows the project to remove any online material at any time that they prefer not to be available to the public. Making personal recordings available online is an exposure of experiences and relationships that would otherwise be private, and recognizing the rights of recordists (and the recorded) encourages trust between the project and the groups engaging with it.

After the pilot study was finished, the following structure for community engagement was arrived at, which, though flexible, has so far proved to be an effective and reflexive model. This outline will inevitably be adapted to suit the requirements of particular groups, and as a response to the research team's own learning experience.

Figure 5.2 Facilitating a LimerickSoundscape training session.

- An initial meeting with the group introduces research team members and the objectives of the project. Those expressing an interest are then asked to engage in a short series of workshops, run at roughly weekly intervals.
- The first workshop introduces the recording devices themselves and discusses both the range of things that might be recorded and how to best capture that sound. It is easy to demonstrate how to use small handheld devices. Together with headphones, participants are able to experience both the amplified "focus" these recorders allow and hear playback of test recordings.
- The group is then left to use the recorders as each individual wishes for a fortnight. Members are not asked to record anything in particular, but to attend to the sounds that are important to them personally or which define the area they live in (the equivalent of Schafer's "soundmarks"). They are asked not to limit their recordings to sounds that they *enjoy*, and to consider both far and distant elements of their soundscape. Groups are asked to complete a short form for each recording, noting its place, time, recordist's name, and subject. There is an associated blog site with supporting information for those with access to the internet or short handouts with pictures are given to members.
- On their return to the next workshop, members of the group play back and discuss what they recorded. If similar material was collected, they are asked to decide between them which is the better recording and why (was it, for

example, technically clearer or was it more accurately representative of the location?).

- The group is then shown how to use basic audio editing software (in order to isolate the most significant features of their recording) and the online uploading system is demonstrated.
- The concluding workshop involves a sound walk, preferably to locations in which some of the recordings were made.
- Crucially, different groups from different organizations and backgrounds aspire to meet to share collected sounds and stories about the process of collecting in order to promote this shared task of doing and to meet with different people.[12]

From a technical and methodological perspective, lots of questions arise from this model regarding media storage, consumption, and filtering. For example, if we are all free to record and upload the sonic minutiae of our daily lives, who would listen to them? (Would even *we* listen to them as researchers?) Liberated from the space restrictions of camera film, how many digital pictures do we take that are never looked at again? Just as with affordable cameras, our ability to sonically reflect and objectify ourselves within our locations could change the way we attend to sound, and perhaps especially to the sounds of others, but only with an effective means of filtering and navigating through a vast field of atomized noise. A second issue is the problem of "future-proofing" recorded material when we are well aware that recording media over the *last* century has changed so dramatically. The LimerickSoundscapes project cannot possibly resolve such issues but, being conscious of them, aims to be responsive to developments in media as to those in wider society. Beginning at this point in time allows the project to record and observe the ways in which community groups record, moderate, and use their own material, and how this will inevitably change over time. The project is, on one hand, introducing Limerick communities to certain technologies and, with a few ground rules, ensuring functionality and alertness to issues of ethics, allowing agency over the material recorded. In the longer term, on the other hand, one of its most fruitful research strands is likely to be a study of how and what people record and listen to, as they become more familiar with the act of sound collection.

From Soundings to Critical Citizenship

All of the people involved in the pilot had ideas about the tangible outcomes of the project. These included expressions of interest in contributing on an ongoing basis to the database to help build up a critical mass. Some thought that it might be interesting to work with a soundscapes composer and turn these sounds into another kind of artistic output. Others suggested creating a CD of Limerick's sounds and distributing them, free, to local schools as resource for sampling, for creative, computer-based projects by young students.

Sustainability would be an ideal outcome from the position of fostering critical citizenship in the field of sound. Following initial workshop programs, which were of broad educational interest, however, we found that a minority of participants in each group were enthusiastic about continuing to record, and a strategy to maintain engagement is an area that the project team is currently being developed. In order to create a sustainable network of Limerick recordists it would be necessary to link these enthusiasts, perhaps through monthly "sound clubs" where a similar process of recording, listening, editing, and uploading could take place, though with as little input from the research side of the project as possible. We also plan to run advanced "train the trainer" workshops for sound clubs, in order for them to run their own workshops, either within their own group on an annual basis, or with communities that are yet to be involved. As groups are also free to develop specialist recording projects autonomously, focusing perhaps on environmental issues, youth, employment, and the like, the project has potential to serve as a platform for a wide range of sonic explorations. In this sense, LimerickSoundscapes might be considered as a catalyst for activity in this field rather than a project with a fixed outcome. With the acquisition of a minimum amount of equipment and software there is no reason the LimerickSoundscapes contributors couldn't take ownership of the practical aspects of the project, and this is an aspiration that the project would wish to encourage.

What the research team came to appreciate during and in the immediate aftermath of this early stage of the project is that that the meaningfulness of sonically mapping the city truly lies as much in the ongoing, collaborative process—the "making" of the work—as it does in the production of an interactive website and other tangible outputs. The work has shown us that this potentially open-ended and community-based model of engagement may be flexible enough to accommodate changes brought about by the flow of people and their music practices and sound environments not just in and through the city in space and time but also to and from shifting local and global hinterlands (Cronon 1991), in movements that shape and recreate the city sonically as well as physically. We had been employing the term "citizen" in our "citizen collector" model in the literal sense of a person who dwells in the city. As we work with different groups with different senses of their place in the city, of belonging and of citizenship more broadly, we have become more and more drawn to the idea of this act of creating soundscapes as having a profoundly critical and engaged dimension. The reflexive process of analyzing and discussing the sounds in one's own neighborhood, and of hearing comparable recordings from other personal spaces across the city, draws a fresh attention to differential environmental and social experiences of the same city.

Based on their applied research at Stellenbosch, in 2012 Nell et al. offer the following definition of "critical citizenship":

> Critical citizenship is based on the promotion of a common set of shared values such as tolerance, diversity, human rights and democracy . . . as an education pedagogy it encourages critical reflection on the past and the imagining of a possible future shaped by social justice, in order to prepare people to live together in harmony in diverse societies. (Nell et al. 2012)

According to the authors, this definition has been adapted from Johnson and Morris's work on critical pedagogy, which places reflection and the opportunity to learn at the center of any social engagement (Johnson & Morris 2010). It is also an approach that we found very much resonates with Catherine WynScully, who offers the following definition of critical citizenship as:

> [a] framework for finding strategies to develop awareness amongst individuals and groups to enable them to combat complacency, and go beyond simple obedient cosmopolitan ways of thinking-acting-and-being, in order to forge a way of living life.

In our experience to date, we have witnessed how citizens of Limerick, from very different backgrounds and life experiences, can develop camaraderie, even friendship, through engaging in the project. An example from the pilot includes a fourth-generation Limerick native and grandmother finding her sonic interests most aligned with a young male asylum seeker from Africa. These two collectors frequently exchanged ideas about the best places to capture sounds in the city and when they met up, they would compare their work and decide whose recording was the best. More recently, students from the National Learning Network in Raheen have expressed an interest in hosting recordists from the Active Retired Citizen's Group based in the city center, in order to offer technical support to some of its members. There are many more anecdotal stories and observations of growing support and engagement that, in time, will be documented. But for the present, the focus is on continuing to provide such opportunities for social awareness and mutual exchange, for their own sake.

There is another important point to make here in tandem with the notion of critical citizenship that undergirds the proposition that simply mapping sounds or representing a geo-acoustics of the city is not enough to aim for in this kind of applied, interdisciplinary research. The writer, composer, and installation artist

Paul Carter has dealt extensively with the concept of the "creative region" as a way of conceiving a place that has both local and global dimensions and flows (Carter 2010). In a personal interview, Carter also posited that, as researchers and critical thinkers, we need to move beyond the concept of mere representation and think more about creation. In other words, the creative potential of each individual needs to be evoked and activated, which essentially mobilizes another facet of the concept of engaged citizenship. Carter makes the following assertion, which resonates with Freire's 1996 work on pedagogies of the oppressed, arguing for students to be active co-creators of knowledge. Carter extends this idea with his own thoughts by insisting that:

> Creativity is not just mapping or "representing" but creating, engaging, dialogue. It's about ambience, between civility and public sociability. New civility emerges through analogical thinking and the simple processes of collaboration, discovery, improvisation . . . in the dialectic between action and reaction . . . focusing on production rather than representation—on production and reflection as a way of conceiving of place. (Carter, personal interview, 2012)

The LimerickSoundscapes project therefore aspires to create the conditions to enable such collaborative exchange, which in turn engages critically with ideas around alternative forms of (re)presentation and active doing, which in turn gives us a particular experience of our place in the world.

Final Reflection

Given Limerick's rich history, its rapidly shifting demographics, and the increased socioeconomic pressures that have come to bear on the town during Ireland's period of economic austerity in the aftermath of the economic crash of 2007–2008, we hope that the LimerickSoundscapes project may be able to re-engage people with their urban environment and with each other. This project offers a way to engage with one's sense of "place," with neighborhood communities, and with the city in multiple ways that promote critical thinking and critical pedagogy. Processes of *listening* and *hearing* are arguably less fraught than *seeing*. Although sound can be intrusive and disruptive, in everyday life individuals perhaps tend to make value judgments based more on the way a person looks or the appearance of a neighborhood than we do on how they/it "sounds."[13] We would like to think that learning and listening activities, collecting and engaging, offer pathways to education, knowledge transfer, and transformation.

Informed by the paradigm of urban soundscapes and critical citizenship, LimerickSoundscapes proposes not just simply to reflect, and literally map, sounds of and in the City of Limerick, thereby giving all citizens of Limerick another means of understanding their city and their place in that city. Instead, in conceiving of the city as being an ever-emergent creative space and region, the associated research *process* is about creating *zones of interaction*, where past and present, as well as future, find articulation, and where the *doing* brings about greater critical understanding of society, place, self, and other. The sound materials, and the pathways of social interaction and active citizenship generated in their collection, should ideally help in forging new relationships between *all* involved, and ultimately, in the development of a sustainable, creative citizenship through this very processes of critical listening and critical (re)production/creation (Dillane & Langlois 2012). If critical thinking is about logical thinking and a willingness to see things from different perspectives, critical listening is also that and more; a somatic response to the environment and a willingness to hear things from different and sometimes unexpected perspectives.

Postscript

At present, the LimerickSoundscapes project is entirely dependent upon voluntary citizen participation in order for it to be sustainable for a hundred years, as we envisage. There is no doubt that its success will also depend on its mutability, as techniques, attitudes, academic theories, technologies, and Limerick's communities themselves develop in unpredictable ways. It is important, then, that researchers not only attend to the material that is accumulating, how this reflects cultural and environmental changes, but how this proposed reflexive and fluid network of recordists also hear their soundscape differently over time. Attention must also be paid to the changing techniques, conceptual perspectives, and context of academic research in this area. It is feasible that the social, archival, and creative aspects of the project could be sustainable without the attention of researchers, but the research cannot take place without a viable recording project. In order to forge a mutually beneficial link between academia and the local community in which it is situated, we are currently working on establishing postgraduate modules at the University of Limerick and Mary Immaculate College that will allow short-term sound projects to take place within Limerick's communities. This would provide much fuller support for voluntary, participating groups while also giving research students the opportunity to explore the sonic environments and perceptions of particular communities in more depth than is currently possible. It would be hoped that this level of mutual engagement would further enhance debate and development within this emerging field. For now, the growth in this area is slow but steady. Finding partners in other cities would also greatly benefit this kind of research, but we are mindful of the dangers of leveraging such work in order to achieve funding that in turn may put pressure on the project to generate "outputs" of a particular kind.[14] But as long as citizens of Limerick continue to show interest in the project, hopefully we will find a way to provide such support.

Notes

1. The LimerickSoundscapes research cluster would like to thank Mary Immaculate College for providing seed-funding support in the project's first years. The team would also like to thank all of the organizations and the people of Limerick who have collaborated in the research so far and remain committed to working with the team into the foreseeable future.

2. While focused upon contemporary recordings, the project will effectively produce a rich archive when maintained for a number of years. Such a collection has considerable potential for identifying changes in language, technology, migration patterns, industry, and uses of space, as well as musical developments. Though an important source for future researchers, the arts, environmentalists, and heritage tourism, our primary intention is to record sonic spaces for the future citizens of Limerick themselves, who may, potentially, be able to hear the sounds and voices of past generations in places they will come to inhabit. Any ethnographic data relating to the recordists is not available on the website, but may, in time, be made available with the consent of the recordists, to researchers wanting to know more about why they chose those sounds. The website functions simply as a repository for sounds themselves. It is in the actual workshops, which we describe later in the chapter, that people talk about why they chose to record certain sound and exchange ideas about the process itself.

3. The LimerickSoundscapes research cluster is led by Dr. Aileen Dillane and Dr. Tony Langlois, and its core members include the following University of Limerick faculty members: Dr. Orfhlaith Ní Bhriain, Irish World Academy; Dr. Martin Power and Prof. Eoin Devereux, Department of Sociology; and Dr. Mikael Fernström and Robin Parmar, Department of Computer Science and Information Systems. Dr. Ciaran Ryan was a graduate of the Department of Media, Mary Immaculate College, Limerick, and key facilitator at sound recording workshops.

4. Initial seed funding was secured by Dr. Tony Langlois, which enabled the group to purchase recording equipment. University of Limerick subsequently provided some funding for the holding of an international symposium entitled "Urban Soundscapes and Critical Citizenship" in 2014. For a full program of this event, featuring urban ethnomusicologists, soundscapes composers, urban sociologists, etc., see www.soundandsociety2014.wordpress.com. For publications from this event, see Dillane et al. (2015) and Dillane and Langlois (2015).

5. "Sonor-Cities—Learning Culture Through a City Soundscapes" was created by Eleni Kallimopoulou, Panagiotis C. Poulos, Konstantinos Kornetis, and Spyros Tsipidis. It is intended for students and researchers in ethnomusicology and cognate disciplines with a stated aim being to set up an interface between the university classroom and

society, drawing from rich archival materials found in libraries, archives, and from contemporary fieldwork activities. As such, the project offers a fine model for specialist, contextually and historically sensitive sound mapping. See http://sonor-cities. edu.gr, and for a review of the project see Dillane (2014).

6. This project may be found at www.soundscapesrostock.de and was run by Barbara Alge and Frances Wilkins. As the website states, it constitutes "an ethnomusicological exploration of sounds which in some way define the city and its suburbs" and draws upon the work of Schafer, while keeping the focus on musical sounds and on the fieldwork and ethnographic methods deployed in their collection by specialist collectors.

7. Recent, entirely online sound projects utilize the potential of recording and uploading directly from "smartphones." Many of these collect large amounts of data from identifiable locations, but most do not filter or curate the material; they simply make it available. The weakness of this model is that although it provides a completely democratic level of access it lacks the editing required to make the collection coherent to listeners. This is an issue that LimerickSoundscapes is attempting to address through the collective sound selection process it advocates. See the following sites for examples of this kind of project: www.mapize.com/soundmap_paiva, www. soundsofeurope.eu, https://socialsoundsproject.wordpress.com, and www.sound-survey.org.uk/index.php/projects/12_tones_intro.

8. In a yet broader current of intellectual trends, a growing awareness of global climate change has brought a new level of attention to the role of environmental factors upon society and culture. This trend brings together the philosophical influences of Deleuze and Guattari (1980), the ecocriticism of Bruno Latour (2017) and Eben Kirksey (2015), and even the post-human anthropology of Timothy Morton (2013). The recent development of soundscape projects and sound theory can possibly be related to an increasing sensitivity to an ecological contextualization of all social phenomena.

9. There are sound physiological reasons why humans pay more attention to the frequency ranges occupied naturally by our own species. We also use sounds, including those of music and speech, to distract, comfort, stimulate, and feel connected to others (Tacchi 1998). The difference between hearing as a passive act and listening and an active intention sheds light upon the nature of consciousness as much as it does on human perception.

10. Contributing recordists have ownership in the sense that they have the right to remove their material at any time, currently through a site moderator, and to offer it for free to the site on the basis of a written understanding that it will be heard in the public domain, thereby avoiding complex copyright issues. Because recordings are often made in private homes and personal spaces, the project aims to maintain some degree of anonymity in the website itself. For example, references to the names of individuals are removed from material, and the location of domestic recordings is generalized to a street rather than a specific house. In order to maintain trust between researchers and community groups a mutually acceptable balance between access and privacy is considered crucial to the success of the project. There is no doubt that managing this in the long term may prove challenging, but it is a starting point.

11. Since the pilot, various groups have approached the research team to come visit and present on the project. The previously mentioned National Learning Network is one such example.

12. There is capacity at this point for gathering ethnographically rich data through interviews and so forth, but we see this as a separate issue for now as we are still more focused on generating sound materials. However, as the project progresses, the desire of the researchers to understand motivations and creative approaches of individual sound recordists will most likely lead us to document, subject, of course, to the agreement of the participant.

13. There are, of course, exceptions to this, including certain sounds from ethnic minority neighborhoods that can conjure up negative value judgments.

14. In 2014, Limerick was designated as Ireland's first National City of Culture and in 2016 sought to become the European Capital of Culture, 2020. While such initiatives raised the possibility of access to generous funding, LimerickSoundsapes remains more committed at this point to grass-roots group involvement without any particular agenda on behalf of participants and funders. However, the degree to which the project can be sustained without some type of regular funding into the future remains to be seen.

6

The Earth Is (Still) Our Mother

Traversing Indigenous Landscapes through Sacred Geographies of Song

Chad S. Hamill (čnaq'ymi)

Indigenous landscapes are brought to life through stories, which form ontological bonds that are culturally constituted and reflect unique ways of knowing and being in the world. In an effort to elucidate the relationship between the Spokane Tribe and our ancestral lands—and demonstrate how deeply environmental degradation has impacted Spokane culture—it seems most appropriate to begin with a story. The following concerns the formation of the Spokane River.[1] It most likely refers to a cataclysmic event that occurred during a series of glacial floods, known as the "Spokane or Missoula floods," some 13,000–15,000 years ago.

> Ages ago the land was devastated by a monstrous dragon of fetid, reeking breath and claws that uprooted in a single stroke the largest pine tree. The people everywhere stood in constant dread and awe of it. An Indian girl, who was gathering berries on a summer day, discovered the monster sleeping in the sunshine on a hillside near the present mouth of the Spokane River. Slipping away, she ran to the village of her tribe and reported the astonishing scene she had witnessed. Instantly, the chief assembled his warriors, and gathering every cord and thong in the village, they stole upon the sleeping dragon and stealthily bound it to a huge adjacent tree and crag. This accomplished, the tribe fell upon the drowsy mammoth with all their implements of chase and war. Besieged, the dragon bestirred himself, and by a single mighty lunge broke all his bonds, and vanished like the wind, tearing as he went a deep gorge and channel to Lake Coeur d'Alene. The imprisoned waters of the lake rolled down the dragon's course, and ever since [then] the pleasant Spokane River has been winding its way to the sea. (Ross 2011: 748)

For millennia, the Spokane and Columbia rivers have been the lifeblood of the Spokane people, the heart-center from which culture is nourished and sustained. Like the rivers, our songs inhabit the landscape; the rivers fed our bodies, the songs feed our souls. Together, they reflect an Indigenous ecology that has

Chad S. Hamill (čnaq'ymi), *The Earth Is (Still) Our Mother* In: *Transforming Ethnomusicology*. Edited by: Beverley Diamond and Salwa El-Shawan Castelo-Branco, Oxford University Press (2021). © Oxford University Press.
DOI: 10.1093/oso/9780197517550.003.0007

shaped Indigenous knowledge in the Columbia Plateau region.[2] The arrival of Lewis and Clark in 1805 signaled the beginning of widespread ecological degradation in Spokane country and the Columbia Plateau region in general. Not long after contact, the life-sustaining arteries of the Columbia and Spokane Rivers were blocked and polluted. The same might be said of our songs, as missionaries sought to obstruct all cultural and spiritual channels of expression. The following account, which took place in the early nineteenth century (before missionaries and industrialists descended upon tribes in the interior Northwest), illustrates an Indigenous ecology in which the land and the prayers operate holistically, linked through a sacred geography of song:

> There was one thing that must be done by the women [near the end of winter], before life started in tree or plant. There must be . . . [a] sweet and solemn invitation to nature for a generous fruitage. The news had been given the day before that a fine dry tree had blown down and this meant wood for all. . . . The women took their straps and started before the dawn cast its gleam upon the eastern sky. They had filled up the hill where snow and mud lay frozen. When one gathered an armful of burrs, she sprang upon the log that was adamant against their puny implements and bare hands. Here she began the Song of Fruitage that swayed and thrilled every woman and girl within hearing distance of her pleading voice. She stroked the burrs saying, "This is the wish of our womanhood. Let the bough bend with fruit and the ground heave up with roots." Then, stooping, she tore a section of bark from the log and waved it back and forth as she sang, "That our bark baskets may overflow and the supplies might flow through our hands." Every act was a sign that interpreted a vast meaning, which was to capture nature in its most tender age and bind their hopes into its growth. . . . Their request was launched at the beginning of the time of flowing sap and would be sent through the grass and vegetation until it ended in the empty cone of next year. All the parts were rehearsed time and again as their slowing ranks moved over the crest of the hill, each holding high a pine cone as a symbol of fruitage and a piece of bark to represent baskets for filling. (Wynecoop 1985: 4–5)

For the women ascending the hill, prayers and songs were an integral part of their ecology, and an "invitation to nature for a generous fruitage" was necessary to ensure the growth that would sustain their community in the coming year. For Indigenous communities the world over, ecology extends beyond scientific approaches to understanding relationships between organisms and their surroundings. It encompasses the immeasurable influence of prayers and songs in shaping those surroundings. An Indigenous ecology, then, is best viewed as a holistic framework inclusive of everything operative within an ecosystem, including spiritual phenomena too subtle for contemporary instruments of science to detect.

At present, baskets in the Columbia Plateau are still being filled with roots and camas, but their arrival has become unpredictable, another environmental consequence of the global colonial project and the climate crisis it has fueled. Like Indigenous communities around the world, we have seen a continual erosion of our traditional foods and natural resources. In the last century, the dams took our salmon. In this century, our roots and berries are at risk, further threatening the sacred continuum at the center of ourselves and our community. Greg Cajete states that, from a traditional Indigenous perspective, "Every act, element, plant, animal, and natural process is considered to have a moving spirit with which humans continually communicate" (2000: 69). Properly maintained, that communication is anything but one-sided, requiring the person to be quiet and receptive if they wish to encounter and behold the movement of spirit in the natural world. This may include one's guardian spirit or *sumeš*. The following is an account of my uncle's first engagement with his *sumeš*, when he was a young boy.

[Gib's] first encounter with his "animals" took place in the hills near Davenport, Washington, where he was digging camas and bitterroot[3] with his mother.... To cover more ground, she sent him out to dig in another spot some distance away. He quickly lost interest. As dusk approached, he pondered his nearly empty bag. It lay under a ponderosa pine, deflated and distant, ambivalent to the expanding pit in his stomach and the lashing that was sure to come. Eli frantically gathered as much camas as possible, stuffing the bag as best he could. Because bitterroot was less plentiful and more difficult to extract, he dug just enough to place a nice layer of bitterroot at the top of the bag. Sheepish but hopeful, he headed back to camp, counting on the deepening darkness to aid in his deception. His plan was quickly foiled. Infuriated at her discovery, his mother took a leather strap to Eli and sent him out again. Terrified, crying, and seemingly alone, he searched for bitterroot in what little light the crescent moon offered. Suddenly, he heard a voice, which said, "Look!" At that moment, he was able to see gleaming bitterroot all around him, its hiding places revealed. The source of the voice then came into view: a small, shaggy animal with coarse black fur, unlike any animal Eli had ever seen. "When you become a man, you will sing this song and help people. Learn the song and sing it right for the people." The animal then imparted his song. Soon after, Eli walked down the hill with a bag full of bitterroot and a song he would use to help countless people in the years to come." (Hamill 2012: 86)

That day Gib became a participant in a sacred continuum that included his spirit helper, the traditional foods, and a song, receiving a teaching tied to the land and Spokane ways of knowing. In *Blackfoot Physics*, David Peat suggests that such knowledge, rather than a "dead collection of facts," "is alive, has spirit, and dwells in specific places. Traditional knowledge comes about through watching and listening, not in the passive way that schools demand, but through direct experience of songs and ceremonies, through the activities of hunting and daily life, from trees and animals, and in dreams and visions. Coming-to-knowing means entering into relationship with the spirits of knowledge, with plants and animals, with beings that animate dreams and visions, and with the spirit of the people" (2005: 65). As Peat suggests, knowledge, including songs, "dwells in specific places." Though it is less common today in the Columbia Plateau, young people wanting to receive a sacred song were often brought to locations where songs were known to reside. If a song was revealed to the supplicant, he would then become a carrier of that song. If, at some point, he wished to pass it on, he might bring someone else to the same location. In this way, songs are intimately tied to the land. In an era of accelerated environmental degradation, Indigenous communities stand to lose—along with their traditional and sacred foods—their sacred songs; both of which are critical forms of cultural and spiritual sustenance.

In Gib's encounter, the material and spiritual spheres merged, like a Venn diagram if you will, revealing the interconnectedness and movement between seen and unseen worlds. Cajete states that "In the Native mind, spirit and matter were not separate; they were one and the same," maintaining that an Indigenous community's connection to "place formed the spiritually based ecological mindset required to establish and maintain a correct and sustainable relationship with place. This orientation was . . . that interaction between the inner and outer realities . . . [among] group[s] of people liv[ing] in a particular place for a long period of time" (2000: 186–187). A central facet of this spiritually based ecological mindset is reciprocity. The climate changes we are experiencing can be viewed as a worldwide failure of reciprocal behavior, where, as Daniel Wildcat puts it, "Humankind has for too long treated the natural world beyond ourselves like automated teller machines (ATMs), and the withdrawals far exceeded the deposits" (2009: 64). In Gib's case, the law of reciprocity meant that he couldn't just take the song and bitterroot and be on his way. His sumesh would require something in return, and if Gib failed to reciprocate, there would be consequences. From that day forward, he continued to commune with his sumeš, who in giving Gib a song, established a conduit for spiritual power that Gib could access and utilize in numerous contexts, including his Winter Dance.

The Winter Dance, also known as the Medicine Dance or Jump Dance, is the oldest ceremony in the Columbia Plateau region, practiced long before non-Native settlers littered the landscape with crosses, small pox, and guns. These dances, taking place in longhouses throughout the Plateau, provide a platform for singers and medicine people to share their sacred gifts with the People. Integral to the Winter Dances are the traditional foods, which are laid upon the sacred floor and honored before they are eaten. These foods, many collected during the previous year, occupy the very space where the dancers dance, the singers sing, and the healers heal, laying the foundation for balance, reciprocity, and renewal. Our Medicine Dance embodies the cycles of life and of nature, where we are active participants in a perpetual process of undeniable interdependence. Contrasting this cyclical process with a Western worldview, Peat asserts that, "In a universe in which time turns in a circle, and in which the ceremonies of renewal are continued obligations of the People, the emphasis is always upon balance and harmony as opposed to progress, advancement, and accumulation" (2005: 118). In much the same way, first-foods ceremonies such as the Root and Berry Feast are held by Indigenous communities throughout the Columbia Plateau, scheduled according to nature's timeline (which, as I indicated earlier, has been shifting). Typically, only foods collected during the previous year can be eaten during this time, with the feast—functioning in tandem with the dancing, singing, and prayers—providing the context for a collective thanks that must be given before the new food gathering season can begin (Hamill 2008: 104).

The Medicine Dances and first-food feasts also function as acts of sovereignty and resistance. Treaties, signed between Indigenous Columbia Plateau communities and the federal government during the mid-to-late nineteenth century, included clauses ensuring the right to "hunt and fish in usual and accustomed places." For the past 150 years, tribes have had to continually reassert that right. The "fish wars" of the Northwest were not limited to the 1970s, but have continued in one form or another from the time of Euro-American settlement. The act of gathering, hunting, and fishing our traditional foods, coupled with their cyclical use in our ceremonies, ensures, at least for the time being, that the foods, the songs, the dances, and our language—essential components of our culture—will be available to future generations. Using Stefano Varese's concept of "bio-cultural sovereignty" within a framework of traditional ecological knowledge, Cutcha Risling Baldy discusses the "steadfast insistence" on the part of California tribes to continue "land-based cultural practices . . . gathering plants and conducting religious, spiritual, and other cultural practices . . . regardless of any concrete acknowledgement by the Supreme Court or the federal, state, or local governments" (2013: 7). Indigenous sovereignty extends beyond boundaries of reservation or state, crosses lines on a map, and reaches deeply into long-held practices embedded in the land.

Referring to a colonial preoccupation with cartography, Patrick Pynes suggests that "a map is always just a kind of symbol for a place, it is not the place it is meant to describe. Indeed, to know any kind of physical landscape you have to experience it directly; that is, to truly know any place you have to live in it and be a part of its life process. Maps also imply a history, and the political and cultural background of its makers" (Pynes, in Cajete 2000: 181). While warning that Indigenous peoples need to "map or be mapped," Joe Bryan suggests that "indigenous mapping should strive to change the profoundly colonial geographical understanding of the world" (2009: 24).[4] As a quiet and insidious form of conquest, colonial mapping has always been followed by occupation and displacement. Rhoda Roberts, in the "Modernity of Songlines" (in the present volume), sees Indigenous mapping in the lands of her Bundjlaung Widjabul people in Australia as a remedy to the colonial legacy, stating that "[t]he old, dreaming tracks, rituals of the creation, ancestors and spirits have been handed down, danced and sung for generations. The singing up of country, and the ceremonies connecting our physical and spiritual embodiment, mapping our spiritual relationship with the land, sea and sky are of crucial importance given the huge impact of colonisation and the missionary era."

The mapping of Spokane Country began in 1805 with Lewis and Clark, the first Euro-Americans in the region, and the occupation commenced not more than three years later, when David Thompson surveyed the area for the Northwest Fur Company. Two years after that, the Spokane House was built, the first permanent establishment by Euro-Americans in Spokane homelands. From there the mapping, occupation, displacement, and construction picked up in earnest.

The year 1881 was a watershed moment in the region: Spokane Falls, a city built upon our traditional lands and ancestral remains, became incorporated; the Spokane reservation was established, some 40 miles away, out of sight of the city that took our name and then our home; and the Northern Pacific Railway cut through the heart of our tribal territory, bringing a torrent of Euro-Americans to the region. To make matters worse, echoing an all-too-familiar theme in Indigenous North America, gold, silver, and lead were discovered in northern Idaho, leading to mining and smelting operations along the Spokane River. With a combination of mining runoff and raw sewage from Spokane (formally Spokane Falls) being dumped into the river, it became too polluted to fish in 1900. The construction of the Little Falls Dam in 1910, which included an inadequate fish ladder, made upstream passage nearly impossible and the Long Lake Dam, rising 200 feet out of the river, further reduced salmon runs. The salmon, who had been swimming up the Spokane River long before people arrived at its banks and had sustained them for thousands of years, began to disappear. From the seemingly benign point of contact in 1805, when two men and their crew arrived in the Columbia Plateau emaciated and starving, it took just 100 years to poison the lifeblood of tribes in the area and remove their primary source of physical and spiritual sustenance. Ironically, without the generosity of tribes nearby, who supplied the Lewis and Clark expedition with fish pulled from pristine river waters, the expedition, and the maps they were making, would have been buried in the Columbia Plateau.

Figure 6.1 Colville Indians Fishing at Kettle Falls (1938), Department of Interior/ Bureau of Indian Affairs. Courtesy of UW Special Collections (L93-75.31).

As vehicles for electric power and profit, dams continued to proliferate throughout the Columbia Plateau in the first half of the twentieth century, distorting the natural flow of many rivers, including the Columbia River and its tributaries. By sheer volume, the Columbia is the most powerful river in North America flowing into the Pacific Ocean. To tribes in the region, one of its most important attributes was Kettle Falls, a primary fishing site utilized for many thousands of years (Figure 6.1). Mourning Dove, born in 1888, reflects on the long-held significance of the falls:

The Indians gathered at the falls every year to spear salmon and dry it for the winter. All the surrounding tribes were welcome at this summer resort in the homeland of my Colvile people. It was a beautiful place to camp, with cliffs overhanging the falls on the west side and trails leading to the water between the high grayish-white rock formations that so often glistened in the sunlight. . . . The falls passed on either side of a large central rock that created a smooth backwater behind it. The area near the falls was filled with mist, ribboned with many colors creating a faint rainbow on a summer evening. A person with an artistic mind could easily draw a beautiful picture of this gift of nature. Our camp was close to the Colvile on the west, beside our Okanagan distant relatives from Osoyoos. The West side was called Lachin (Woven Kettle or Bucket) because of the many depressions made by the whirlpools there. The east side was known as S-calm-achin (Dug Ground) because the ground was rough with boulders and looked as though nature had dug it out in places. The east side encampment included the Kalispel, Spokane, Coeur d'Alene, and Flathead, while on the west side were the Okanagan, Sanpoil, Squant, and Wenatchi. . . . As soon as we arrived and my parents worked to set up camp, I ran down the side trail overlooking the falls. I could see the thirty-foot drop to the river, which was dotted with many Indian men with spears getting king or chinook salmon. Large log scaffolds extended over the foaming river where men stood to spear or net fish fighting to get up the falls. . . . Periodically, the salmon that had been caught were gathered into a big heap under the shade of the cliffs. There a man called the divider or Salmon Tyee took charge of giving fish to all the campers according to the size of the family in each lodge. It was equally divided among all, both workers and visitors, regardless of how much labor they had put in, every day at noon and dusk. Everyone got an equal share so that the fish would not think humans were being stingy or selfish and refuse to return." (Dove & Miller 1990: 100–101)

Apparent in Mourning Dove's account is the respect and reverence Indigenous communities had for the falls and the salmon that sustained them. Nothing was taken for granted and every family received an equal share, reflecting a worldview oriented toward collective balance rather than individual enrichment. It was understood that selfishness would disrupt that balance and that true abundance was something granted by the natural world, not amassed and measured at nature's expense through financial profit and material gain. In 1940, the tribes would meet at Kettle Falls one last time, before the Grand Coulee Dam would drown them and reduce the roaring river to a lifeless lake. Between 8,000 and 10,000 tribal members attended what became known as the "Ceremony of Tears," a time to grieve as well as an effort to comprehend, to the extent possible, how a shared history shaped over thousands of years could disappear in a matter of days (Figure 6.2).

Figure 6.2 Indigenous leaders of the Colville Indian Reservation gathered at the soon-to-be finished Grand Coulee Dam (1941). Photograph by William S. Russell, US Bureau of Reclamation.

In addition to flooding vast swaths of land that held traditional foods and bones of their ancestors, the Grand Coulee Dam ended salmon migration through the upper Columbia and Spokane Rivers, robbing thousands of tribal members, the salmon, and rivers they navigated of their primordial meaning and purpose. Violence toward the Spokane River continues today. Owing to the Bunker Hill Mine and Smelting Complex, a Superfund Site,[5] and pollution from Lake Coeur d'Alene, it contains more heavy metals than any river in the state of Washington. It's as if the monster from the river's creation story has returned from the lake after 200 years of industrial poisoning, a wild-eyed toxic beast spewing waste into the river, mirroring the self-destructive behavior of its non-Indigenous captors.

Tribes in the region have been anything but idle, using contemporary "implements of chase and war," including the courts, to drive the monster out again. In January 2014, the Spokane Tribe adopted strict water quality standards for the length of the river that runs through the Spokane Reservation, spurring a federal judge in March 2015 to order the Environmental Protection Agency to come up with a plan to adequately address cancer-causing PCBs in the Spokane

River. On May 21, 2015, the Coeur d'Alene, Kalispel, Kootenai, Spokane, and the nine Confederated Tribes of the Colville Reservation received the Ralph Johnson Hero Award for "their leadership in restoring salmon" through tribal fisheries. After the removal of two dams on the Elwa River, our neighbors to the West, the Klallam tribe, have seen salmon return for the first time in over a century.

For these tribes, ecologically based adaptation predates contact. The following, shared by Chief Lot in 1907, has its origins in the formation of the Spokane River:

> One summer morning the entire population were startled by the rumbling and shaking of the earth. The waters of the lake began rising, and pitching, and tossed into mountainous waves, which threatened to engulf the entire country. To add to the horrors of the situation, the sun became obscured by an eclipse, and darkness added its horrors to the scene. The terror-stricken inhabitants fled to the hills for safety. The shaking of the earth continued for two days, when a rain of ashes began to fall, and so heavy was the fall of them that there was little difference between night and day. The fall of ashes continued for several weeks. The game abandoned the country, the waters of the lake receded and dry land filled its place, and desolation spread over the entire country. . . . The remnant [of Indians] who escaped starvation followed the course of receding waters until they arrived at the Falls (now Spokane)." (Whis-tel-po-sum, aka Chief Lot, in Ross: 747)

Today, Indigenous communities in rural Alaska, while seeing air temperatures increase twice as fast as the global average, a reduction of summer sea ice, thawing of permafrost, and a shortening of the snow season are well positioned to observe the ecological and societal consequences of climate change and develop strategies to respond accordingly (Lynn et al. 2013: 551) because of their intimate connection to an environment in which changes in weather, plant, and animal populations have been the norm. Indigenous communities around the world are similarly prepared to adapt, relying on Indigenous epistemologies rooted in the land and the traditions formed from it. The Intergovernmental Panel on Climate Change appears to agree, stating in its 2014 report that "historically, indigenous peoples have had a high capacity to adapt to variable environmental conditions" based on their "intimate relationship" to the environment and age-old "livelihood activities" "dependent on climate and weather conditions" (765–766). While earth-centered Indigenous communities are drawing on these age-old relationships, large segments of the dominant settler society have shown no interest in developing that connection, destined to repeat the cycle of environmental degradation. They will continue to feed the monster, consuming the gifts of our Mother Earth with reckless abandon while chasing illusory forms of wealth that will become worthless as exploited resources dry up and vanish.

Meanwhile, just as our ancestors followed the receding waters to the Falls through air thick with ash, we will continue to make our way through the photochemical haze of the colonial legacy. Following a sacred geography of song, we will walk along well-worn ancestral pathways, traversing the landscape, filling our baskets with sacred foods that will be placed upon the sacred floor, where we will continue to sing, dance, and pray our Indigenous ecology and Spokane world into being.

Notes

1. A tributary of the Columbia River, the Spokane River is located in the interior Northwest United States, stretching 111 miles through present-day northern Idaho and eastern Washington.
2. The Columbia Plateau is a region composed of 63,000 square miles of lava basalts, encompassing parts of present-day Washington, Idaho, and Oregon.
3. Camas and bitterroot have been important traditional foods for tribes throughout the Columbia Plateau region for many thousands of years. Camas is a type of lily with a nutritious bulb that, when cooked, has a sweet quality. Bitterroot is a small flowering plant with a similarly nutritious taproot that has many medicinal properties.
4. An Indigenous map would dissolve geographic boundaries and emphasize important cultural sites, stories, and songs tied to the land. Rather than denoting territory and dominion, it would reflect the respect and reverence the People have for the land and all that it provides.
5. Superfund sites are areas identified by the federal Environmental Protection Agency as significantly polluted, requiring cleanup of hazardous contaminants that pose serious health risks to nearby populations. Nearly 25 percent of the over 1,300 Superfund sites are located on American Indian reservations.

7

The Modernity of the Songlines

Rhoda Roberts

I am a Bundjlaung Widjabul woman, the founding director of the Boomerang Festival and also head of Indigenous programming for the Sydney Opera House. Our programs endeavor to revisit ancient cultural elements and undertake reclamation work, creating new works across all platforms and commissioning international First Nations collaborations while considering certain risk factors such as exploring the intersection of art and social change.

I have titled this chapter "The Modernity of the Songlines." For me, the songline is about your clan, your boundaries, water resources, obligations; it is a road map of history and spirituality. The interconnecting stories, the song cycles, were, for some, the first sound that began our ancient creative process and marked the lore as well as marking trade routes on the ground. Songlines were also paths in the sky; our cultures contain evidence of a detailed understanding of tides, eclipses, and the cosmos.

Along with the massive environment changes globally, our local communities are facing a time like no other. While we are an ever-adapting culture, with the passing of our cultural custodians—lore men and women who carry the ancient degrees of knowledge—our traditional knowledge is slipping away. With each death a library of profound knowledge, eternal worth and timeless customary value is lost.

Our elders only told the anthropologists what they wanted to hear. Some things were/are secret: sacred material and public knowledge ceremonies they kept to themselves. It was the responsibility of each generation of children to know, learn, listen, and hear country.

For the last decade our landscape across the creative industries has changed in Australia for Aboriginal people. That change has come in many forms, including new technology and the internet. We have also seen political change. On April 3, 2009, the Australian government announced that it would become a signatory to the United Nations Declaration on the Rights of Indigenous Peoples. This document recognizes the importance of respect for Indigenous knowledge, cultures, and traditional practices and affirms that Indigenous people have individual and collective rights. The Declaration had been adopted by the General Assembly of the United Nations in September 2007. This was the culmination of more than

Rhoda Roberts, *The Modernity of the Songlines* In: *Transforming Ethnomusicology.* Edited by: Beverley Diamond and Salwa El-Shawan Castelo-Branco, Oxford University Press (2021). © Oxford University Press.
DOI: 10.1093/oso/9780197517550.003.0008

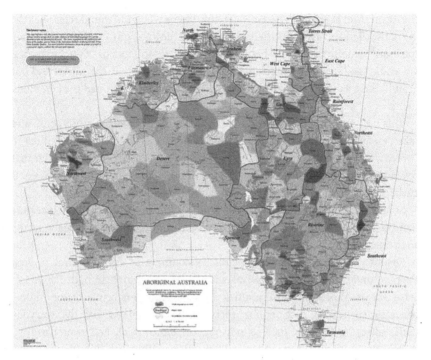

Figure 7.1 Map of Aboriginal Australia.

twenty years of negotiations between the Indigenous peoples and governments of the world. The Australian government at the time under the Howard regime had voted against the declaration and it took two years of strategic approaches and discussion for the government to sign.

The Declaration notes that Indigenous people have the right to maintain, control, protect, and develop their intellectual property over cultural heritage, traditional knowledge, and traditional cultural expressions. It calls on signatory states to take effective measures to recognize and protect the exercise of these rites. Since Australia signed the Declaration, we have seen a groundswell of growth across the creative industries, and through education and capacity-building initiatives, a two-way approach of working has developed. Most significantly, the revitalization of knowledges of Aboriginal peoples has strengthened intergenerational transmission.

But to get here in the last decade it has been an ongoing battle. The struggle began back in the 1700s when Pemulwuy of the Burramatagal Clan declared war on the new arrivals. He was one of our greatest custodians and his resistance fighters led the way in what became known today as the years of the Struggle. Sadly after his beheading, an era of terror reigned over our peoples in the form of the Aborigines Protection Act: it was a time that my Granny would refer to as the era of the silences. "Don't let them hear you talk the lingo girl, don't sing that song too loud." Quietly she took us behind the sugar cane and told us of the time when we would "go bush for women's business"; my father told me the stories and our grandfathers sang the ancient songs, while the women drummed the ceremony to life.

This was done in secrecy. There was fear the mission man would come and take you away. Over the years there were many policies that basically aimed to "breed out the problem," by assimilating the Blacks. Our cultural knowledge that related to our kinship lines, moieties lore, and societal structures were seen as barbaric, our practices of maintaining country as uncivilized savagery.

So as a Bundjalung woman I today still feel the connection to my ancestors and the cultural obligations and responsibilities to continue the legacy of the song line.

Dispossession and assimilation policies continue to affect Australia's First Peoples, undermining community, leadership, and cultural strength. There is a crisis across Aboriginal communities resulting from our brutal history, inter-generational trauma, and ongoing racism, when combined with the everyday issues affecting families such as poverty, unemployment, and overcrowding. A certain social isolation and marginalization within the dominant society becomes a reality. We constantly hear the negative: we are said to be the problem, the Aboriginal disadvantage.

But actually the reality is that we have the advantage: our culture, the oldest living and adapting culture on the planet. It is the advantage. So rather than con-sistently bombard our artists with the usual statistics that I am sure many readers have heard—higher rates of infant mortality, incarceration, unemployment—I see the positive. If I was a young man I wonder if I would wake up with hope.

The statistic on which I like to focus is that 92 percent of Australians con-sider our First Nations arts an important part of Australian culture.[1] In addi-tion, 64 percent of Australians have a strong or growing interest in art created or performed by Aboriginal or Torres Strait Islander peoples. However, only 24 per-cent have attended Aboriginal or Torres Strait Islander arts events and activities in the last year.

So we have a lot of work to do at home, and there are many challenges with developing our arts, engaging the diversity of our communities, developing audiences, and creating a sustainable economic future.

There is still a major imbalance between efforts to provide a Westernized edu-cation and better lifestyle that has seen many of our people relocate off country. This has created a generation of children who are missing out on Aboriginal ed-ucation and understanding of how biodiversity directly affects their connection to country and access to traditional cultural knowledge. This is due to a number of reasons, from access to sites, lack of leadership, isolation, and a feeling of help-lessness with new federal policies, as well as a failure to recognize the vital impor-tance cultural and language revitalization can bring.

This cannot be solved unless partnerships are formed with the broader sector, allowing the choices in delivering the solution to be informed by First Nations' international perspectives and dialogue. I have watched our Canadian and Maori brothers and sisters to see how they have created a viable ethical cultural tourism industry.

But while we tread the paths that have been created by the ancestors we are operating in a new world and there is often a sense that many Aboriginal arts workers, performers, and cultural custodial practitioners feel pulled between our two worlds. We need to be mindful of this and challenge many assumptions of what is authenticity, what are taboo subjects and appropriate material. It is what our artists tackle on a daily basis within their own communities and clan structures as well as with elders and leaders. But again we need to focus on the positive while understanding those damaged and disenfranchised members of community. With almost 40 percent of the Indigenous population under the age of fifteen years, compared with 20 percent for the non-Indigenous population, we have a very bright future if it is mapped and nurtured appropriately.

We have over 70,000 years of Indigenous story-telling. Aboriginal Australia presents, therefore, a diverse cultural and creative mix that is dynamic and highly valuable to the national social and economic life of Australia. Our art forms cannot be boxed into one specific genre: music is not music without other forms of expression. Our extensive heritage of cultural production has been tradi-tionally combined in many forms such as painting, wood carving, rock etching, weaving, body adorning, and other performative practices. These traditions have been retained and, at the same time, transformed in an exciting contemporary artistic paradigm. Contemporary Aboriginal and Torres Strait Islander art and culture is in new media, music, contemporary dance, literature, acrylic paint on canvas, and glass work, among other genres. The cultural embodiment of who we are, where we belong, and our spiritual connection to land and kinship has informed us as communities, and now through artistic and performance oppor-tunities contributes to a collective cultural identity for all Australians.

As expressions of the world's longest continuing living culture we need to re-visit what the assumptions are. We must ask whether the recording of stories, music, and other cultural expressions from the old people translated well. There is now a huge reclamation work across all sectors of the creative industries. In music new works are exciting, bold, and at times a fusion of many modern styles. But we must ask: is this still Aboriginal cultural work?

While greater representation of Aboriginal and Torres Strait Islander people across the arts is sought, there are challenges. Some non-Indigenous audiences have preconceptions and perceptions about the content of Aboriginal and Torres Strait Islander art that may inhibit their engagement with Aboriginal and Torres Strait Islander art. Marketing that focuses on audience education is a recognized need.

Achievements and Challenges

I turn now to recent initiatives to consider the achievements as well as the challenges. It is all about commitment. The commitment that the Sydney Opera House makes, for instance, is to continue to provide support to all art forms. This makes a huge difference where the First People's perspectives are concerned.

In my current position as head of Indigenous programming at the Sydney Opera House, we have developed a framework that:

- Encompasses and builds a sustainable program, to showcase the depth, diversity, and excellence of culture and to attract new audiences by creating an Indigenous experience.
- Grows and embeds projects across the House through a program that observes Indigenous protocol and reflects integrity, authenticity, and diversity while remaining true to its vision as a leading cultural venue.
- Ensures audiences are given new cultural experiences that reflect both the change and continuity of First People's lives.
- Engages artists, cultural custodians, and Indigenous companies—both international and national—from rural, remote, and urban areas.

Each art form faces slightly different challenges. Our visual art faces some challenges in the commercial art market, but is strengthening its presence in large-scale exhibitions. The depth and quality of dance being developed and performed is very strong. The challenges relate to the underdeveloped audience and the need to build public awareness of Aboriginal and Torres Strait Islander dance. Theater is viewed as a mature art form, which has made significant inroads in developing audiences. There is a great sense of optimism and a sense of momentum behind the growth and development of Aboriginal and Torres Strait Islander theatre. Aboriginal and Torres Strait Islander literature is particularly strong in its ability to tell diverse stories. Awareness and literacy levels, particularly in remote and regional communities, are identified as two critical challenges to developing audiences.

Music has enjoyed great success in recent years, with a number of breakthrough performers. Music has the potential to be an accessible entry point for

Aboriginal and Torres Strait Islander art. Recent projects include Gurrumul's gospel album[2] and the Sydney Symphony collaboration on a project to present Prison Songs featuring singer/songwriter Shellie Morris[3] at the Darwin Festival.[4] Other projects include performer and producer Jessie Lloyd's *Mission Songs* project[5] and the Country Song Theatre show, both of which are reconnecting modern history to practices that over the decades have also become traditions. Our most successful theater projects have been musicals such as *Bran Nue Dae*[6] and *The Sapphires*.[7] While musicals are not one of my favorite genres, they have allowed our modern history of color bars and living under the Protection Act along with the nineteenth- and twentieth-century Aboriginal music traditions to be told to new audiences. A new form of aural/oral tradition!

Festivals, including the Boomerang Festival[8] which I founded and direct, are also identified as a major opportunity for engaged and potential audiences to experience a range of Aboriginal and Torres Strait Islander art. Festivals that are produced by Aboriginal and Torres Strait Islander people are particularly important in celebrating communities and providing people with opportunities to develop new skills.

We have seen a groundswell of creative work as more and more projects across the globe are controlled and created from an Aboriginal and/or First Peoples perspective. Much of the work retains language and revitalizes ritual forms. It is exciting and can be edgy to see the fusion of our traditional dance, the maintenance of our mother tongues, first instruments and song practices, with Western creative disciplines, techniques and multimedia. At the Sydney Opera House, we would argue this is a good thing.

Critical practice and repatriation are redefining the false myth of our "lost cultures." Our creative practices have enabled Indigenous arts industry workers across all genres a relevant voice, better employment prospects, community outcomes, and, most important, the control of how we are perceived. Portrayals of the "primitive" or "noble savage" as in the static museum exhibitions of the past now receive ridicule.

With our creative control has come enlightenment, there is depth and a layered comprehension, enabling the viewer an awareness of the sophisticated and complex societal structures we have developed and lived for thousands of years.

But what of the continuing cultural obligations and clan /nation responsibilities that are the cultural inheritance of the oldest living race?

I believe it is vital for the next generations of First Peoples to build bridges, to develop Indigenous capacity, employment in the workplace, and health and wellbeing for our communities. But is there enough importance placed on ensuring that our youth experience the old ways of traditional intergenerational knowledge transmission. Do we respect the relevance of these forms of transmission in the twenty-first century? Are we in a dangerous predicament of unconsciously conforming to a "mainstream" perspective and, to a certain extent, devaluing our own ancient ways?

Is there room for the unchanging knowledge and traditions of the songline and the *Corroboree*? Continuing the Songline interchange through social and cultural intergeneration transmission has become vital. The old trade routes, dreaming tracks, rituals of the creation, ancestors and spirits have been handed down, danced and sung for generations. The singing up of country, and the ceremonies connecting our physical and spiritual embodiment, mapping our spiritual relationship with the land, sea, and sky, are of crucial importance given the huge impact of colonization and the missionary era.

At the Sydney Opera House we have had the opportunity to explore many dynamics through programming and international exchanges. We have built capacity through outreach projects such as Song Rites and Deadly Voice projects.[9] We now move forward with a new annual event designed to bring the songlines back on country and to create sustainable employment practices. We are doing what all societies—from those of Aristotle to Mozart, for example—must do to highlight their traditions, culture, and music forms. It is a given that each civilization nurtures and treasures their culture.

Notes

1. Australian Council for the Arts (2014: 17).
2. Geoffrey Gurrumul Yunupingu (1971–2017) was an acclaimed artist in Australia. He received numerous awards for his recordings and performances. A film has been produced about his short life.
3. https://www.shelliemorris.net/music.html, accessed December 11, 2018.
4. https://www.darwinfestival.org.au, accessed December 10, 2018.
5. http://missionsongsproject.com, accessed December 10, 2018.
6. A 1990 musical that tells stories of life in the 1960s in Broome, Western Australia, written by Jimmy Chi and Kuckles.
7. A 2012 production about an all-girls group—The Sapphires—who entertained US troops in Vietnam in the late 1960s.
8. https://www.boomerangfestival.com.au, accessed December 11, 2018.
9. Descriptions are available online: https://www.sydneyoperahouse.com/events/sydney-opera-house-presents/first-nations.html, accessed December 10, 2018.

8

Music Endangerment, Repatriation, and Intercultural Collaboration in an Australian Discomfort Zone

*Sally Treloyn and Rona Goonginda Charles**.

In 2011, the Australian and New Zealand Regional Committee of the International Council for Traditional Music issued a statement that describes Australia's Indigenous music and dance traditions as "among the oldest and most endangered in the world" and estimates that up to 98 percent have been lost (ANZ-ICTM 2011). Not surprisingly, many ethnomusicologists in Australia have sought to address music endangerment. Recording has long been an approach to this task. However, responding both to recognition of Indigenous rights to cultural heritage and rights of Indigenous peoples to self-determination in the conduct of research and management of research outcomes (AIATSIS 2002 [2012]),[1] the repatriation of recordings has increasingly entered the practice of many Australian ethnomusicologists (cf. Treloyn 2016b). The prevalence of repatriation in discourse around preservation in Australia is exemplified by the 2002 Garma Statement on Indigenous Music and Dance, which recommends that: "[t]he preservation of performance traditions is . . . one of the highest priorities for Indigenous people" and "the recording *and repatriation* of songs . . . be supported by universities and other institutions" (GFIPR 2002, emphasis added).

The growing prevalence of repatriation and the dissemination of legacy records in the work of Australian ethnomusicologists is evident. Both early-career and senior ethnomusicologists, such as Linda Barwick, Clint Bracknell, Reuben Brown, Genevieve Campbell, Aaron Corn, Grace Koch, Fiona Magowan, Allan Marett, Peter Toner, Sally Treloyn, and others, have woven repatriation of and dissemination of legacy recordings into their research agendas. Indigenous musicians and researchers in the academy and community, such as Joseph Neparrnga Gumbula, Payi Linda Ford, Rona Goonginda Charles, Matthew Dembalali Martin, and Bracknell, have pioneered repatriation in collaboration with these scholars and independently. Marking the increasing prevalence of repatriation as a documented research tool and/or activity, two of the four doctoral dissertations on Aboriginal song completed in 2014–2016 (Campbell 2014,

Sally Treloyn and Rona Goonginda Charles, *Music Endangerment, Repatriation, and Intercultural Collaboration in an Australian Discomfort Zone* In: *Transforming Ethnomusicology.* Edited by: Beverley Diamond and Salwa El-Shawan Castelo-Branco, Oxford University Press (2021). © Oxford University Press.
DOI: 10.1093/oso/9780197517550.003.0009

Brown 2016, both at University of Sydney) extensively examine processes and effects of repatriation within the song tradition under examination.

In the history of ethnomusicological research that has sought to address the problem of how to sustain endangered music, there has been a broad shift from salvage, collection-based approaches toward approaches that also seek to understand and reinforce the social fields in which musical traditions are created and thrive (Grant 2015). This shift is demonstrated by new approaches to the assessment of music endangerment centered on music vitality that take into account: social creative innovation, change as a factor in continuity, opportunity to practice, and social attitudes to the health of traditions (Grant 2014). Insofar as intergenerational knowledge transmission is a factor in music vitality and access to legacy records has been shown to be an important factor in the social production and transmission of knowledge in Australia (Marett & Barwick 2003, Toner 2003, Campbell 2012, 2014) and elsewhere (see, e.g., Hilder 2012, Kahunde 2012), it is logical that repatriation and dissemination may contribute to music vitality. Repatriation has emerged as a widely used intervention and method to address the question of how to maintain the vitality of endangered musical traditions and the linguistic, epistemological, and ontological diversities that they sustain.

Repatriation studies also produce substantial knowledge about the modern contexts in which music and musical styles are produced, shared, learned, and performed. Moreover, repatriation studies have also begun to produce knowledge about the political and social underpinnings of applied ethnomusicology, particularly that which has employed recording, archiving, and repatriation as methods to address preservation and cultural rights agendas. Speaking of the repatriation of the Klaus Wachsmann collection from the British Library Sound Archive to the Makerere University Klaus Wachsmann Music Archive in Kampala, Uganda, and to relevant materials to the Bagisu community, Nannyonga-Tamusuza and Weintraub (2012) suggest that "the study of repatriating" has forged a new transformative ethnomusicological praxis (cf. Seeger in Volume I of this compendium):

> Repatriation is a form of cultural critique: a critical and reflexive discourse about the social relations of power in cultural representations, and a model for dissembling and potentially undoing those relations. (2012, 209)

Scope for critical and reflexive discourse on the power relations in the intercultural repatriation that occurs in the context of ethnomusicology in Australia is similarly marked by the idea that repatriation can fulfill a rights-based research agenda. Repatriation may indeed support cultural equity and be one way for cultural heritage communities to control records of cultural heritage and lead revitalization efforts. This is particularly the case in collaborative approaches to repatriation. However, any uncritical assumption that intercultural collaboration via repatriation somehow redresses the problems of past collection-orientated research methods risks reinforcing relations of power that originate in the colonization of First Nations and Peoples. Gregory Bateson's notion of the "double bind" (1973: 173–249) as applied by Australian anthropologist Deborah Bird Rose in her critique of the pathological "passive violence" (1986) and "deep colonising" (1996) in contemporary Australian society, including in uses of the trope of self-determination, is useful here. In Rose's model:

> 1. a "victim" chosen by those who have the power to choose; 2. [there is] a primary coercive injunction; 3. [there is] a secondary injunction, also coercive, and conflicting with the first (usually communicated at a more abstract level); 4. [there is] a tertiary injunction which prohibits the victim from escaping from or commenting upon the pathological communication of the first two injunctions. In short, a "victim" is faced with the paradoxical necessity to act in a no-win situation and is denied the opportunity to escape or to represent this situation to others. (Rose 1986: 25)

In the Australian situation, the actors involved in the rollout of policies that served to kill off Indigenous linguistic and cultural practices can be seen to have enacted the first criterion of the double bind: "a 'victim' chosen by those who have the power to choose." An account provided by Chester Street, a linguist at the Centre for Aboriginal Studies in Music (CASM) in the 1980s, illustrates this:

> Confronted by force, ignorance and arrogant contempt, by the sheer weight of white numbers, by new authorities replacing the old, and by the illusory hope of white man's ease, the music and its embodied authority, power and cohesion were wounded, often to death. . . . Aboriginal people were dispersed from the places where songs ought to be sung, often by direct prohibition of performances or by the death of too many of the song owners. The songs could no longer be passed on. As an initiated Flinders Ranges man said in the 1960s:
> "We see everybody going to the pack boys and even girls—they just do what they like. The old people that went through the rules, they know better. White fellas interfered in our rules, stopping us from doing our corroborees. No songs—no rules." (Street, in Breen et al 1989: 12, Ellis 1968: 5)

The "primary coercive injunction" was the requirement that, in order to survive, Indigenous peoples were compelled by the state to "assimilate," not speak Indigenous languages, or practice ceremony, song, or other cultural activities. This is fundamentally paradoxical, in that song and language are held to be essential for survival. For singers who survived to the early 1900s, a "second co-ercive injunction," contradicting the first, came into play as outsiders sought to record and preserve song. Then in the late twentieth century and into the twenty-first, with the rise of Applied Ethnomusicology, a concern for cultural equity, and self-determination, Indigenous peoples are compelled to engage and collab-orate with outsider-researchers and archives if they wish to retrieve their songs and cultural practices: we see "a tertiary injunction which prohibits the victim from escaping from or commenting upon the pathological communication of the ... injunction[s]" (Rose 1986: 25).

Working from this problematic ground of deep colonization, there is substan-tial scope for ethnomusicologists and cultural heritage bearers and stakeholders engaged in repatriation for the purposes of revitalization to feel deep unease. Contributing to a broader body of critically reflexive research on intercul-tural collaboration in Australian ethnomusicology (Mackinlay & Barney 2014, Mackinlay & Chalmers 2014), repatriation on this problematic ground provides scope for collaborating researchers and community members to critically ex-amine the power relations of the past and present in which they are entangled, thereby—it is hoped—disrupting the "bind" through present action. Such re-flection is also seen beyond Australia. In the case of the Hopi Music Project, for example, Trevor Reed describes how examination of the processes of repatria-tion led to the development of a critically and culturally informed "community-partnered repatriation" that supported social networks in the cultural heritage community, allowing recognition of local views on intellectual property and a more equitable practice (2009: 9).

For Rose in the 1980s, it was the responsibility of the anthropologists (and presumably others engaged in forms of ethnography) to reveal something of what they witnessed in Indigenous communities in the action of their disci-pline, to "develop a distinctive discourse based on a non-violent analysis of the power relationships in which these communities are embedded," and thus push back against the tendency of scholarly disciplines to become complicit in the passive violence that pervades the academy and other institutions in the settler state (Rose 1986: 24). An ethics of witnessing in ethnomusicology emerges (cf. Wong in Volume I). Elsewhere, we (the authors) have approached our intercul-tural collaboration as a site of productive discomfort, drawing on Somerville and Perkins's reframing of the postcolonial contact zone (Pratt 2008 [1992]: 7) as a "discomfort zone" (Somerville & Perkins 2003: 257) where a tendency to homog-enize experience is resisted and there is potential for new and hybrid knowledge to be produced (Manathunga 2009: 166, Treloyn & Charles 2014).

In this chapter, we recount some of the outcomes and discomforts of The Junba Project, a project based in the Kimberley region of northwest Australia (which has run since 2009) supported by AIATSIS, the Australian Research Council, and numerous Aboriginal organizations—the Kimberley Aboriginal Law and Culture Centre, the Kimberley Language Resource Centre, the Mowanjum Aboriginal Art and Culture Centre, Winun Ngari Aboriginal Resource Centre, the Dambimangarri Aboriginal Corporation, and the Wilinggin Aboriginal Corporation. The project has emphasized collaborative reflection on research methods and assumptions, with an aim to identify strategies to sustain endangered Junba dance-song practices through recording, repatriation, and dissemination. The successes of the project, in terms of how it has supported music vitality and addressed endangerment, are reported in a number of recent publications (Treloyn, Charles & Nulgit 2013, Treloyn & Charles 2015, Treloyn, Martin & Charles 2016). We have also reflected on the contested, intercultural spaces of our relationship and collaboration, and the relationships between individuals in cultural heritage communities and archives (Treloyn & Charles 2014, Treloyn, Martin & Charles 2016). In this chapter we revisit this conversation, looking now to the roles that the recordings and a local epistemological framework to understand the departure and return of the voices of ancestors play in intercultural collaboration to address music endangerment. The chapter is in three sections. The first provides a brief introduction to the Kimberley region and lifeworld in which Junba is composed and performed and repatriated, with some insight into its revitalization. The second turns to discomforts. The third turns to the local epistemological framework for approaching, listening to, and conceiving of the return of recordings of Junba for the purposes of revitalization.

The Junba Project: Repatriation and Music Endangerment

The Kimberley is an expansive region of over 400,000 square km in the northwest of the Australian continent. It is culturally diverse, with approximately thirty language groups and a population of approximately 40,000 people, approximately 50 percent of which is Indigenous, living in towns and remote communities. Junba is a diverse genre of dance-song that is Indigenous to almost all of the language groups of the region. It is a public genre and performed at events such as festivals, art gallery openings, and exhibitions, as well as at more private events. The composition, performance, and sharing of Junba is done to teach young people, to honor and carry the legacy of deceased family members, maintain and reinvigorate connections with creative ancestral beings, and, intertwined with each of these, maintain connections with land and demonstrate cultural practice to strangers. These connections are enacted through the composition and performance of song texts, performance practice, choreography, and the carrying of elaborate *ornod jirri* (dance boards) upon which important stories, ancestral beings, and places are painted. Junba has been a primary tool for the families of the Mowanjum Aboriginal Community to negotiate their displacement from traditional country further north and inland through the twentieth century to the present. The singing is done by a mixed-gender ensemble, within which men and women have distinct, alternating melodic parts, led by a composer and accompanied by clapsticks and clapping.

The primary aim of the Junba Project has been to respond to concerns voiced by elders about the attrition of Junba songs and dances from current repertories and a reduction in participation by young people. As has been documented elsewhere, the project involved teaching events in which elders pass knowledge and skills to young people (see Figure 8.1); community-led discovery, research, and repatriation of recordings of Junba from national archives and legacy collections; the recovery of songs from recordings and reconstruction of dances from archival photos and videos, supplemented by knowledge of elders and associates; community-led recording and documentation; production of knowledge through Junba-based iMovie workshops; creation of databases of Junba dance song recordings for community use and dissemination; and use of these materials and their production as part of Indigenous ranger and art center programs.

Data on the number of songs and repertories performed at the annual Mowanjum Festival between 2010 and 2016 suggest that repatriation-based

Figure 8.1 Elder Pansy Nulgit teaching young dancers at Mowanjum Festival, Mowanjum, Western Australia, July 7, 2016. Photo: Sally Treloyn.

activities of the Junba Project have supported the task of addressing the health of the tradition. While there was attrition up to 2010, over the five-year life of the project and through 2016 there was a recovery and increase in the quantity of songs and repertoires. With this increase comes an increase in the musical and linguistic diversity. An increase in factors such as the age of singers, and opportunities for performance and knowledge transmission, can also be observed.

While a fine-grained examination of the link between particular acts and histories of repatriation and the revitalization indicated in Figure 8.2 is needed, it might be asserted that the Junba Project exemplifies how repatriation can support music vitality. In assessing the role of repatriation in countering music endangerment in neo-colonial Australia, however, we must turn to how participants—the authors of this chapter and others—have approached and experienced the transactions and its products. To do this, we approach the contact zone of our intercultural collaboration as a "discomfort zone," looking upon the intellectual and social spaces of our project as defined by both difference and as an opportunity for intersubjective identification that allows for transcultural, postcolonial knowledge production and cultural maintenance. Second, we approach the legacy recordings according to local regard for them as subjective participants in knowledge transmission, rather than as objective relics of past research and research relationships; and, we approach our collaboration for cultural maintenance via an Indigenous epistemology, as an enactment of the northern Kimberley Law and ethos of Wurnan.

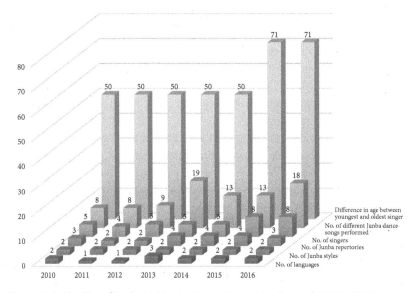

Figure 8.2 Vitality of Junba in Mowanjum: Mowanjum Festival, 2010–2016.

The Discomfort Zone: Double Binds
of Intercultural Collaboration

The Kimberley region has a violent history marked by attempts to depopulate the territory for townships and pastoral leases: massacres, war and resistance, slavery, and human rights violations. The injustice of this persists today in the re-traumatization of non-recognition, ongoing struggles for access to land, equitable health, housing, education, and representation. In the Kimberley, the work of ethnomusicologists shares a particularly uncomfortable history with research that was complicit in this violence. On the same expedition that Swedish zoologist and ethnographer Eric Mjöberg stole remains of descendants of Ngarinyin and Nyikina peoples (the two groups to which Charles belongs) from burial platforms in 1911, Yngve Laurell made the first recordings of song in the region (Treloyn & Charles 2014). The reverberations of this are felt by Charles with the steady stream of researchers who have come through her communities from the 1930s onward. Charles has previously reflected on her initial concerns of Treloyn's presence in the Mowanjum community in 2000 to 2002, when Treloyn was a graduate student working almost exclusively with elders:

> Sally . . . was doing a lot of recording with some of the older people, [a] lot of the seniors. . . . I thought to myself, "She gonna come in there, get all this stuff, take him [the recordings and research] back, and lock it up somewhere," you know. That [was] what I was thinking. (Treloyn & Charles 2014)

While recording does not necessarily remove a song from a cultural heritage community, it is the experience of many that *something* is taken when a song is recorded and when that recording is transported away. This concern is not remedied by simply ensuring that communities have access to the end products of research. Charles's concern was that Treloyn was claiming a possibly unique opportunity for transmission of song knowledge that comes about when an elder feels that are ready to pass on:

> I used to always think that "They are preparing themselves to die, when they want to give their knowledge." . . . I used to say to myself, "They'll ask me to be part of them when they are ready." I used to think [that] they want to put all that knowledge . . . in the CD with you, because they might be running out of time. (Treloyn & Charles 2014)

For Charles, Treloyn's presence compounded her difficult task of repairing the ruptures in intergenerational knowledge transmission that were caused by policies that harmed people, language, and cultural practice.

As a non-Indigenous researcher in Australia, Treloyn's discomforts centered on the risk of perpetuating the passive violence of intercultural research. Critical discourse on music endangerment, and music revitalization, has become nuanced by corresponding awareness of the political connotations of the deficit language that is often used to describe the state of musical traditions: preservation suggests that song practice is separable from living people; loss connotes a lack of care on the part of heritage communities; endangerment connotes association between Indigenous peoples, and animals and plants; the notion of "dying cultures" connotes Aboriginal Protection Acts predicated on the notion that Indigenous peoples were of a "dying" race—a discourse that featured prominently in the early twentieth-century anthropological work in the region (see, e.g., *Sterbende Welt in Nordwest Australien* [The Dying World in Northwest Australia], Petri 1954). As such, as discussed in the opening section of this chapter, collaboration and repatriation risks a pathological double bind. At best, such terms also risk positioning the ethnomusicologist—typically from outside a cultural heritage community—as coming in to save or protect. As Grant (2014: 3–4) has pointed out, such notions point to the paternalistic notions that underpin discourse of music endangerment.

In practice, when thinking of the harm of the coercive injunction of the double bind, Treloyn's concern centers on the impact that she has on intergenerational knowledge transmission. Today she finds herself in the position of holder of song knowledge. This manifests in numerous ways, but the most recent is that emerging singers aged seventeen to thirty-five have come to her to elicit the lyrics of Junba songs. Singers—old and young—have called on her to support performances as a backup singer and sometimes female lead. She finds herself contributing to the search and identification of photographic and video materials to support the recovery of dances. Digital Heritage Officers turn to her to populate community databases, which she has supported the establishment of, and that are inadequate in their structure when faced with the complexity of the song system. Treloyn has produced documents—namely her 2006 dissertation—that culture bearers have used to support their learning lyrics. While she is pleased to have produced and mobilized knowledge and products that are of use in the community, this is perhaps a striking example of the symbolic violence of colonial Western discourse described by Edward Said in action, wherein "knowledge about Indigenous peoples . . . [is] collected, classified and then represented in various ways back to the West, and then, through the eyes of the West, back to those who have been colonized" (Tuhiwai Smith 2012 [1998]: 31).

Thus, while supporting music vitality, the applied collaborative project is marked by discomfort and risk, for both of the authors. For Charles this could understandably result in her abandoning the notion of research—as Māori scholar

Linda Tuhiwai Smith notes, for many, research is a "dirty word" (Smith 1999). For Treloyn, like others, it could be easy to feel paralysed (see Lancefield 1998).

So, we (the authors) ask ourselves, how do we proceed? For Charles, supporting younger generations as emerging singers, dancers, composers, and researchers is essential, as is listening to the wisdom of elders and country. For Treloyn, a way forward has been paved by new modes of reflexive, collaborative, applied ethnomusicological practice, and the willingness of Indigenous stakeholders to engage with her and her institutions, coupled with generous funding support and mentorship. For both of us, along with increasing community agency in research design, process, and outputs, our collaboration is framed by a local epistemological basis for dealing with strangers and strange things: the subject-status of repatriated voices and the Law and ethos of sharing known as Wurnan.

Relational Repatriation and Revitalization

As repatriation becomes a subject of ethnomusicological research, rather than just a tool, so too recordings—tangible receptacles such as tape, disc, USB, computers, holding instances of song and voices of singers—have a subject-status. In the course of Treloyn's work in the Kimberley, beginning in 1999, sharing of materials has developed from cassette tapes, to compact discs, to USB sticks and hard drives, and increasingly shared cloud-based folders. The media in which materials are returned is significant—durability, compatibility, currency of technology, ease and cost of access, and access control—are all important factors to consider. The power and efficacy of a recording resides in its potential to bring the voices and sounds of family now deceased into the present. The elder Ngarinyin and Wunambal singer and teacher Matthew Dembal Martin has explained:

> The old people beside you sitting, you can feel the spirit. Makes you remember songs too—songs you don't forget. You get them back on your mind; the old person that is singing there—you get the words off him. That's how it worked. . . . The spirit it is like a magnet that goes into your mind. It might be that the composer is beside you. The songs that you pick up, he put them in your mind. You think you have the words and you have the tune. You pick it up, like a magnet in your mind. . . . It's like a recording. It's like that spirit is singing that song in the recorder while you are singing, picking the words up, and the tune. (Martin, in conversation with Treloyn, 7 December 2014)

Similarly, speaking of the recordings of Hopi singers and song recorded by Laura Boulton at Columbia University, Reed notes that "the item being repatriated is not simply a historical object, but a "performable" voice" (2009: 9). The subject-status of legacy recordings for cultural heritage communities has emerged as a common theme in repatriation-centered ethnomusicological scholarship, by virtue of the presencing of the voices, messages, humor, and affect, of deceased family members stored in the recordings, when recordings are auditioned (see, e.g., Toner 2003). Several community leaders in repatriation initiatives have articulated the presence of the spirits of deceased singers in legacy recordings. The association of repatriation of legacy recordings with the repatriation of stolen human remains is also articulated (see Treloyn & Charles 2014, Treloyn, Martin & Charles 2016).

In bringing attention to the subject-status of recordings, our intent is not to suggest that they are a third party in the repatriation transaction, from archive to community. However, the subject-status of recordings does bring attention to the relational nature of singing, listening, recording, and repatriating. To explore this, we turn to the local framework of Wurnan.

Wurnan refers to a network of trade routes linking groups and clans throughout the Kimberley region. Wurnan underpins social institutions and collaborations such as the skin system, marriage, intergroup negotiations, land care and management, the distribution of goods, and dissemination of knowledge. It was laid down in the ancestral present—the Dreaming—but, far more than a rigid system of trade, Wurnan is flexible and inclusive. As the anthropologist Anthony Redmond has explained, Wurnan continued through the colonization of the region by what he terms "strange relatives," including pastoralists, displaced groups, governments, and other outside entities, who entered the social and economic world (Redmond 2005). Not surprisingly, Wurnan also accommodates its strange relatives that appear in the form of ethnomusicologists and archives. Matthew Martin was the first to explain this:

> Wurnan only coming to [us] for sharing. Share a lot of things, like food, Junba. Share, sharing with spears, woomeras, it's sharing. Wurnan is for a gift, you know. Free gift. Like you [Treloyn] are working with me and I got a Wurnan for you. I go, I Wurnan with you see. You do the recording for me and I do the talking and I'm, it's just like Wurnan giving us. I giving you the stories and you work with me and it's a gift. Recording—that's a gift. You record things. (Martin, in conversation with Treloyn, 7 December 2014; see Treloyn, Martin & Charles 2016)

In this passage, Matthew is referring not just to Treloyn recording his voice, or contributing to skill development in his community, but also to their cooperative responsibility to continue Wurnan that was started by singers and researchers, who recorded their voices, of the past. Looking back to archived recordings,

Matthew explains that these singers of the past, whose voices and spirits are present in recordings, left the promise of a gift for their future generations; a promise that he and Treloyn through their collaboration now fulfill. Key to this is that, in the Ngarinyin life-world, recordings carrying the voices of ancestors must be returned to their homeland, just as stolen human remains are:

> [The] old people are gone but their spirit is still there. What you call that archive place? They still there, they still remain. [We need to] bring the whole lot back, . . . bring them back to Country. (Martin, in conversation with Treloyn, 16 January 2014; see Treloyn, Martin & Charles 2016)

Such a formulation of Wurnan as a model to understand relational recording, repatriation, and revitalization resonates with other Indigenous research methodologies that foreground the importance of accountability, connection, and responsibility, namely "relational accountability" (Wilson 2008).

Reflections on the relational status of repatriated recordings, such as those provided by Martin, illustrate some of the ways in which digital heritage items and the metadata that guide their discovery and use circulate and generate complex social and political environments and relationships that cross histories and tensions of ethnomusicology, nation-states, and personal relationships. These relationships stretch across time (from past research relationships to the present), across institutions (archives, university and community organizations), and individual people (Indigenous and non-Indigenous, researchers and singers, elders and young people). In so doing, repatriation in the Australian settler state is at once an opportunity for empowerment, resurgence, and reclamation, but also references a number of boundaries or ruptures: cultural materials taken away, paternalism, deep colonization, and passive violence. Repatriation references a field of loss, for some grief, for many anger, and disconnection, that extends well beyond the removal of tangible objects, to the loss of song practice, children, language, land, and connection. In resisting an evaluation of repatriation that rests solely on markers of revitalization, notions of equity, and self-determination, and recognizing the limitations of our endeavors, we find ourselves conducting our research in the post-colonial territory of relational discomfort.

The Australian anthropologist Deborah Bird Rose came to understand boundaries (geographical, temporal, and personal) in the Victoria River District (to the east of the Kimberley) as a productive zone in which relationships are affirmed:

> Tracks and songs are the basis to Aboriginal maps and are often called "boundaries." To say that there are boundaries is to say that there are differences; the universe is not uniform. Unlike European maps on which boundaries are lines that divide, tracks connect points on the landscape, showing relationships

between points. These are "boundaries" that unite. The fact that a Dreaming demarcates differences along the line is important to creating variation, but ultimately a track, by its very existence, demarcates a coming together. Dreaming creativity made possible the relationships which connect by defining the differences that divide. (Rose 1992: 52)

Similarly, through Wurnan relationships, Indigenous people in the Kimberley have been able to overcome massive differences between their lifeworlds and those of others. Redmond's description of Ngarinyin peoples' adaptation to the pastoral industry in the east Kimberley in 1930s is eerily reminiscent of the repatriation today:

The operation of Wurnan helped sustain an uneasy accommodation between the original landholders and those who appropriated the country for cattle grazing.... The expectations of reciprocity ... helped to shape the tenor of these relationships, incorporating the alien behaviour of the intruders into a local social reality that contained its destructive effects to some extent. The exchange relationships that were an integral part of Wurnan, and the prestige of introduced goods that were obtainable only by working for station bosses, promoted some stability in the decades following the extreme violence of invasion. The station bosses were largely oblivious to the importance of Wurnan, allowing it to continue as a relatively autonomous form of governance.... For decades after white settlement at Karunjie, Aboriginal people maintained the prestige of a traditional system of trade, sustaining a parallel economy within a system designed to strip them of any economic power. (Redmond & Skyring 2010: 84)

Similarly, Charles explains that the use of Treloyn by elder singers in 1999–2002 to record songs and song histories may have been a strategy to ensure that their gifts (that is, their knowledge of song, history, and country) could be held for forthcoming generations of singers yet to emerge. That is, knowledge is not transferred through the movement of tangible recordings, but through the minds, bodies, and intent of the participants in repatriation, including of Treloyn.

Read this way, through Wurnan the discomforts that arise between culture bearers and strange researcher-relatives allow for productive intercultural collaboration that supports cultural maintenance. Such a view can also be seen to emerge in singers' and emerging singers' negotiations of Treloyn's song knowledge. In the position of being asked to sing at the Mowanjum Festival in 2017, riling concerns within Treloyn about her own acts of neoliberal cultural appropriation and homogenization, Treloyn said, as is appropriate in the situation, "I can't put myself front!" (i.e., with no shame; as an unsocialized person, or dog for that matter, would). Elder singer Lucy Ward said to her, "You *have* to sing, because you have followed me all the way." Treloyn had followed Lucy since 1999 and spent the previous week with her, singing more and more with the high, loud tone preferred by the elder singers. She did this because it in turn brought Lucy's voice up, giving confidence to young learners to also sing. So, in the festival, Lucy considered that Treloyn had to sing, for Lucy, for Lucy's grandchildren and Lucy's country, and for their shared relationship. Relational accountability can be seen where Treloyn is a privileged guest and Lucy, we might suppose, ensures that there is benefit through this relationship for her community. Echoing this, Charles explains that secondary products of research such as Treloyn's 2006 dissertation similarly became a subject of Wurnan:

> You went and worked with Scotty [an elderly singer]. You got a lot of his stuff and wrote it down, you know, but he is also teaching about his culture to you. You returned it back to us, we're younger ones with technology and writing. So *he* [is] giving it back to us, and we [are] learning off that. We [are] learning both ways, we [are also] learning from him. (Treloyn & Charles 2014)

Conclusion

As observed by the Australian education researcher Catherine Manathunga (2009: 166), the production of knowledge in the post-colonial intercultural research contact zone is contingent on boundary crossing, wherein difference is treated as productive, rather than something to disavow, allowing mutual identification, cultural exchange, and transculturation to enter the research process and product. In Wurnan epistemology, hereditary, cultural, ecological, and linguistic difference and diversity—embedded in the kinship system that guides marriage, the distribution of food and knowledge, and so on—are essential for life. This extends to the modern lifeworld of strange researchers, strange ethnomusicologists, and strange archives. In terms of Wurnan, Treloyn's withdrawal from collaboration—or the inability of an archive to release legacy recordings—would not be read as a closure of the matter, but rather a stagnation or ossification that results from a temporary failure of participation (Redmond 2012): a denial of intersubjectivity and relatedness. The vitality of Junba has been stimulated and sustained not simply by the repatriation of the legacy recordings, but by:

1. The relationships past and present that brought the recordings into being and that mobilizes them through repatriation today;
2. An applied approach to ethnomusicology that acknowledges histories of research violence, and,

3. An applied approach to ethnomusicology that embraces heterogeneous intercultural research epistemologies, in this case postcolonial notions of productive difference, and a local epistemological framework for relational accountability that encompasses recordings, singers, researchers, archives, and the academy past and present.

Notes

* The research presented in this chapter is a part of the project "Singing the Future: assessing the effectiveness of repatriation as a strategy to sustain the vitality of Indigenous song" supported by the Australian Research Council (FT150100141).
1. Self-determination is a trope of the Australian Indigenous rights movement that emerged in the late 1960s as a response to the dominant colonial assimilationist policies (see Kowal 2008). The Guidelines for Ethical Research in Australian Indigenous Studies (AIATSIS 2002 [2012]) cites Article 3 of the Declaration on the Rights of Indigenous Peoples (United Nations 2007), noting that researchers must "[u]nderstand the meaning of self-determination in relation to Indigenous peoples and their rights to maintain, control, protect and develop their cultural heritage, including their traditional knowledge, traditional cultural expressions and intellectual property" (AIATSIS 2002 [2012]: 2).

9

Dancing *Domba*

Intersections of Ethnomusicology, Music Education, and Research with Children and Young People

Andrea Emberly and Mudzunga Junniah Davhula

In Vhavenda communities in South Africa, initiation schools for girls and boys have historically marked transitions from child to youth to adult. Initiation schools connect education, music, and well-being, these three layers intersecting to imbue children with the knowledge, culture, and foundations necessary for healthy development. This collaborative chapter examines the critical relationships between music, education, and well-being in the lives of children and young people in Vhavenda communities. It aims to explore the emotional, physical, and socio-cultural transition from childhood to adulthood that is embodied musically in initiation schools and through the transmission of musical arts practices (song, dance, instrumental performance).

Current community efforts to document and revive initiation school musical arts practices aim to preserve Indigenous knowledge systems that are viewed as increasingly endangered. These efforts have led to our current collaborative project—The Dancing Domba Project[1]—that explores how research and documentation can be used, not only to preserve endangered, intangible cultural heritage, but also as a means to support community efforts to reimagine and reframe the cultural practices and musical systems of initiation schools. This revival includes community efforts to teach and sustain musical arts both in and outside the classroom and a commitment by community elders and leaders to find pathways for transmitting musical knowledge systems that safeguard the intangible cultural heritage of Vhavenda communities.

The Dancing Domba Project has built a research agenda shaped by the concerns of cultural leaders about what happens when young people no longer attend initiation schools, as is the case at present because most initiation schools are no longer performed in their entirety. This is a difficult task given that much of the knowledge surrounding initiation schools is considered sacred and secretive even if it is shared with members of the research team. Although detailed descriptions of all aspects of the ritual schools have been published at length (see, e.g., Blacking 1969b, McNeill 2011, Stayt 1931, van Warmelo 1932), it has

Andrea Emberly and Mudzunga Junniah Davhula, *Dancing* Domba In: *Transforming Ethnomusicology.* Edited by: Beverley Diamond and Salwa El-Shawan Castelo-Branco, Oxford University Press (2021). © Oxford University Press. DOI: 10.1093/oso/9780197517550.003.0010 been the goal of our research to take an approach that does not document the sacred parts of initiation. Rather, our approach considers community interests in reviving initiation schools in creative and diverse ways that recognize both the musical significance and the educational and cultural identity aspects of the tradition. Community safeguarding of the endangered traditions of initiation schools requires a more fluid approach to sustainability because, for many reasons, the schools can no longer be performed in their entirety as they were in the past. Given the present-day challenges that young people face in Venda communities, leaders and elders are searching for ways that the revival of initiation schools might support young people in connecting with their cultural heritage as a means to support them in their everyday lives.

As longtime collaborators in an ongoing project to document Venda children's folk songs (most of which are typically outside the purview of the politics that tend to surround initiation schools), we were challenged by community leaders, in particular female community members, to include the songs of initiation schools in our research, given that they are in much greater danger than most genres of Venda music. In particular, female leaders wanted to see their knowledge represented as authoritative in the dominant realm of male authorship on the subject. In addition, given our background of work with young children, it was imperative to us to include young people in the project in a meaningful way. Although this has been a challenging task, the research collaboration has begun to unveil some of the connections between Indigenous technologies for preservation and music sustainability. Through collaborative writing, we have been slowly working towards transposing community knowledge into accessible scholarship that is paired with community events (both small and large) that showcase community efforts to integrate the music of initiation schools into public and private events. In addition, the research team has participated in several different types of initiation schools to increase their understanding and awareness of what it means to go through initiation and how knowledge is shared from one generation of women to another. The goal of our approach has been to transform research into a collaborative space with outcomes and agendas that address both community and academic interest and, in particular, the interests of young people who are faced with the immense task of supporting these traditions into the future (see also Impey, Tan, and Titon in this compendium for related discussion on the linkages between ethnomusicology, communities, public organizations, and activism).

Vhavenda initiation schools, and in particular the initiation schools for girls, have been declining since the arrival of the Berlin missions in the nineteenth century. Although still present in various forms, the systematic educational system that initiation schools once provided has been dismantled in order to accommodate missionary and governmental school systems. Thus, at present, there has been a localized drive to promote greater access to, and participation in, initiation schools in many Vhavenda communities. This chapter will present community concerns regarding the lack of access to initiation schools and community-driven efforts to maintain the learning that is embodied in musical practices within these schools. This echoes the work of Impey in Volume I, who argues for "innovative partnerships and collaborative action" that cross the academic-public divide. Focusing on initiation schools for girls, this chapter examines how various educational systems (cultural, religious, and governmental) have intersected and become important sites for examining childhood, especially with regard to emotional, socio-cultural, and physical well-being.

A Brief Introduction to Vhavenda Culture

The Vhavenda live primarily in the most northern area of the Limpopo province of South Africa (Vhembe district), bordering Zimbabwe and the Limpopo River. The Vhavenda language, Luvenda, is one of the eleven official languages of South Africa and it is concentrated only in the northern part of Limpopo province. Luvenda is spoken by only about 2.4 percent of the total South African population (about 1.2 million Luvenda speakers throughout South Africa), making it one of the least-spoken languages in the entire country. The Vhavenda have retained their culture through music and language as well as through an established and maintained royal dynasty and kingship system that recognizes chiefs as cultural and political leaders. There is currently one recognized king of the Vhavenda people (Khosi Khulu)[2], and twenty-eight chiefs (Mahosi), who have regional authority within the area. Each chief also has many headmen (Vhamusanda), who carry out the wishes of the chief and look after specific areas in the chief's territories (Emberly & Davhula 2016). The royal dynasty system also differentiates between different lineages, including those who are considered from the royal family and those who are commoners.

John Blacking's well-known work in Vhavenda communities from 1956 to 1958 highlighted the role of music in the lives of children and young people (Blacking 1964, 1967, 1988, 1990) and became the cornerstone of his theories on human musicality (Blacking 1973). Utilizing the archival records of Blacking's work (housed at the Callaway Centre at the University of Western Australia and the International Library of African Music [ILAM]) provides a framework to examine changes in musical arts practices between the 1950s and today. His extensive documentation of Vhavenda girls' initiation schools in particular (Blacking 1969, 1969b, 1970, 1985, Blacking & Huffman 1995, Blacking, Bailey & Grau 2002) provides focus on continuities and change in cultural practice in the lives of children and young people. As such, repatriation and access to Blacking's archival materials has become a process that is increasingly critical, given the highly endangered and/or obsolete state of many of the musical practices embedded in the initiation school system (Emberly 2015, Emberly & Davhula 2014, 2018, Emberly & Post 2019, Emberly & Treloyn 2013). While access to these materials is limited for Vhavenda community members, efforts to connect Blacking's (and his Vhavenda field assistants') documentation to community driven efforts to revitalize these practices began with an exhibition in 2014 at the University of Venda of materials from his archival collection (Emberly & Davhula 2014).

A Legacy of Education

The state and role of Vhavenda initiation schools have faced significant change. As is recognized in neighboring countries, the "movement towards urbanization, modernization, and a focus on formal education introduced both physical and time constraints on holding prolonged ceremonies that had served as the primary root for sex-education" (Bulled 2016: 85). While some genres of performance traditions for children and youth have been successfully sustained and maintained within governmental school systems, the music of initiation schools faces critical endangerment. The practice of embedding traditional musical arts in the classroom is more challenging and problematic for the music and songs of initiation schools. As a result, the musical practices found in initiation schools have seen substantial and detrimental decline in Vhavenda communities since the early 1800s.

There are several major historical landmarks for Vhavenda communities that have had particular impact on the delivery of education through traditional initiation schools that have led to their dramatic decline. The first major documented change in education systems in the area came during colonialism and the arrival of the Berlin Mission Society in Venda during 1872. As a result of missionary proselytization, Vhavenda people who converted to Christianity were not allowed to practice their initiation rites, which were the primary means of education for young people. During this period the Berlin missionaries banned all cultural activities, attire, cultural music, dance, rites, rituals, and religion (see, e.g., Kirkaldy 2007, Kruger 1999, Mathivha 1986, Muthivhi 2010, Van Warmelo 1932). This period of history saw a steep decline in cultural practices that were referred to as heathenism and witchcraft. The arrival of the Berlin Mission Society was a critical moment for initiation schools that quickly went from the central system of education to a banned practice.

Almost a century after the arrival of the Berlin missionaries, the formation of the Venda Bantustan in 1969 gave semi-independence to Vhavenda people and provided a turning point in the downward spiral of loss of cultural practices. It was recognized by the prime minister of Venda, Thovele Vho P. R. Mphephu, that the cultural practices of Vhavenda communities had been decimated by colonization, the arrival of the missionaries, and the ensuing and oppressive apartheid regime. Thovele Vho Mphephu prioritized cultural practice and introduced competition as a means to "re-transmit" culture to young people who had suffered a gap in generational knowledge transmission. This renaissance of cultural practices, and in particular, musical arts practices, supported the revival of many musical genres that had previously been practiced covertly and primarily by elders during times of cultural banishment. As a part of the cultural renaissance, group music genres such as *tshigombela* (girl's group dance), *malende* (solo dances of joy and happiness), *tshifashi* (courtship dance), and *tshikona* (reed pipe ensemble) saw substantial revival through the introduction of competition to the area. Competitions take place at every age level, from young children to elders, and groups advance from local levels to province-wide finals (Emberly & Davidson 2011). Musical arts competitions are particularly prominent in school-based competitions where local primary and secondary schools compete in various genres. In addition to musical competitions, school learners compete in drama, poetry recitation, cultural practice, and varying other school subjects.

In 1990, the end of the apartheid regime was marked by the release of Nelson Mandela from prison. The rapid change that this brought was visible for children and young people in particular who had suffered through the oppressive apartheid education system. By 1994, there was an overhaul of the entire South African education system and a South African national curriculum was introduced (Abdi 2002, Chrisholm 2004, Mouton et al. 2012). This national curriculum has since been overhauled several times in an attempt to find balance in delivering content to a diverse student body across the country. In 2000, the South African Department of Education OBE (outcomes-based education) policy introduced arts and culture as an area of study in the curriculum. However, the OBE curriculum did not focus on any one cultural practice and did not give space for schools to incorporate their own cultural practices into the classroom. In 2002, the national curriculum statement (NCS) was released, with little change to the arts and culture learning area, still ignoring a need for, cultural activities within the classroom (Department of Education 2002). In 2012, a curriculum assessment policy statement (CAPS) was introduced and arts and culture was changed to "creative arts," with reference to Indigenous dances and cultural music (Department of Education 2012). However, while peripheral acknowledgment is made, there is still minimal recognition of the value of integrating cultural practice into the school classroom even given the research data that demonstrate its value in the South African classroom (see, e.g., Carver 2014, Herbst et al. 2003, Nzewi 2007). At present, musical practices in Vhavenda communities are often integrated into the classroom by teachers who value their importance for children and young people. Dance ensembles practice for annual competitions, Vhavenda children's songs (*zwidade*) are sung to teach various subjects, and historical songs such as grinding songs (*mafhuwe*) are taught to relay to children the hardships endured by their ancestors.

The introduction of different types of curricula since the end of apartheid has impacted Vhavenda cultural activities and, in particular, the role of initiation schools and their musical practices within communities. While recognition of cultural practice has been outlined in CAPS, the role of initiation schools complicates the integration of cultural practice into the school classroom. The songs and dances of initiation schools have been taught less often in the school classroom; however, public genres of song and dance, such as *tshigombela*, *malende*, *tshifashi*, and *tshikona*, have been successfully integrated into school competitions and activities. This division of genres taught in the classroom is due to complex factors, including the sacred and secretive nature of initiation schools, the content and context of information taught at initiation schools, and community resistance to integrating the songs and dances of initiation schools into the classroom because of the nature and significance of the musical genre.

A Brief Introduction to Initiation Schools for Girls

The content delivery in initiation schools is done primarily through songs and dance. Each level of initiation incorporates the teachings and education of young girls into music and dances learned through participation and often hardship, such as in songs that require the initiates to dance in a squatted position for long periods of time. Historically, all girls would undergo initiation in order to learn the cultural norms and practices of her community; she would learn information through song and dance and from the symbolism of the material objects used in the schools. However, at present, initiation schools have been interrupted and, to a large extent, dismantled by outside forces such as those briefly mentioned earlier. In order to understand the impact on these systems it is important to know the general framework of some of the main stages of initiation schools for girls.[3]

Musevhetho

Musevhetho is the first initiation school for girls between the ages of nine and thirteen. This school is three months long and teaches girls the basics of doing simple household chores that she will be expected to do such as sweeping, washing the dishes, and carrying water, for example. Other educational values are also introduced at this school as the basics of societal behavioral expectations. These include respect for elders, obedience, loyalty, listening, hospitality, and kindness.

Vhusha

The *vhusha* initiation school is for girls between the ages of fourteen and sixteen who have started menstruation. There are two different schools, one to be danced by girls from the royal lineage and one for commoners. For royal girls the school is called *u fhisa* or *u tamba* (depending on which area it is danced in) and for commoners it is called *vhusha*. This is a short initiation school of five to seven days that can be done in any season but preferably in the winter. At present, *vhusha* is the initiation schools that girls would be most likely to attend because it is the most accessible and can be done during the winter school holidays. However, very few girls attend this initiation school.

Vhusha is considered one of the most important stages of initiation because it sets the course for the final stage of initiation—*domba*. It is also considered an essential part of initiation due to the subjects that are taught during this phase. Among other teachings, the girls are taught how to look after themselves during menstruation, advised of the consequences of sexual relationships and of precautions, and instructed how to date and remain abstinent. In addition, girls are taught more complex household chores such as how to cook for large groups of people at her household. During *vhusha*, girls face immense hardship including singing and dancing all night long, dances that include squatting and kicking, sitting in the river for extended periods of time, and withstanding humiliation and taunting. The hardships that girls face during *vhusha* are an indication of the hardships she will endure as a woman, and the songs, dances, and rituals are meant to mimic many of these. Growing strong through *vhusha* means learning patience, endurance, and acceptance for milestones in their lives including childbirth, married life, and negative treatment from your in-laws. The Tshivenda proverb—*vhuhadzi ndi nama ya thole, ya fhufhuma ri a fhunzhela*— where the meat of the game animal is hard to chew—is related to this endurance of hardship that initiates face, meaning that although things are difficult, you must be patient and calm in order to cope with the difficulties you must endure.

This stage of initiation, with its vital well-being curriculum (physical and social in particular), is one of the most important transitions for young girls becoming young women in preparation for their graduation into womanhood that will come in the final stage of initiation. At present, *vhusha* is the most prevalent initiation school because it is accessible in a few villages during school holidays. Because *vhusha* is so vital it has also been adopted by Zion Christian churches who hold *vhusha* initiation schools with an emphasis on Christian doctrine. Thus, a young girl might attend a "cultural" *vhusha* (*vhusha ya musanda*) or a "church" *vhusha* (*vhusha ya vhatendi*). Although the content, including the songs and dances, are predominantly the same, in the church *vhusha* some of the vulgar language that is historically used during *vhusha* is changed and several rituals that precede the initiation school have been replaced by prayer. The church *vhusha* replaces veneration of ancestors with God, and an emphasis on morality, ethics, and virginity is stressed.

Domba

Tshikanda is a short preparatory course that is considered the introduction to *domba*. It is very important because of the rituals and the rites that are to be performed during this stage of initiation. *Tshikanda* lasts for only two weeks, during which initiates are provided with information about the process of *domba* and they undergo an initial test of fitness that girls must pass in order to enter the *domba*. This stage involves difficult exercises and dances, in one of which initiates hang upside down while singing and moving. These dances and rituals are done to teach about the hardships that women must endure once the young girl moves into adulthood. Each particular initiation school focuses on different hardships according to age, gender, and social status.

The final initiation school for girls before they marry is called *domba*. It is during this initiation school that the girls will pass their final rites transforming them from being a girl to becoming a woman. It is considered the university education of a Vhavenda woman. This initiation school teaches girls the final preparations for womanhood, including how to have a relationship with their husband, how to handle in-laws, childbirth, the rites and rituals of childhood, and how to take care of their family.

This initiation school lasts one year and must be staged by the relevant chief whose firstborn daughter (the princess) must "cry" for *domba* to start (e.g., she must be the correct age and at the correct stage to call for *domba*). Once this initiation school has started it must be danced every day until an entire year has passed. However, at present, *domba* initiates never attend the school for the entire year but the drums must still be beaten every single day. The initiates will attend on the weekends and during school holidays to accommodate the governmental and post-secondary school system that they must attend during the weekdays. When *domba* is about to be completed, the final rites, called *ludodo*, must be performed. These rites teach the final hardship that the girls must endure before they leave: the girls sit on the floor with their head resting on the thigh of the girl next to her. *Ludodo* lasts all night long and the girls must endure the pain of lying in this position without moving. During this segment, the initiates sing the rites that signal the end of *domba*. In the morning, each initiate will be forced to gather water in her mouth and endure the taunts of elders without spilling any of the water—if she can keep the water in her mouth it means she is strong enough to graduate from *domba*.

The *domba* initiation school, well known for the *domba* dance that mimics a snake through the synchronization of the dancer's arms and legs (Figure 9.1), has not been performed in its entirety for many years; the last documented *domba* took place in the early 2000s and was incomplete according to local accounts (personal interviews 2016).

In addition to the sex education curriculum in *vhusha* and *domba*, some have argued that all initiation schools could be used to enhance HIV/AIDS education (Bulled 2016, McNeill 2011). Contribution to lessening health risks such as HIV/AIDS is implicitly present, given that *vhusha* and *domba* place emphasis on virginity, shaming initiates through song who are found not to be virgins upon entry into the schools. For example, during the stage known as *matano* during

Figure 9.1 *Domba* dance, Dopene village, Noriah Ralinala (group leader), August 2, 2015.

the final school of *domba*, initiates who are found to be virgins are carried upon the backs of elders who sing joyful songs while dancing and ululating; initiates who are found not to be virgins are not carried and receive no ululations. While communities have resisted stating candidly that initiation schools should be used for HIV/AIDS prevention, their educational frameworks do center on physical well-being that many community members endorse has having healthy outcomes for participants.

Arts, Culture, and Tradition in the School Classroom

While musical practices embedded in the initiation schools have seen dramatic decline, other musical practices remain extremely strong and community members have worked within the system to maintain musical arts activities. In the genres mentioned in the previous section (*tshigombela, tshifashi, tshikona, malende*), which were "revived" in the 1960s, community members continue to maintain high levels of proficiency with high levels of participation and mastery (Emberly & Davhula 2014, Emberly & Davidson 2011). These genres have flourished within the school curriculum because they are public dance forms and they have fluid styles that allow for adaptation of lyrics, melody, and dance. In addition, competitions (both local and national) support the maintenance of these genres, with schools competing annually for recognition (Figure 9.2).

While cultural revival in the classroom presses forward, the musical practices of initiation schools remain marginalized and largely inaccessible to students in the classroom. Given the complex nature of the initiation school curriculum, focusing primarily on the body, relationships, and sex education and their connection to cultural practices tied to ancestral worship, the songs and dances of initiation remain firmly on the outside. In addition, because children cannot miss school to attend initiation schools, it means the practices have been in rapid decline since the arrival of the Christian missions.

There has been some attempt to integrate particular segments of initiation schools into the classroom, namely the *domba* dance and certain cultural practices including socio-cultural behavioral expectations (e.g., *u losha*—showing respect by lying low on the ground) and traditional clothing. These are common at local gatherings, *zwisevhesevhe*, where women and girls wear traditional clothing (*minwenda*) and often perform the *domba* dance alongside other traditional performance genres. School competitions now include a cultural parade where students dress in the outfits used during different phases of initiation schools (e.g., *shedo*[4] and *musisi*[5]) and parade past judges (Figure 9.3). These parades also include other traditional tasks such as grinding mealies (corn) and sweeping with traditional brooms. There is no music during

Figure 9.2 Dzondo circuit primary school competition, May 28, 2015, Tshimbiluni Senior Primary School grounds.

Figure 9.3 Cultural parade, Dzondo circuit competition, August 19, 2015, Tshimbiluni Senior Primary School.

the cultural parade and students are silent while they walk past the judges, demonstrating their command of cultural norms through dress and action.

While cultural parades and competitions may include reference to *domba*, the songs and melodies of initiation schools are not performed. Some cultural celebration events at schools and in communities might include songs or melodies from initiation schools, but these songs are always "public" or "play" songs that initiates would historically have sung in front of visitors to the *domba* school. For example, the song "*Thi nayo ya u rengua domba*" ("I don't have money to buy the *domba*") is most commonly sung at schools while students dance the *domba* snake dance. This song talks about how some young girls do not attend *domba* and thus have to pay a fine while others do not have money and so they have no choice but to attend *domba*. While public *domba* songs are considered acceptable, the sacred music of *domba* is never used and some schools in the Vhembe district have discouraged teachers from using any songs from initiation schools (personal interviews 2016). It is not unheard of for teachers to relay stories of being chastised by local elders for singing songs of initiation schools in the classroom. The politics of who can teach initiation songs is also prevalent, with evocation of royal lineages and rights to teach being evoked as a means to keep the songs and melodies out of the school classroom. In addition, participation in the *domba* dance is reserved for children of appropriate ages, so that young children are not participating in this style of song and dance.

Initiation Schools Today

As we have discussed briefly, there are many reasons initiation schools have seen rapid decline over the past two decades. The introduction of a governmental school system has overridden the cultural curriculum that initiation schools once provided. Clashes between those who advocate the introduction of controversial subjects to learners in primary school (such as body parts, relationships, sexual health, etc.) and the age-graded stages of initiation underscore the incongruous relationship between the two curricula. The education that is embedded in the songs and dances of initiation schools is meant to introduce culturally appropriate learning at particular phases in life, thus shuttling girls from children to young women and upon graduation, full adult members of a community. There is much discussion among community members about current health-related issues (such as teenage pregnancy, drug and alcohol abuse, and HIV/AIDS) that may be attributed to the loss of initiation schools (personal interviews 2016; see also McNeill 2011) and to the introduction of a school curriculum that does not reflect culturally relevant stages of learning. One of the primary teachings in initiation schools is abstinence, with initiates vowing abstinence until marriage. Thus, correlations are often drawn between the lack of initiation schools and issues facing the physical, social, and cultural well-being of young people today (personal interviews 2016).

Although there has been a decline in initiation schools as a complete educational system, re-traditionalization of young women has been a means to rework cultural practices into present-day activities for young people (Bulled 2016, McNeill 2011). Performance groups such as Nyavhumbwa Wa Dagaila in Lwamondo, Limpopo, strive to revive cultural practices in an attempt to model moral behavior for young people who are faced with socio-cultural, financial, and health hardships, particularly in rural communities. Nyavhumbwa Wa Dagaila has over twenty-three branches throughout Limpopo and over 1,500 female attendees at their Saturday cultural schools. Music and dance is the primary mode of education and traditional melodies from initiation school are reworked with new lyrics to emphasize chastity and respect for the body that intersect with Christian models of morality. Thus, musical traditions are being sustained and maintained as culturally relevant to present-day youth. Leader Mrs. Livhuwani Ngwana started the group in 2007 as she realized that the decline in cultural practices correlated with a decline in well-being, in particular for young women who suffer long-term health risks and other consequences from teenage pregnancy, as well as drug and alcohol addiction. Ngwana stated that "this unique and important group teaches culture and values to girls from the age of 10 in order to promote, preserve and enhance Vhavenda culture and tradition. By learning about cultural, social and heritage issues in their communities, young women are prepared to become responsible adults with high moral values and ethics. Their participation in this group demonstrates how young people are the backbone for strong, resilient and sustainable communities around the world" (personal interview June 28, 2016). Ngwana also runs initiation schools such as *vhusha* and is dedicated to staging a full *domba* in the future. Her revival of cultural practice demonstrates a meaningful pathway for the musical language of initiation to be sustained, and young women in the group articulate that their participation provides support and creates community. In addition, Nyavhumbwa Wa Dagaila connects culture and Christianity, drawing connections between the mandates of initiation schools and the doctrines of the dominant religion (Figure 9.4). Thus, participants are not forced to choose culture or religion, but rather can connect the two, which is fundamental for communities that have extremely high rates of participation in Christian-based religions.

In addition to the incongruities between the curricula in the school classroom and initiation school, there are a myriad of other factors that have had contributed to the decline of initiation schools and the musical practices embedded within them. Young people today do not attend initiation schools in high numbers, even when access is available. For example, *vhusha* is typically offered during winter school holidays but factors such as religion, availability, politics, and youth priorities all influence attendance at these schools. When a *domba* can be staged also relies on the politically motivated chiefs who oversee each village/

Figure 9.4 Mrs. Livhuwani Nfwana (*center*) and Nyavhumbwa Wa Dagaila participants, Lwamondo village, June 28, 2016.

area. Chiefs can only stage one *domba* during their reign (*Zwifaro*) as a means to communicate to the ancestors that he or she is completing a cycle of culture. Chiefs are now living to older ages and do not take as many wives and thus do not have as many girls ready to cry for *domba*. Therefore it is not unusual to find that *domba* in some form (perhaps shortened) has happened only once over the past ten to twenty years.

Conclusion

The complexities of re-imagining and re-embedding the cultural practices of initiation schools highlights the importance of considering issues that impact the cultures of childhood and youth in Vhavenda communities today. While this chapter has not discussed research methodologies, incorporating young people into the research process has been an important aspect of understanding how communities are aiming to sustain traditional musical practices such as those embedded within initiation schools (Emberly & Davhula 2018). Thus, privileging collaborative ethnographic practices that include children and young people as participants and knowledge bearers initiates a shift away from tokenistic representations of children to informed, child-directed, and child-initiated research participation. Recognizing that issues with sustainability must be addressed by children, youth, and adults in communities promotes participation and long-term sustainability. However, this presents additional challenges for researchers interested in musical participation, as young people can only participate musically in appropriate stages of initiation schools that include sacred/secret processes. Participation in initiation schools is challenged with issues of timing with regard to government school regulations, but perhaps more important, pressures between Christian religious practices and "traditional cultural practices" also dampen participation and musical mastery.

This chapter has begun to reveal some of the issues facing community leaders and young people in retaining the cultural practices of initiation schools by understanding how people negotiate within the structure of the current South African education system. As we have seen, there has been a historical dismantling of Vhavenda initiation schools in order to privilege colonial education systems, which has directly resulted in the endangerment of the musical arts practices associated with initiation schools. In addition, community members have argued that the connections to the ancestors are also threatened by the lack of initiation schools, as venerating ancestral spirits is a key part of initiation school processes. Like many of the chapters in this compendium, our work underscores how the loss of musical arts practices has rippling effects, as is the case in Vhavenda initiation schools where a loss of song is related directly to the loss of identity in terms of the symbolic, socio-cultural, and physical transitions from childhood to adulthood. As Titon suggests in the present volume, a sound economy values a communal approach to sustainability that moves beyond capitalizing on a musical tradition. Vhavenda initiation schools face a myriad of challenges in terms of music sustainability that cannot be addressed by simply documenting or commodifying the cultural practice. Instead, as Titon observes, a "participatory, cooperative, diverse group whose exchanges of sound presence affirm identities and maintain cohesion" invokes Indigenous technologies for sustainability that negotiate within and between the socio-political and educational landscape. It is clear that the cultural markers of Vhavenda childhood have been impacted by the interruption and dismantling of initiation schools by larger, dominant educational structures in conjunction with urbanization and globalization. However, communities have found pathways to embed cultural knowledge inside and outside the governmental school classroom in order to negotiate space for Vhavenda tradition and identity through a pluralistic response to indigenize education systems in order to support the sustainability of musical arts practices.

Notes

1. Dancing *domba*: an ethnomusicological study of childhood, musical arts education, and well-being in contemporary Venda communities. Social Science and Humanities Research Council of Canada Insight Development Project (SSHRC

IDG 430-2014-00031). This project is a collaboration between ethnomusicologists, educators, community leaders, and children and young people that aims to create resources for teaching and learning and for documenting the musical practices found in initiation schools for girls.

2. At the time of presentation/writing (2015) there was one recognized king of the Vhavenda people but at the time of publication (2020) there has been a challenge to the kingship that has gone through the highest courts in South Africa to recognize a queen of Venda.

3. It should be noted that these initiation schools have been described in detail by scholars (Blacking 1969b, McNeill 2011, Stayt 1931, van Warmelo 1932) but that the information detailed here comes from the authors through the research project and through Indigenous cultural knowledge (author Davhula).

4. As seen in Figure 9.3, the six girls on the left of the photo are wearing *shedo*, a small piece of cloth worn by young girls and by girls undergoing initiation.

5. As seen in Figure 9.3, the two girls on the right of the photo are wearing *musisi*, a traditional dress worn by girls who have undergone *domba*. When a girl gets married and becomes a woman, she would then change to wear a *gwana*, which was historically made of the skin of a goat.

10

Ethical Friction

IRBs, Ethnomusicological Ethics, and Music in an American Jail

Andy McGraw

In this chapter I describe a music program I facilitate in the Richmond, Virginia, city jail and the ethical ambiguities arising from my overlapping roles as organizer and observer. I examine the vague boundaries between applied and academic ethnomusicology, voluntarism and work, and personal and institutional ethical standards. From the perspective of most IRBs (Institutional Review Boards) in the United States,[1] research involving incarcerated populations is unethical if any critical consequences (e.g., punishment or reward) result from inmates' participation in a study. An ethnomusicological study of a jail as a total institution, coercive in nature and populated by various kinds of actors (inmates, staff, and visitors) with complex roles and motivations, presents more nuanced ethical dilemmas. Such a study would consider, among other things, how music is possible (or not) within the institution, the uses to which it is put, and its contested meanings. An ethnomusicological approach to music in jails and prisons exposes ethical frictions between policies, methodologies, and codes espoused by IRB (or other ethics review) boards, ethnomusicologists, and their academic societies.

The tension between my status as a volunteer and ethnographer has raised a number of questions: How is ethical knowledge differently defined? Which definitions have more authority and how is that authority established? Where are the epistemological and ethical boundaries between academic and applied ethnomusicology? How is knowledge connected to action?

As a volunteer in the American criminal justice system I have come to believe that mass incarceration, and possibly incarceration itself, needs to be abolished. IRB ethical guidelines arguing that research should not change the lives of "human subjects" suggests that such an activist stance is inappropriate. However, the very practice of ethnomusicology is activist inasmuch as it acknowledges, archives, and publicizes (often minority) cultural traditions, extends access to musical expression, and critiques socio-political structures that inhibit musical expression. Ethnomusicologists often change the lives of their research

Andy McGraw, *Ethical Friction* In: *Transforming Ethnomusicology.* Edited by: Beverley Diamond and Salwa El-Shawan Castelo-Branco, Oxford University Press (2021). © Oxford University Press.
DOI: 10.1093/oso/9780197517550.003.0011

participants. As an academic observing the criminal justice system, I am unsure if my personal and disciplinary ethics are in irreconcilable conflict with those of the IRB system. What kind of ethical beings are we if we find ourselves pragmatically shifting between personal, disciplinary, and institutional ethics as it suits our needs?

In this chapter I first outline my voluntary activities in the Richmond City Jail (RCJ) beginning in 2013 and the transformation of the music program following a move to a new facility, the Richmond City Justice Center (RCJC), in 2014. I present an anecdotal account of the potential impacts of the music program as seen from my perspective as a volunteer. I then describe how my attempt to account for or measure the program represented an ethically ambiguous shift in my status from volunteer to researcher. From the perspective of my university, this shift necessitated the arbitration and approval of an IRB. I discuss the contentious and complex place of social science and humanities research in the historic development of IRBs in the United States and I analyze how ethnomusicology as a discipline does not adhere neatly to IRBs' medicalized models of research and human subjects. Finally, I draw on Cheliotis (2014, 2016) to demonstrate the ways in which arts programs can be instrumentalized by carceral institutions to obscure the institutions' essentially punitive functions. I argue that ethnographic accounts of criminal justice systems as total institutions would produce more accurate, nuanced understandings less susceptible to instrumentalization and that IRB prohibitions on such research may represent an unethical restriction of academic freedom.

The Richmond City Jail

In May 2013 I received an email from the jail's education director asking if the gamelan orchestra I directed in town could perform in the jail's mess hall. I suggested that a performance might be a possibility, but that I could first conduct a workshop to "warm up" the residents to what they would hear in performance. The first workshop led to invitations to provide weekly music sessions in the facility's education room, at that time called the "Sanctuary." My experiences in the Richmond City Jail conform to Irwin's (1985) description of the jail as a particular kind of social tool rather than an effective deterrent for serious crime. After getting to know several of its residents, I came to understand many as refugees of poverty and dispossession, rather than immanently dangerous and violent criminals. This perception is supported by recent indictments of the use of jails in America as a "modern day debtor's prison" (Subramanian 2015). The contemporary American jail houses many populations—petty and serious criminals, the poor, mentally ill, and addicts—that might be served by different facilities in other countries. As a group, this population is the "rabble" that the modern American system of mass incarceration is intended to remove from civic life.

Besides the highly discretionary nature of arrest (which targets the poor, the addicted, and minorities), special provisions such as bail and OR (own recognizance)[2] ensure that most members of Richmond's middle and upper class never experience the inside of the Richmond City Jail, an institution more dangerous than most jails, as demonstrated by its higher-than-average mortality and HIV rates (due in part to Virginia state laws forbidding contraception in prisons and jails).[3] The Richmond City Jail was built in 1964, immediately adjacent to the low-income housing intended for the Black communities displaced when the construction of the Interstate 95 highway destroyed their historic neighborhoods and business centers, primarily in the Jackson Ward area, known for decades as the "Black Wall Street" for its high concentration of African American–owned banks and businesses.[4] Built atop the ruins of slave shacks and down the street from the notorious Lumpkin's Slave Jail, the Richmond City Jail is located at the nexus of African American dispossession in Virginia, and many of its residents hail from the adjacent low-income housing developments. In their conversation, poetry, and song many members of the Sanctuary referred to the jail as a "housing program."

By July 2013 I had established a small recording studio in the Sanctuary and by August Sanctuary residents were producing over an hour of original music and recorded poetry each week. Collaborations between musicians, lyricists, engineers, and singers cut across all categories of race and gender. In our weekly group sessions, we sometimes listened to fully recorded tracks while at other times a singer or poet would perform live with a pre-recorded backing track.

In response to a Centers for Disease Control report suggesting that overcrowding in the Richmond City Jail represented an existential threat to its population, the city approved the construction of a "cutting-edge" new facility, the Richmond City Justice Center. The new facility, built adjacent to the old Richmond City Jail and designed to accommodate 2,000 residents, replaced overcrowded tier housing with triangular "behavior modification pods" sometimes staffed by a deputy at a touchscreen. Each pod cell, housing one to four residents, as well as all bathrooms, hallways, and multipurpose rooms, are continually monitored through video and audio surveillance devices.

Musical activity was greatly hampered by the move into the new facility due to new administrative rules that restricted residents to the pods, or cells, for most of the day. These tighter restrictions on resident movement, the hiring of a new education director, and the use of multi-purpose rooms rather than a dedicated education room meant the end of the Sanctuary community. The portable music studio was moved to a small square room that could only accommodate a maximum of five individuals. By 2015, only select residents had access to the studio only when I was in the facility, roughly two hours a week. In the old RCJ Sanctuary, a wider range of residents had access to the studio for as much as eight hours a day. Nevertheless, as of the fall of 2017, a wide range of music continued to be produced weekly in the space by both men and women. Residents and I persistently lobbied for expanded access such that, by summer 2019, engineers (around four individuals) each had roughly eight hours of access a week and a roster of around twenty participants who cycled through their sessions every week.

Observed Impacts

A decisive shift in the music program occurred when I suspended my education sessions (oriented around a university-level music appreciation course), and invited residents to make music of their own. My role shifted from teacher to facilitator as I helped them acquire instruments and studio gear, guided introductory recording and production sessions and hunted down backing tracks they requested for their rap or spoken word. Because it incorporated easy-to-learn music software pre-loaded with hundreds of samples, loops, and beats, the studio provided a musical outlet to a wide community, beyond those with technical training in instrumental performance or singing. Within three months the studio's hard drive was overloaded and files had to be regularly downloaded to external drives to free up space. My role had shifted from volunteer music teacher to that of witness and archivist.

As an observer, it appeared to me that the music program was having palpable impacts on participants. This was reinforced through informal conversations with released participants in the program. Many cited the program's open-ended, indeterminate character as a key to its impact. Within the context of the highly regimented, overdetermined schedule of incarcerated life, the opportunity for any form of choice is unusual. Access to relatively unscheduled time is a rare privilege in all so-called total institutions (Goffman 1961: 97). When new participants asked me what they should do and how they should begin, some seem temporarily paralyzed by my practiced response: "I don't know what's going to happen. It's up to you." Within the context of incarcerated life, to be faced with choice can be both powerful and overwhelming.

The music program encourages participants to imagine themselves differently. Through music, some participants have discovered as yet hidden or unrecognized aspects of their personality and ability. To understand one's self as possessing specialized, restricted knowledge (of software, engineering, musical theory, performing techniques, composition) over which one has exclusive control contradicts understandings of the self as controlled by institutions (e.g., criminal justice, poverty, racism), pathological behaviors (e.g., addiction), or disabilities (e.g., mental illness).

Re-imagining one's self also encourages a rethinking of one's relationship to others. The music program seems to have encouraged forms of empathy rarely displayed in jails and prisons. Both music and empathy require imaginative reason, the ability to follow (and cultivate) a mood we are not necessarily experiencing ourselves at the time. According to Laurence (2008), empathizing is a process by which we retain a sense of ourselves as a distinct consciousness while simultaneously being able to: "enter . . . actively and imaginatively into others' inner states to understand how they experience their world and how they are feeling, reaching out to what we perceive as similar while accepting difference" (2008: 24). In both the old RCJ and the RCJC, residents in the music program often collaborated across comparatively segregated populations, for example, Black residents producing beats for rappers (and vice versa), and men producing backing tracks for women's spoken word pieces. Teamwork and collaboration in the studio are far more common than solo musical projects. Ostensibly, this encouraged concrete experiences of empathy between historically self-segregating and often antagonistic populations in the jail.

The music program also appears to encourage empathetic understanding across the staff-inmate boundary. One of the primary purposes of total institutions is to stage a "difference between two constructed categories of persons—a difference in social quality and moral character, a difference in perceptions of self and other" (Goffman 1961: 111). Within this context, "irregular contact" (Goffman 1961: 93) between staff and residents in the music program can be highly charged, potentially liberating, or frightening. In a recent recording session, female rappers invited a male deputy into the studio to give a "shout-out." Placed in front of the microphone with residents at the controls, the normally imposing deputy suddenly became nervous and shy, doubling over in nervous laughter after a failed first take. As the residents laughed along with him, the atmosphere radically shifted from hierarchical tension to relaxed camaraderie. This friendliness makes some staff nervous; musical interaction erodes the hierarchy many of them feel is necessary. Empathy humanizes and makes the job of incarceration more painful.

Volunteer or Researcher?

Jail staff, including the sheriff, have enthusiastically praised the music program. Some have suggested that I conduct a formal, longitudinal study of the program's relationship to recidivism and infractions and have encouraged me to collect bibliographic evidence of the supposed positive effects of arts programs in other carceral institutions. However, such activity would fundamentally change my position in the facility from one of volunteer and witness to academic researcher and require official approval from my university's IRB. At this juncture I realized the ambiguity of my status in the facility. I am not a trained music therapist, approved to practice in the facility, and yet many of the music sessions appeared to be therapeutic.[5] I was not actively taking formal field notes, but caught myself taking note of especially powerful social interactions and musical expressions. I was not recording ethnographic interviews, but was helping to archive a large body of expressions of a unique population.

As a facilitator and informal observer, the public statements I could make about the impacts of the program would be limited to the abbreviated anecdotal account provided earlier. I had learned from my volunteer experience and many casual conversations with staff, residents, and released inmates that an adequate description of the music program could not be limited to the activities I observed in the studio during my weekly sessions. An adequate explanation would require situating the program within the jail's systems of social control and the broader context of the American criminal justice system. Every person that intersected with the program continuously negotiated a web of real and perceived incentives, punishments, subterfuge, and conflicting agendas. If I was to understand the meaning of my own activities in the institution, and to find ways to make it more meaningful and useful to inmates, an ethnomusicology of the institution itself was required.

IRB

Institutional Review Boards were mentioned only in passing during my graduate education and none of my advisers suggested or required that I seek approval for my ethnographic projects in America or abroad. To date, none of the journals or presses that have published my work has requested any documentation related to IRB approval, confidentiality, or informed consent. Based on informal conversations with colleagues, I believe my limited experience of IRB is common within the field. It appears that faculty and students at large state universities have been required to submit their research programs for IRB approval more often, primarily after the late 1990s.[6]

Many ethnomusicologists appear to perceive IRB as a nuisance. Those required to work through IRBs often must undergo mandatory online training programs, fill out numerous forms, and wait up to several weeks to proceed with their fieldwork. They must accept the IRBs' proposed changes to their research program and some are required to fill out annual reports listing all informants, tabulating them by sex and race. Many IRBs require interview and follow-up questions to be submitted in advance. However, it is often impossible for ethnomusicologists to predict whom they will meet and what questions they will ask. In almost all cases, ethnographers follow the grain of their research rather than pre-determining its pattern. IRBs are primarily concerned with the a priori management of research structure, whereas ethnography is focused on process.

IRB: A Short History

Anthropologists and social scientists began publishing codes of conduct through their professional societies beginning in the 1960s. The National Research Act of 1974, which governs IRBs in the United States, was drafted shortly after the abuses of the Tuskegee Syphilis Study were revealed.[7] The scandal led to broad national interest in limiting the powers of doctors and biomedical researchers and encouraged the drafters of the National Research Act to frame their conception of research and the human subject within a biomedical framework. With their considerable political power, medical professionals ensured that they played key roles in authoring the new national guidelines. As Schrag describes in his history of the IRB system, social scientists and ethnographers were largely excluded from the process (Schrag 2010: 8).

The 1974 report was debated and revised several times. Following new federal hearings in 1977, congressional staff explicitly advocated the exemption of several categories of research, including ethnomusicology, from IRB and federal oversight (Schrag 2010: 68). The revised regulations of 1981 appeared to include several concessions for social scientists, but vague language allowed federal regulators to gradually reimpose medicalized paradigms over the following decade.[8] According to Schrag, by 1979, "when the applicability of the regulations did become subject to public debate, it was too late for a fresh examination of the problem" (2010: 68). Universities accepting any form of federal funding (that is, nearly all) began to apply the national guidelines to all research conducted through the institution—including social science research and ethnography—although it was unclear if this was federally mandated. Local IRB boards strained to fit policies designed for biomedical research to proposals from the social sciences and humanities. The ethicist Albert Jonsen referred to IRBs' misapplication of biomedical ethical models to a range of dissimilar disciplines as "ethical imperialism" (2010: 9).

In 1998, government regulators temporarily suspended federal funding from several universities for lax IRB oversight. This encouraged IRBs around the country to tighten control and restrict research, fearful of federal crackdowns. Many institutions responded by hiring full-time IRB administrators certified by professional agencies. The expansion of IRB as an industry has shifted power from researchers and faculty-populated IRB committees to professionals invested in the expansion of their oversight. Within this context, IRB administrators may prioritize the needs of their employer—protecting its public image, insulating it from lawsuits, ensuring the flow of federal dollars—over the needs of researchers, research participants, or the expansion of public knowledge.

Ethnomusicology and IRB

Many scholars and organizations have critiqued the apparent "mission creep" of IRBs beyond biomedical research over the past three decades. One of the most articulate critiques was summarized in the Illinois White Paper, the result of a 2003 conference on IRB oversight (Gunsalus et al. 2007). The report cited IRBs' concerns over lawsuits and federal shutdowns for the expansion of oversight to fields that appear to pose virtually zero risk for subjects, including ethnomusicology, ethnography, oral history, journalism, and history. If my own training is any indication of the approach in the field, many ethnomusicology departments appear to have taken a "heads down," and "ask for forgiveness rather than permission" approach, based in the belief that IRBs are often irrelevant to the field's methodologies and topics.

As a discipline, ethnomusicology does not neatly adhere to the standard IRB model of research, knowledge, and the human subject. The *Federal Register* of 1978, a guiding document for IRBs, defines a human subject as: "a person about whom an investigator . . . conducting scientific research obtains 1) data through intervention or interaction with the person or 2) identifiable private information" (quoted in Schrag 2010: 74). The IRB model assumes that researchers will define and identify a finite and specific set of research participants prior to beginning their project, which will apply only to those predefined individuals. Ethnographers often do not know whom they will meet during the course of their research and who will be most relevant to the questions and frameworks that evolve over the course of their project. In the case of biomedical research, investigators may know more about their subjects' condition (as it pertains to the research) than the subjects themselves do. This is not a condition of ethnography, in which informants often know better than the ethnographer the consequences of their interaction.

The American IRB concept of informed consent is modeled upon a biomedical understanding of the human subject and his/her relationship to the researcher. In 1966, Margaret Mead argued that anthropological research does not have "subjects;" instead, anthropologists: "work with informants in an atmosphere of trust and mutual respect." As opposed to biomedical models of informed consent, Mead suggested the appropriate model for anthropological research was one of "voluntary participation . . . in a collective enterprise" (1969: 361).[9] The definition of research provided by the federal government characterizes research as "a systematic investigation, including research development, testing and evaluation, designed to develop or contribute to generalizable knowledge" (quoted in Schrag 2010: x). This model assumes the construction of a testable hypothesis and specific procedures used to evaluate it.[10] In 2007, the Association for the Accreditation of Human Research Protection Programs began advising IRBs to ask if proposed "research design[s] [are] sound enough to yield the expected knowledge" (Schrag 2010: 140). Ethnographers, by contrast, are often interested in documenting and explaining the diversity of cultural phenomena and human experience. At the preliminary stages of their research, they might not know what knowledge to expect.[11]

IRBs and Incarcerated Populations

Almost every university IRB submits a Federalwide Assurance pledging to follow the guidelines regarding the protection of human research subjects as outlined in the Belmont Report, a 705-page set of guidelines and case studies originally published in 1978. The terms "music," "ethnomusicology," and "ethnography" do not appear in the report; "anthropology" appears only four times. Like other documents guiding IRB policy, the Belmont Report takes medical experimentation as its model and confuses participants with patients; its applicability to social science and ethnography are ambiguous at best. Nearly all of the federal guidelines regarding work with "vulnerable populations" (including prisoners) are outlined in the Belmont Report.[12]

Incarcerated persons are vulnerable because they have experienced expulsion from the community. The over-incarceration of poor, minority populations in America is an indication that they possess, in the eyes of power, lives unworthy of being lived, lives no longer politically relevant (Agamben 1998: 139,142). Stripped of humanity-as-community and apparently possessed only of "bare life," incarcerated populations are extremely susceptible to coercion and mistreatment as guinea pigs. According to Agamben:

> What the well-meaning emphasis on the free will of the [incarcerated] individual refuses to recognize . . . is that the concept of "voluntary consent" is simply meaningless for someone interned at Dachau, even if he or she is promised an improvement in living conditions. From this point of view, the inhumanity of the experiments in the United States and in the camps is, therefore, substantially equivalent. (1998: 157)

According to the authors of the Belmont Report, research with incarcerated populations can be ethically valid only if there is a "separation of critical consequences and activities" (106). For instance: "In a prison situation, when earlier parole is independent of whether or not an inmate participates in a program, then consent to participate in that program is not related to the release which the penal-judicial system made critical" (106). Participation in a research program must not affect the status of an inmate within the institution as a whole. The Belmont Report appears to make an exception in the case of programs that might lead to "nonrecidivism." "Under appropriate precautions, such programs may be characterized by noncoercive mutuality of outcomes as well as by congruent contingencies for program-relevant behaviors of professionals and inmates/patients/students/research subjects" (Belmont Report: 120). Here, the authors of the Belmont Report assume that inmates would enter such programs voluntarily and that any critical consequences for the inmate would not be governed by the institution, but by society as a whole (through the general concept of criminal activity). Nevertheless, based on my experiences in the RCJ, issues of consent, coercion, and social contingencies remain ambiguous in such situations.[13]

The question of prisoner consent hangs upon a society's theory of imprisonment. If the goal is rehabilitation, then it would be unreasonable to deny the prisoner the right to consent, in principle, and the exercise of that right may aid rehabilitation. If the goal is punishment through the exercise of sovereignty (in Agamben's sense), then consent is more ambiguous because it would be more difficult to ascertain if it was ever truly voluntary or simply a reflection of control. I believe that the latter is the case in the contemporary American context because the incarcerated population is overwhelmingly made up of a particular segment of a society—African American men—whose genuine criminality is often in doubt. American jails function as a form of social control in the service of neoliberalism's need for structural poverty and labor precarity. The legacy of racism and oppression make urban African American men a convenient target population in this scenario.

Modeled upon biomedical notions of research and the human subject, IRB guidelines are often unnecessarily restrictive when applied to most ethnographic and ethnomusicological research. However, regarding research focused specifically on incarcerated populations, IRBs help researchers think through the complex relationship between power and research. The ethical veracity of the Belmont Report guidelines, however, remains ambiguous. Some passages appear to allow for research on incarcerated populations when "compensation" is provided. How such an arrangement avoids problems of coercion is unclear.[14] Other passages appear to question the ethical validity of any research on incarcerated populations. In the face of this ambiguity, many university IRBs play it safe, preemptively disallowing research with incarcerated populations.

SEM and IRB

As compared to American social scientists and anthropologists, Society for Ethnomusicology (SEM) members have engaged in relatively little public debate and conversation on IRBs or on ethics in general. SEM's ethics committee was established in 1972, seventeen years after the society's founding. According to Slobin, until the late 1970s the field displayed "apparent and overwhelming apathy . . . towards the public airing of such issues" (1992: 330–331). Writing in the early 1990s, Seeger stated that "[n]o major figure in the field of ethnomusicology ever defined the object of our study in terms of rights and obligations, conflict, or adjudication. The issues simply were not raised by our 'ancestors' and have rarely been part of our theoretical reflections since" (1992: 346). Shelemay echoes this point in a 1999 essay, stating that considerations of the ethical implications of musicological research "emphatically [have] not" been discussed in the field (1999: 531).

A short flurry of emails to the society's listserv appeared in January 2008 in which some members complained about IRB restrictions, bureaucracy, and the inappropriateness of its models to the discipline. According to Schrag, many IRBs preemptively restrict social science research without demonstrating compelling cases in which social scientists have harmed subjects in ways comparable to notorious biomedical cases such as the Tuskegee experiments. The "worst-case scenarios" contributors to the SEM listserv could provide were possible cases of copyright infringement.[15] However, as Eliot Bates describes, this scenario is not covered by IRB guidelines. In his "voluminous" doctoral research proposal submitted to the UC Berkeley IRB, Bates "did not need to prove in any way that [he] had a system for assuring fair payment of royalties in the event that a field recording [he] made ended up being commercially used" (email of January 12, 2008). Alternately, we could imagine hypothetical cases in which ethnomusicologists reveal authors of banned music to repressive governments, potentially exposing the author to imprisonment. I have been unable to identify any actual cases of such a scenario.

Official SEM statements on IRB, posted to its website, are dated from 2008 and 2013. In protesting the inappropriateness of standard IRB models to the methodologies of the field, SEM's 2008 statement aligns with protests made by social scientists first articulated in the mid-1970s.[16] According to the 2008 SEM statement:

> The Society for Ethnomusicology joins other scholarly societies in calling for changes in the application of IRB guidelines to ethnographic research. We seek a review protocol that acknowledges our scholarly objectives and methodology and that will be more consistently and appropriately applied. The Society views

the current situation as a threat to academic freedom as well as a detriment to the spirit and practice of the ethnographic endeavor.

The document continues to argue that notions of consent are culturally relative and that the application of an American biomedical concept of consent to foreign musical cultures is inappropriate.[17]

The 2008 SEM document argues for "exemption" of IRB review of ethnomusicological research. By 2013 the Society appeared to have moved from protest to accommodation. Rather than arguing on principle, it pleaded for "expedited" IRB approval in most cases and suggested that IRBs include ethnographers, a situation that Schrag states is very rare. The document further requests that ethnomusicologists be exempted from the requirement to obtain formal written consent and to delete their records, which might represent important cultural patrimony.

SEM's attitude of accommodation is widespread in other academic departments and professional societies (Schrag 2010: 144–148). IRBWatch.org, once an active website dedicated to documenting and protesting abuse by IRBs, now appears defunct. An SEM Newsletter article of 2008 argues that changes brought about by following IRB interview processes can lead to positive new insights in fieldwork (Amado 2008). The rise of medical ethnomusicology has increased the intersection of scholars with IRBs and accounted for the three additional mentions of IRBs in the Society's publications (Bakan et al. 2008, 2015; Stankova 2014).[18] However, many more ethnomusicological articles published in *Ethnomusicology* and similar journals discuss incarcerated populations, children, and mental patients, all considered "vulnerable populations" necessitating special IRB oversight. Because ethnomusicologists are generally not obligated to demonstrate IRB approval or exemption in their publications, the ethical status of research projects regarding vulnerable populations may be ambiguous.

While it is likely that many ethnomusicologists have quietly proceeded with their research independent of institutional review, others have creatively interpreted loopholes within the regulations themselves. By framing his activities in Louisiana's Angola prison as "artwork" rather than formal "research," Benjamin Harbert succeeded in receiving IRB exemption from UCLA's board. The "artwork" Harbert produced was a video documentary of the facility's music program (Harbert 2010: 26–27). Because framing our work as "art" as opposed to "research" sits uncomfortably with (ethno)musicology's historic appeals for scientific rigor, it is unlikely that many ethnomusicologists would adopt Harbert's creative approach to IRB. Furthermore, it is probable that many of the issues of coercion and consent raised earlier apply as well to artistic activities in prisons. As I have suggested, IRB clearance does not necessarily clarify or remove all ethical ambiguities or conflicts of interest.

IRB guidelines generally prohibit deceiving human subjects. In the case of ethnography, however, what counts as deceit may be unclear. At the beginning of new projects, most ethnographers likely experience phases of ethical confusion and discomfort. In my work in the jail I have struggled with a range of questions: Am I going to write about these people? Do I ask them now if I might? When is it appropriate to ask permission to "make note" of our interactions? What is the epistemological and ethical status of my memory of interactions before the temporal boundary of the formal approval to conduct research? Is an unexplained hypothesis or interpretation in my mind a form of deceit?

For some researchers, the dividing line between "informal observation" and "approved research" may be the receipt, or not, of official funding. Seeking approval and announcing research prior to that time exposes the academic to the potentially embarrassing situation of canceling or substantially changing research programs due to a "failure" on his or her part (i.e., not being awarded research funding).

Since the original draft of this chapter was composed in 2016, new and substantially different ethics and IRBs statements have been published (in 2018), guided by myself as SEM's Ethics Committee chair. Nevertheless, to echo Slobin's and Shelemay's frustrations described earlier, it remains a considerable challenge to formally engage the general membership in issues of ethical concern within the discipline. This is ironic considering that the liveliest conversations on social media sites related to ethnomusicology often concern ethical issues.

IRB and the Richmond City Jail

I teach at a small, private liberal arts university with a comparatively easy-to-navigate IRB. Its chair is the full-time director of the university's Office of Research Compliance and Integrity and the board is made up of full-time faculty, currently including one anthropologist, one sociologist, and one political scientist, all engaged with forms of ethnography. Despite my IRB's unusually friendly stance on ethnography, I carefully limited my initial research application concerning the jail music program to interviewing released participants no longer attached to the criminal justice system. In addition to an open-ended interview I submitted an eight-point questionnaire limited to rather generic and "safe" questions. I did not include any questions that might elicit responses critical of the jail or its staff. In addition to the questionnaire I requested permission to document my personal "reflections" on the music program that would not include any personally identifiable information.

The director of my IRB determined that this proposal was appropriate for expedited review, which required completing a simple twenty-eight-question form, submitting a sample consent form explaining to subjects the potential "risks and benefits" of participating in the study, and providing the IRB a copy of the questionnaire and interview topics. The proposal was approved within three days with the caveat that follow-up questions required further IRB approval and that "any adverse reaction or other complication of the research which involves real or potential risk or injury to subjects must be reported . . . as soon as possible." Additionally, although my interview subjects were no longer associated with the criminal justice system, because of high rates of recidivism I was advised to keep interview topics "on point" and to disregard potentially critical or fractious information that interviewees might offer voluntarily. This was to avoid potential retribution by facility staff against any re-incarcerated critics.

In contrast to researcher-directed questionnaires, the conversations that emerge through participant observation in ethnographic contexts are participant-guided interactions in which trust between researcher and research participants can gradually develop. The establishment of genuine trust built up over time is necessary for all successful participant observation. This is all the more crucial when working with incarcerated populations, for whom trust is the most valuable asset. But the term "participant observation" (and its correlates "fieldwork" or "ethnographic fieldwork") does not appear anywhere in the medicalized paradigms of IRB guidelines, and my efforts at convincing my IRB to allow for more open-ended interactions with residents were not successful.[19]

Although I successfully received IRB approval to conduct research *associated with* incarcerated populations, the process led me to prospectively censor the scope of my research in order to win approval. If my proposal is followed to the letter, the research will enable me to discover the potential positive impacts and experiences of music itself on a highly restricted number of past participants (approximately five people). However, I will have adhered to institutional ethical guidelines and its biomedical model of research and I will have followed my discipline's official ethical guidelines by seeking approval from an IRB.[20]

IRB ethical guidelines designed to protect incarcerated (and potentially incarcerated) individuals paradoxically restrain the possibility of co-producing public knowledge about carceral institutions. The effort to protect vulnerable individuals, an effort most researchers are sympathetic to, can have the paradoxical effect of protecting the institutions that oppress those individuals. When IRBs designed to protect "human subjects" suggest that some segments of society are *perpetually* vulnerable to coercion (due to a high likelihood of re-incarceration), the researcher may perceive a higher ethical obligation to examine and understand the structures of power themselves, placing institutional, professional, and personal ethics into friction.

The Ethnomusicology of Jail as a Total Institution

As it is typically framed, music therapy programs in carceral institutions are designed to "give voice" to underserved populations (Abrahams et al. 2012) while lowering both violence within the institution and recidivism. In response to the ambiguous data on the effectiveness of such programs (Cheliotis 2014), more recent research claims that music therapy assists in the vague aim of "secondary desistence," a more long-term, processual transformation that guides individuals away from the behaviors that resulted in their incarceration (Crossick & Kaszynska 2016, Cheliotis & Jordanoska 2016). However, research on the effectiveness of therapeutic interventions in carceral institutions rarely consider the ways in which such programs are institutionally framed and instrumentalized and they rarely take into account residents' reflections on mass incarceration. For instance, music therapy's investment in secondary desistence is based on the assumptions that: (1) the inmate did what they are accused of doing; (2) that act is in fact wrong; and (3) their punishment is just. In my view, mandatory minimum sentences for minor marijuana possession may violate all three of these assumptions. Because my role in the RCJ is as a listener, I often witness residents reflecting on the ethical failures of the criminal justice system itself. That is, they may critique the very structures that condition our interaction and the dominant philosophies of criminality, justice, trauma, recovery, punishment, and the interlocking "nonprofit industrial complex," including universities and their faculty, that enact and support such dominant philosophies.[21]

Conclusion: Decorative Justice and Changing Lives

While it is popularly celebrated as a "universal language," music can be highly unethical. I am not referring here to the potential for musical sounds themselves to produce behaviors deemed unethical[22] but to the ways in which sound can be unethically instrumentalized. The arts program in the Theresienstadt concentration camp enabled the Nazis to fabricate a positive image of their treatment of Jews to outside observers. Inmates were forced to sing cheerful and carefree songs in a perverted mockery of their actual mistreatment (Gilbert 2005: 117, Cheliotis 2014: 17). More recently, in Philippine prisons residents are sometimes forced to practice mass dances and music for hours and are reportedly physically mistreated if they refuse. The most widely known recent example involved over 1,500 inmates at the Cebu prison dancing to Michael Jackson's "Thriller" (Cheliotis 2014: 18).[23]

Criminological research on the relationship between arts programs and imprisonment overwhelmingly focuses on their ostensible effectiveness in empowering and rehabilitating prisoners. Cheliotis critiques this research for ignoring "the socio-political dimensions of . . . context, content, conduct and consequences" (2014: 16). Instead, he argues, arts programs in prisons often amount to a kind of "decorative justice," instrumentalized to "mask the injustices and painful nature of imprisonment behind claims of fairness, benevolence and care" (2014: 16). These programs expanded in the United States and Europe beginning around 2008, in tandem with the global economic downturn and "heightened public punitiveness" (2014: 21). This counterintuitive development predated the recent proliferation of academic studies such programs,[24] the overwhelming majority of which argue for their therapeutic impacts and cost-benefit effectiveness. According to Cheliotis, their expansion is not in response to research on their effectiveness. Instead, prisons and jails have realized the potential of these programs as advertisements for the institution as a site of humane treatment and rehabilitation.

Prison arts programs also abet a subtle form of control independent of malign instrumentalization. Arts activities may remind residents of the strict hierarchies of the institution and the impenetrable boundaries between inmate and staff. The common use of music in prison talent shows and other events recalls the annual fete of a "great house" with its masters (represented by the sheriff and staff) and servants (represented by inmates playing music).[25]

Inasmuch as music can be instrumentalized towards malign ends and forms of social control, it contains no absolute value or ethical good. Within this context an ethnomusicological study of a jail as a total institution would produce more valuable and rich knowledge about the meanings and uses of music in the institution than any bounded research on the therapeutic effects of particular music programs.

If I had examples of instrumental uses of music in the RCJ, I would be bound by my IRB not to present them here in order to protect my "human subjects." IRB guidelines require me to go to great lengths to protect confidentiality in response to a hypothetical scenario assuming an improbable chain of events: (1) results from my study will include damaging critiques of the facility by identifiable persons; (2) the study will be published; (3) staff from the facility will read the study (likely appearing in an esoteric academic publication); (4) the identifiable persons will be re-incarcerated; and (5) the staff will be vengeful.

How do incarcerated individuals benefit from such considerable caution? How does such caution serve the production of public knowledge, contribute to an informed citizenry, and further the cause of social justice? Who benefits most from this caution? The legal scholar Philip Hamburger argues that federal human subjects regulations violate the First Amendment by placing a prior restraint on speech, regulating the possibilities of new knowledge before they emerge (Hamburger 2005). In what ways do IRBs function as a new form of censorship that impedes the production of public knowledge that would serve the ethical demands of social justice?

In the federal Common Rule that guides local IRBs, "vulnerable populations" are categorized in terms of a priori types of people (e.g., "prisoners," "children," the "physically disabled," the "economically or educationally disadvantaged"). However, depending on cultural and social context, such populations may or may not actually be vulnerable. A better approach would be to define vulnerable populations as those people whose safety and freedom are imminently vulnerable to coercion by an outside power. Practically everyone is vulnerable to some form of coercion; from persistent cajoling from a boss trying to persuade, to prison violence. The argument that young Black men in Richmond are a vulnerable population (in or outside of the jail) is certainly true, but must be balanced with the particular situation of each individual and their own informed wishes. In such cases, IRBs should remember the Belmont Principle of Justice, which calls for equal opportunities to participate in research and the necessity for IRB boards to seek board members with the expertise to comment on particular populations described in research proposals.

There is widespread consensus that America has an incarceration "problem" (Subramanian 2015). A broader examination of the RCJ as a total institution, involving ethnographic interviews with current and former inmates and staff, would help us better understand how incarceration and the criminal justice system themselves function in Virginia. Greater understanding of the systemic injustices within the criminal justice system might contribute to their dismantling. I have been told directly by released program participants that they would run the risks described earlier, which they characterize as minor, if information they provided offered any possibility of improving the system. Ethical caution in this context benefits institutions. My university is protected from federal accusations of code violations, and the criminal justice system is protected from any substantive, specific critique.

Changing Lives

What is the ethical duty of individual researchers in such situations? IRB guidelines suggest that researchers should produce neutral, generalizable knowledge (Schrag 2010: 4,13,18, 41) and not (intentionally or not) change the lives of human subjects. Many social scientists, anthropologists, and ethnographers seek both to expand knowledge in general and further the cause of social justice. Inasmuch as IRB codes are absolute, these dual roles may be in ethical conflict. Researchers may perceive a consequentialist ethical duty to deceive some of their informants in the name of social justice. When the anthropologist van den Berghe deceived the apartheid government of South Africa about the nature of his research, this was in the greater ethical aim of abolishing apartheid (cf. Foster et al.). A former resident at the RCJ responded to my description of the ethical challenges posed by IRB by saying: "but questions, just questions, does, *must* change people!" In an atmosphere of conspiratorial community, both sympathetic staff and inmates, interested in "getting the word out" about the American criminal justice system, have volunteered ways in which I should "spin" (i.e., mislead) my activities to both my IRB and the jail administration (suggestions I have disregarded).

In 1975, Ithiel de Sola Pool, a strident critic of IRB at MIT, distinguished between journalists and academic researchers. While journalists are subject to the whims of their corporate employers, academics *are* their universities, as opposed to being employees of them (quoted in Schrag 2010: 103). In Pool's estimation, academics must exercise the special freedoms of their situation to further the cause of an ethics beyond the university.[26] If I were to closely follow IRB guidelines it is highly unlikely that I would receive approval to conduct an ethnomusicology of the RCJ as a total institution. The consequence is that I cannot know if the "anecdotal impacts" of the music program I have outlined are real or apparent. I cannot discover ways in which to improve it. I cannot detail abuses that may or may not be occurring. I cannot bring to public awareness the stories of resident's experiences of incarceration as expressed in their music.

Even in its most "academic" (as opposed to "applied") strains, ethnomusicology is a form of action that changes lives. Because an increasing number of ethnomusicologists work in refugee camps, war zones, or with endangered cultures and "vulnerable populations," it is time to reconsider the SEM's accommodationist approach to IRB review in the Unites States.[27] For inspiration, we might examine the ways in which journalism departments and academics involved in Participant Action Research manage their relationship to IRBs. Alternately, the SEM might consider establishing its own IRB. Because concepts of research, research participants, consent, confidentiality, and authorship differ between disciplines, the quality of research and the well-being of the individuals and communities involved are best ensured by discipline-specific ethics oversight. A disciplinary IRB would be guided by the discipline-specific guidelines and unique history and culture of ethical behavior, as described in the Society's ethics statement. While there are serious practical, bureaucratic, and legal hurdles to developing a disciplinary review board, such a body would be better equipped than local IRBs to, according to the Society's definition of ethnomusicology: "promote the research, study, and performance of music in all historical periods and cultural contexts."

Notes

1. I am primarily concerned in this chapter with IRBs in the United States, which are overseen by the federal Office for Human Research Protection (OHRP). Ethics review boards in Canada, the United Kingdom, and European Union have more local autonomy. On the situation in the UK and EU, see Reigersberg (2016). On the situation in Brazil, see Seeger (forthcoming). Neither the British Forum for Ethnomusicology (BFE) nor the International Council for Traditional Music (ICTM) has published position papers on IRBs or RECs (Research Ethics Committees), and none is being considered (Reigersberg 2016: 91).

2. When a suspect is arrested and then released on their "own recognizance" they are not obligated to pay bail or post bond. The suspect instead promises, in writing, to reappear in court for future proceedings. Often the granting of OR is at a judge's discretion and informed by his/her personal prejudices.

3. These conditions were more acute in the old Richmond City Jail. When residents were moved to the Richmond City Justice Center in 2014, mortality rates declined and a greater number of White middle-class residents began to appear, primarily as a consequence of America's opioid crisis of the late 2010s.

4. The historic capital of the confederacy, Richmond's post–Civil War history is pockmarked by a series of racist housing policies and attempts to extend Jim Crow laws. This included race-based grading of property values through the Home Owners Loan Corporation, racist zoning and "redlining" procedures employed by the Federal Housing Administration, and the use of public housing projects and school district gerrymandering to further segregate populations. In the 1930s, Virginia's "racial integrity laws," which prohibited interracial marriage, were used to segregate neighborhoods by disallowing a person from living in an area whose residents he or she could not marry. The Nazis borrowed these policies to develop their own Aryan purity laws. The civil rights movement succeeded in enacting the 1968 Fair Housing Act, which opened some suburbs to non-white populations. In practice. this largely furthered the already ongoing process of "White flight" out of the city, toward the west, further depleting Richmond of its tax base.

5. The skills I had developed as an ethnomusicologist, primarily to listen and witness, were possibly more powerful and transformative in the jail population than the predetermined lesson plans a music therapist might utilize. Despite my original fears of accidentally harming the population due to my lack of formal training in music therapy, there is evidence that artists not trained in therapy or in work with at-risk populations have achieved positive results in such situations (Cheliotis 2014: 27).

6. According to Beverley Diamond, all graduate student and faculty research is reviewed in Canadian universities, and faculty must confirm that ethics are taught in all classes involving ethnography. This system has been in place since the 1990s (personal communication, October 2016).

7. The Public Health Service conducted a clandestine research project documenting the effects of syphilis on 399 African American men for forty years, without providing treatment.

8. By the late 1990s, anthropological textbooks on research methods included sometimes contradictory information and advice on IRBs (Schrag 2010: 127).

9. By 2008 the National Science Foundation began critiquing the indiscriminate use of biomedical concepts of informed consent as formal, written consent, suggesting that in ethnographic projects this might "seem suspicious, inappropriate, rude and perhaps even threatening" (National Science Foundation 2008).

10. This definition of research was proposed by the Belmont Report and is narrower than earlier IRB definitions, which included qualitative research not defined by a hypothesis (cf. Schrag 2010: 92).

11. The state of affairs remains extremely fluid and ambiguous. Between 2002 and 2004, many universities concluded that oral history and ethnography were subject to IRB review. However, simultaneously, the OHRP (Office of Human Research Protections), which currently provides guidance to IRBs, initiated its own oral history project and determined its research was exempt from IRB review, because their project "did not represent research as defined . . . because the activity was not a systematic investigation, nor was it intended to contribute to generalizable knowledge . . . [but] designed merely to preserve a set of individuals' recollections" (OHRP, quoted in Schrag 2010: 158).

12. IRB committees and directors also often refer to Bankert and Amdur's (2005) interpretation of these guidelines.

13. For instance, residents' concept of criminality may differ from that of the criminal justice system; arrest for minor marijuana possession is a frequently cited example. Additionally, residents may be coerced into programs associated with (or assumed to be correlated with) reduced recidivism.

14. Based on my experience of the highly complex relationships of power within the RCJ, the Belmont Report's guidelines occasionally seem naïve and opportunistic. The report appears to allow for compensating inmates participating in "voluntary" research programs for their "time and discomfort." This is because their participation would be related to "opportune" rather than institutional coercive control (Belmont Report: 108–110, 681). This perspective underestimates the complexity of prison economies, the ways in which they interlock with the coercive structure of the institution, and the extreme value of apparently nominal amounts of compensation within carceral institutions.

15. Marc Perlman cites John A. Lomax Sr.'s sharing the official songwriting credit for Huddie Ledbetter's "Goodnight Irene" as an example (email of January 10, 2008).

16. These critiques were voiced most energetically by the MIT faculty member Ithiel de Sola Pool (Schrag 2010: 102)

17. This argument is open to criticism because those invested with power in any culture may inhibit the self-determination of individuals. Staff at the jail encouraged me to use inmates as human subjects and intimated that the institution's consent stood in for those of the inmates. Powerful individuals in other cultures may dictate that talking at any time to women or children, for instance, is acceptable, even if the informants themselves may not feel that way.

18. The references to IRBs in Bakan et al. (2008 and 2015) are passing affirmations that the medical ethnomusicology discussed received IRB approval.

19. This is the case both for the OHRP's "Common Rule" and for the proposed "Final Rule," an updated version of the IRB guidelines which took effect in 2018. However, the change did not significantly address or resolve the issues regarding consent described earlier, nor does it fundamentally change the definition of vulnerable populations. It does exempt all oral history and classroom projects, which may make life easier for some in the field.

20. Since the original draft was composed I have also become a member of my institution's IRB committee. This "inside view" has not substantially changed the positions I have outlined here. I serve as the "non-scientist" required for a full quorum, a designation that tickles the "social scientists" on the committee with whom I share many of the same methodologies.

21. Some universities have realized the potential of such programs to function as a form of "virtue-signaling" that can be instrumentalized in public relations as a form of penance for contributing to gentrification or for a lack of socioeconomic and racial diversity among student and faculty bodies.

22. On this see topic see Cobussen and Nielsen (2012), Johnson and Cloonan (2008), and Plato (2007).

23. See Cheliotis (2014: 9) for more international examples of the negative use of the arts programs in prisons.

24. See Cheliotis (2014) for references to several studies.

25. Goffman elaborates on this similarity (1961: 109).

26. See Massumi (2002: 208–256) for a similar, more recent, and theoretically sophisticated argument.

27. As noted, ethics review boards are configured differently in different national contexts. Whereas IRBs in the United States are subject to federal oversight by the OHRP, local institutions have more autonomy in Canada, the United Kingdom, and the European Union (see Reigersberg 2016). In Canada, specific communities at risk maintain their own ethics boards and require that research benefit the community in some way (personal communication, Beverley Diamond, October 2016).

11

Ethnomusicology and the Meeting of Knowledges in Music

The Inclusion of Masters of Traditional Musics as Lecturers in Higher Education Institutions

José Jorge de Carvalho[1]

The Eurocentric and Monoepistemic Basis of Our Academic Discipline

The purpose of this chapter is twofold: firstly, to offer an account of the Meeting of Knowledges, a movement that began at the University of Brasília in 2010 with the aim of inviting masters of traditional cultures, such as Indigenous, Afro-Brazilian, and popular groups (including masters of music), to act as lecturers in universities, regardless of the fact that they don't have formal schooling; secondly, to connect this movement with the wider international effort toward an applied and engaged ethnomusicology, in order to propose a radical transformation and renewal of the discipline.

Like any other movement of participation, collaboration, advocacy, commitment, and other similar exercises of an engaged discipline, the Meeting of Knowledges has to be understood within the specific social, political, racial, and academic context in which Latin American ethnomusicologists operate.[2] Nonetheless, I believe it can be of interest to colleagues engaged in activism on other continents, even if they institute different kinds of collaboration and solidarity with the Indigenous, immigrants, minorities, refugees, or other oppressed and discriminated groups, peoples, and communities. However, as it will be developed later, the Meeting of Knowledges is an intervention in at least three spheres of knowledge production: in the communities of the masters of musical knowledges, in ethnomusicology as a discipline, and in the university as a whole, in both its epistemic and institutional foundations. This third sphere of intervention involves an exercise of decolonization of the prolonged Eurocentric regime of academic knowledge in Latin America, which means to analyze how disciplines such as anthropology and (ethno)musicology were created and form part, to a certain extent, of a general neocolonial project of defining a modern

José Jorge de Carvalho, *Ethnomusicology and the Meeting of Knowledges in Music* In: *Transforming Ethnomusicology*. Edited by: Beverley Diamond and Salwa El-Shawan Castelo-Branco, Oxford University Press (2021). © Oxford University Press. DOI: 10.1093/oso/9780197517550.003.0012 university institution that still operates within the same modern Western epistemic paradigm worldwide.[3]

In the case of Latin America, universities were established during colonial days as a full copy of European academic institutions modeled after the Napoleonic and Humboldtian reforms around 1800.[4] Native traditions of knowledge, especially those of Indigenous, African, and other traditional peoples, were denied as legitimate sources of knowledge and therefore became absent from the university curricula. This pattern of epistemic exclusion was particularly severe in the arts and the humanities, as evident in our music schools today, which only teach, with a few exceptions, the erudite European musical genres. Thus, if we want to include the national musical diversity in our faculties of music, we will have to invite master musicians of those traditional genres to act as temporary or visiting lecturers in regular courses. This is the general background that motivates the existence of the Meeting of Knowledges.[5]

Genesis of the Meeting of Knowledges

The project was created out of two distinct and complementary social and intellectual movements: (a) the struggle to meet quotas for Black and Indigenous students in universities; and (b) the movement created by a national network of masters of traditional knowledges, agents, producers, and researchers, who demanded public policies for the groups, communities, and masters of those traditions. As to the first movement, our Brazilian academic environment has been marked, since its beginnings, by a truly racial *apartheid*: although the Blacks represent 50 percent of the country's population, the percentage of Black professors in the year 2000 was only 1 percent; and of Black students, not more than 5 percent. To confront this extreme racial inequality we started a national struggle for quotas, racial and ethnic, which is still going on.[6]

The system of quotas, now fully established for undergraduate entrance, posed a profound challenge to the chronic racism of Brazilian society. Following dramatic racial discrimination suffered by one of my doctorate students, we formulated in 1999 a system of quotas for Black and Indigenous students at the University of Brasília (UnB). After UnB approved the quotas in 2003, a series of other universities also started to establish their own models of affirmative action, so that by 2008 about 100 different universities already had some form of quotas for different categories of historically excluded subjects.

That campaign for racial and ethnic inclusion involved the entire academic community (professors and students), as well as social movements (Black, Indigenous, network of popular cultures), state institutions, the political sphere (deputies and senators), media, and other sectors of Brazilian society. Finally, the

Congress passed a law, in 2012, which makes it mandatory for all federal universities to implement quotas in their undergraduate courses.[7] In recent years, the struggle has been extended to demand quotas in graduate programs, in hiring new faculty members and also of new researchers in research institutions. The central role of UnB was once more acknowledged when the National Council for Scientific Research installed the Institute of Inclusion in Higher Education and Research inside its campus.

The issue of academic colonialism and epistemic racism appeared right in the beginning of quotas, when some critics of the policy argued that Black and Indigenous students would be alienated from their cultural and epistemic traditions if they entered an academic environment that is basically white, Eurocentric, and racist. Our answer was that we urgently need an epistemic inclusion, parallel to ethnic and racial inclusion. Here, I can bring three examples of epistemic racism from another historical process, different from the Brazilian: the boarding schools of the United States and the residential schools in Canada and Australia, where young Indigenous students were forbidden to speak their languages and to practice their cultural traditions.[8] Similar situations occurred with various Indigenous groups in Brazil, and that is why the Meeting of Knowledges can fulfill a need put forward by the traditional communities submitted to state violence and epistemic exclusion.[9]

Thus, what started as an intellectual argument to demand an expansion of the inclusion model through quotas was transformed into a political challenge to the colonized way institutions of higher education were constituted in Brazil. Taking the case of music, for example, the exclusion of musical traditions was shown to be a form of musical prejudice parallel to racial exclusion and racial prejudice. It was then possible to formulate the idea that musical Eurocentrism was an expression of social and musical racism: not only Black and Indigenous faculty and students were excluded from music schools, but Black and Indigenous musical traditions were also excluded from them. The opportunity to include non-Western musical traditions in music faculties finally came when we opened the institute in 2009; and, soon afterwards, we opened the Meeting of Knowledges.

The Meeting of Knowledges is one of the research projects of the Institute of Inclusion in Higher Education and Research, located at the UnB and which forms part of a federal program of National Institutes of Science and Technology, dedicated to expand the frontiers of scientific knowledge. Our institute is classified as applied social sciences, counting on an interdisciplinary group of researchers, which includes ethnomusicologists and anthropologists. Its goal is to promote what I call a politics of double inclusion: on the one hand, to expand quotas in all universities and research institutions in order to achieve ethnic and racial equality; on the other hand, to invite masters of traditional knowledges (including master musicians) as temporary professors in regular courses and as researchers, in order to achieve epistemic equality; or, as I call it now, epistemic quotas.

The demand to widen the epistemic horizon beyond Western science, culture, and the arts started to grow more effectively when the first generation of Black and Indigenous students finally entered higher education through quotas. In classes on literature, they questioned the absence of Black writers in the bibliography of the courses; in classes of history, they questioned the absence of African, Afro-Brazilian, and Indigenous history. Finally, in classes of music, they also challenged the curriculum, which included only erudite European music: no Indigenous nor Afro-Brazilian musical genres and no traditional instruments were taught, and Black instrumentalists and composers were not included, neither as professors nor as important musicians in musical history classes. Some of the most obvious exclusions were the percussive and choreographical traditional genres of Afro-Brazilian music, such as *maracatu, jongo, tambor de crioula, congado, capoeira,* or the various styles of *candomblé* drums,[10] as well Indigenous music. This way, since the first years of quotas, the extreme Eurocentrism combined with the negation of traditional genres of Afro-Brazilian and Indigenous music in music faculties was exposed and criticized by the newly arrived Black and Indigenous students.

It must be added here another move, simultaneous to the quotas, which was the Law 10.639, of 2003, that made mandatory the teaching of the history of Africa and Afro-Brazilian culture in all schools. This law put a positive pressure on the universities to open new courses in order to prepare the teachers to transmit these cultural elements to students. I regard this law as the first decolonizing law in the history of Brazil. It was complemented in 2008 by the Law 11.645, that also included the teaching of the cultures of the Indigenous nations. Quotas for Black and Indigenous students, together with the inclusion of Afro-Brazilian and Indigenous cultures in the curricula, strengthened the argument in favor of the inclusion of masters of traditional knowledges as teachers in the public schools and in the university system.

The foundational moment of the project occurred during the Lula years, when the Ministry of Culture, headed by the popular musician Gilberto Gil, organized two seminars in Brasília to discuss public policies for traditional popular cultures. The first one, which happened in 2005, gathered around 600 masters and their disciples, and the second one gathered over 1,000 masters and disciples. The second seminar was simultaneously called the First South American Meeting of Popular Cultures. Various masters and groups of music and dance, researchers, and state civil servants from Argentina, Peru, Colombia, Venezuela, and Ecuador shared their experiences and their arts with their fellow Brazilian participants. Finally, in 2008 a third International Seminar was held in Caracas, Venezuela, widening the scope of the demands for the inclusion of Indigenous and Afro-Ibero-American cultural traditions in higher education and research institutions.[11]

Since the seminars took place during the height of the national debate on quotas for students, quotas for masters appeared among the numerous demands that were discussed and put forward by the various collectives involved. The first time I formulated an explicit demand for the masters' presence in universities was in an event preparatory for the first seminar, held in December 2004 in Rio de Janeiro at the National Center of Folklore and Popular Culture: "Music Departments of all public universities should incorporate, from now on, Afro-Brazilian musicians as students and as professors. The only plausible way I can envisage in order to dismantle this racial and symbolic hierarchy that is omnipresent and established for such a long time is to take the decision of ceasing to reproduce Eurocentric white institutions. If we want to transform Brazil into a truly multicultural nation, then the masters of *jongo, capoeira, candomblé, tambor de mina,* and *congado,* must also be academic masters and professors in our public universities."[12]

During the first seminar, in 2005, the masters and the network of popular cultures presented the following demands to the Ministry of Culture: "To include popular cultures in the curricula of higher education" (164). And: "To invite masters to transmit their knowledges to the teaching community" (172).[13] After the First Seminar, a workshop was organized in Rio de Janeiro in March 2006 to prepare the second seminar. In that occasion, I established a connection between the previous demand of quotas for Black professors to the new one for masters of traditional knowledges: "we can make a list of masters, each one of them with their artistic and scientific singularities, and try to devise a format to place them, by means of innovative criteria of adequacy, as professors in federal and state universities" (Carvalho 2006: 18). Finally, in the third seminar of 2008 in Caracas, I organized the production of a collective manifesto called "South-American Chart of Popular Cultures," signed collectively by masters, professors, journalists, producers, and civil servants from Brazil, Argentina, Paraguay, Bolivia, Ecuador, and Venezuela, which included, among other recommendations, the following one: "We need to promote and preserve popular cultures, gathering and letting flow new creations. In order to do this, there should be in all countries a marriage between culture and education, valorizing the masters as teachers in schools and in universities, and also teaching the teachers how to dance, perform and play" (*Carta Sul-Americana das Culturas Populares,* in Carvalho 2010). Thus, with the three seminars, the demand to include masters of traditional knowledges in higher education (including master musicians) was made explicit by the four main actors involved: state institutions, the academies, the communities, and the masters themselves.[14]

Basic Characteristics of the Meeting of Knowledges

The seminars helped to consolidate two concepts that are central to the Meeting of Knowledges as a theory and as a practical movement: the concepts of *mestre* and *mestra* (male and female master) and of popular cultures. As to the first one, *mestre* became the established word to represent the whole range of people of great knowledge in all the different traditional communities. This way, *mestres/as* are shamans of Indigenous nations; priests and priestesses of the various forms of Afro-Brazilian religions, such as *candomblé*; leaders of the different genres of popular cultures, such as master musicians; artisans; healers and specialists in medicinal plants; and so forth. Furthermore, whereas in our academic system there is a clear distinction between the professor and the researcher, the *mestre* is both the one who teaches and the one who researches.[15] Added to this double capacity of the master is the idea of someone with authority—personal, communitary, and epistemic—being close to the meaning of a wise person.

It is based on this condition of a living treasure of knowledges that the master becomes unrepresentable: neither the university professor nor the master's disciple can teach that which the traditional master teaches. The knowledge accumulated by the master is always transmitted in presence, in the here and now of his or her performance in the classroom, without the mediation of books, manuals, or virtual replicas of that direct encounter with students and academic professors in the position of a teacher, a researcher, and a sage.

The pedagogic and epistemic revolutionary turn generated by the Meeting of Knowledges is the concrete act of placing Indigenous and Afro-Brazilian masters of traditional knowledges in the position of academic authority that Jacques Lacan used to define as the "subject supposed to know."[16] By granting full epistemic recognition to a master we are, at the same time, transferring a similar new power to his or her community, through various mechanisms of either mediation or direct representation. We should bear in mind that the recognition given to the master is not made in terms of the Western individualistic ideology, which would only benefit him or her; on the contrary, the aim is to reinforce his or her role as representative of the communities and ethnic groups that hold great cultural traditions that were denied and censored as a consequence of colonialism and racism. This way, as the master enters our prestigious academic environment, it is the entire community or ethnic group that finally becomes also present, affirming its traditions with the same importance as the Western-based traditions of knowledge. This new and important recognition strengthens the master's community in its demands against the various levels of injustice they suffer.

In the classrooms, the masters not only teach specific elements of their knowledge, but also present themselves as someone who belongs to a people, narrating their biography and describing the dramatic problems faced by his or her community. In fact, traditional peoples, such as Indigenous, Maroons, Afro-Brazilian communities, and other groups who live on the basis of traditional cultures, are under great danger nowadays, with violent neoliberal attacks on their territories and their means to reproduce their unique and autonomous ways of living. In short, the masters come from the oppressed side of the global South, and coming to universities is a precious opportunity to denounce injustices they suffer to an audience capable of reproducing their voice to spheres of power and decision making, nationwide and also internationally.

Another key term is "popular cultures" (in plural), whose meaning is quite different from the established usage of "popular culture" (in singular) in the English-speaking academia. The latter is normally used to define the vast universe of cultural expressions connected with the culture industry, sometimes on a global scale.[17] In the so-called developed countries of advanced capitalism, popular culture operates with a radical distinction between producer and consumer,[18] partly as a consequence of the decline of the communitary oral traditions over the last two centuries. On the other hand, "popular cultures" in Brazil and in the other Latin American countries are defined as those artistic and symbolic expressions that are mainly produced, controlled, and consumed by the communities themselves.[19] The majority of them are expressed in non-commercial musical genres—usually family-based, communitarian, orally transmitted, connected with local festivals and celebrations, and many of them created through syncretism with Catholic celebrations. Their social bases are mainly in rural areas, small towns, or the suburbs of the major cities, and they resist being fully transformed into commodities or bound to strict commercial rules. Moreover, popular cultures, in the sense the term was employed in the seminars mentioned earlier, mean not only traditional popular genres (some of which used to be defined as folklore), but also Indigenous and Afro-Brazilian. In short, *mestres* and popular cultures are two signifiers that have acquired a general, aggregatory meaning, to express an enormous variety of scientific and symbolic forms that were never present in the national cultural canon of the Brazilian social elite (including academia, which is part of that elite).

After the 2006 seminar, in order to attend the demand expressed by the masters of popular cultures, the Ministry of Culture proposed an interministerial agreement with the Ministry of Education with the specific goal of "reintroducing the art and crafts of traditional knowledges in the formal process of education."[20] As soon as the Institute of Inclusion was installed in 2009, a memorandum of understanding was signed between the Institute and the Ministry of Culture to put into practice, for the first time, the interministerial proposal. The project was then given the name of Meeting of Knowledges.

The main focus of the project is the creation of a new regular course taught by masters and that can be offered to both undergraduate and graduate students.

The procedure to offer this unprecedented course required a specific model of academic organization that we had to invent before its first edition of 2010. Together with the research group of the Institute of Inclusion, we devised the entire project, with its theoretical foundation, its methodology, and its intercultural pedagogy. Since its inauguration at UnB we chose to offer the course as a series of modules, either four of five, each of them given by one master by a particular area of knowledge, who usually comes with his or her disciple and/or with a group of performers. In 2010 we had five modules taught by masters of five areas of knowledge: a master of Indigenous architecture; another Indigenous master of reforestation and permaculture; a female Maroon master of medicinal plants; a master of *Congado*, a sacred Afro-Brazilian performative genre; and a master of *Cavalo Marinho*, a traditional folk play involving music, dancing, masks, recitation, and singing. What we did, in fact, was to expand fully the meaning of "arts and crafts" to encompass all areas of traditional knowledge.[21]

To complete this pedagogic experiment, we invited, for each module, what we define as a "partner professor," a colleague who is a specialist in the academic area close to the subject the master is teaching and who will establish a dialogue with him/her. The role of the partner professor is to build bridges between the topics taught and explained by the master during classes and draw examples and illustrations from the established Western academic knowledge in that same area. In other words, the two systems of knowledge will be taught simultaneously in the classroom, in most cases for the first time ever in our universities. The new scene of placing together the two kinds of lecturers in the same class requires necessarily the creation of codes or protocols adapted to all the different areas of traditional knowledges, which will facilitate an interepistemic dialogue—or, in Bakhtinian terms, epistemic dialogism, providing, this way, the space for a true meeting of knowledges.[22] Another revolutionary effect of those courses of Meeting of Knowledges, as I will discuss in the last section, is that the partner professor who holds a PhD will be placed in the position of being a special disciple, or student, of the master who, although illiterate, certainly is a higher authority in the field of knowledge he or she has chosen to teach.

As UnB offered the pioneering course, the Ministry of Culture required that we invited masters from the five regions of the country. However, the other universities have invited the masters of their own states, taking the chance of promoting their own living treasures. The initial format of modules was also modified. For example, the University of Pará, in the Amazon region, offered a course called "The Meeting of Knowledges in Music," simultaneously for the BA in Music and for the graduate program in arts. Luckily, it provided the opportunity to introduce in that School of Music three traditional musical genres of the state (Indigenous, Afro-Brazilian, and popular cultures) that had never been taught there before.[23]

Although the ethnomusicological community works most of the time with a more restricted definition of "music" in order to confine ethnomusicology as an academic discipline (distinct, therefore, from dance, theater, literary theory, visual arts, etc.), most of the Brazilian traditional performative genres of popular cultures may not fall exactly into the category of "music," that is, as an exclusive artistic expression. And very few of the masters of traditional performing arts can be classified solely as "musicians" in the modern Western sense of the term.[24]

Of the 140 masters who have already taught in the Meeting of Knowledges, almost half of them can be categorized in the terms of our academic departments and faculties, as masters of performing arts and celebrations—musicians, dancers, actors, storytellers, etc. Since most of the traditional masters are polymaths, some are effectively master musicians—quite different from Western music masters, who are mostly an elite subclass of the class of musicians. In this sense, the idea of the partner professor is, as we said before, only approximate. Apart from that, parallel to the integrative knowledge of the masters as musicians, the vast majority of the traditional musical genres of Brazilian communities, be it Indigenous, Afro-Brazilian, or popular cultures, are performed as part of celebrations and are, as such, not only artistic, but also ritualistic and spiritual. Instead of separate genres with specific aesthetic languages, these traditional genres can be conceived as integrative cultural expressions. Consequently, Brazilian music schools will possibly be, in the future, transformed into schools of integrated arts once they start to invite *mestres* as teachers on a regular basis. Of course, this integration in the arts already exists in schools of music in other parts of the world; in Brazil, however, this process is just starting now, provoked by the Meeting of Knowledges.[25]

Another issue that has been present since the beginning of the project is the dimension of spirituality, an area of knowledge (both of transmission and of reception) that is absent from the modern Western public universities. Practically, all of the masters who have been invited so far exercise some form of spirituality, and many of them are spiritual leaders themselves. So, apart from being musicians, most of them are shamans, healers, leaders of Afro-Brazilian religions (such as *candomblé*), leaders of popular Catholic traditions (such as *reisado, folia de reis, taieiras*, etc.), and other so-called syncretic forms such as *maracatu, jongo, congado, tambor de crioula*, among others. All of these genres have an external, performative side, with drumming, dancing, singing, and folk play, combined with an internal sacred side, usually hidden from the public.[26] So if we want to transform our musical schools from Westernized institutions to integrative and plurimusical ones, they will also have to accept the dimension of spirituality as a component of this totality of aesthetic and symbolic expressions the masters of music are now presenting to us in their classes.[27]

Expansion of the Meeting of Knowledges

After its beginning in 2010, the course has had consecutive annual editions in UnB. In 2012 it was expanded to Colombia, in the PhD program of cultural studies of the Javeriana University of Bogotá. In 2014 it was duplicated in five other Brazilian universities: in the federal universities of Minas Gerais, Juiz de Fora (Minas Gerais state), Pará, and South of Bahia, and in the State University of Ceará. In 2016 it was offered at the Federal University of Rio Grande do Sul; in 2017 it started at the Federal University of the State of Rio de Janeiro (Universidade Federal Fluminense); and in 2019 more editions are being offered in the federal universities of Rio de Janeiro, Recôncavo of Bahia, Roraima (Roraima state), and Vale do Jequitinhonha and Mucuri (Minas Gerais state). Besides, the universities of Minas Gerais and of South of Bahia have already made the Meeting of Knowledges an obligatory component of the basic cycle for all the fields of study offered.

Besides the expansion of the Meeting of Knowledges, we have fulfilled another demand made by the masters, namely, the Cartography of Masters and of Genres of Popular and Traditional Cultures.[28] The map we built provides an idea of the gigantic scale of Brazil's cultural traditions, a universe partially unknown in academia in its proportion and diversity.[29] It can also be used as a guide to identify which masters will be invited to teach in the universities of our network. We have already mapped around 2,200 masters, organized according to the various areas of knowledges in which they excel. Of those, around 140 of those have already taught in some of those universities mentioned earlier.

Once we started receiving the masters to teach regular classes, it was necessary to legitimize their position as invited, or temporary professors, basically because they don't have schooling, and many are practically illiterate. So, our next move in the way of decolonizing and reorganizing the Brazilian academic institution is to demand universities that form part of the movement to assign the title of *Notório Saber* (which can be roughly translated as "socially recognized higher knowledge") to the masters who taught in them. This title has been used by a few Brazilian universities to grant academic recognition to scholars and artists who hold only an undergraduate degree, in spite of having outstanding knowledge in their areas. With the title, they are recognized to be formally equivalent to professors who hold PhD degrees, so that they are able to teach in graduate programs.[30]

Inspired by the opening of the Meeting of Knowledges there in 2014, the State University of Ceará (UECE) granted in 2016 the award of Higher Knowledge to all the masters who already had the previous title of Living Treasures conferred by Ceará's State Assembly. Among the sixty masters who received the diploma, forty of them are masters of various performance genres and celebrations. The

Figure 11.1 *Mestre* Biu Alexandre.

Figure 11.2 Zé Bengala Ensinando, 2017.

granting of this award is, in my view, the most radical epistemic revolution in Brazilian universities of all time.[31]

We can now foresee a highly positive perspective in our struggle toward a pluriepistemic university because the masters will be able to start a new lineage of future academic professors who will learn those genres directly from them and later teach their students with an inside knowledge of their traditions. If the Meeting of Knowledges is turned into a continuous program, we can finally achieve radical musical diversity in our academic music schools after one generation, because the students will learn directly from the masters while doing their Bachelors in music, and then their MMus, followed by their PhDs, and finally, when they become professors of music, they will be able to effectively combine their Eurocentric background with their knowledge in traditional genres based on direct transmission. In other words, we will be able to finally overcome the centuries-old monomusical and monological model of our schools of music and transform them into polimusical and dialogical institutions of learning and performing.

Meeting of Knowledges as Social Participation and Collaboration

After the Meeting of Knowledges was established, various kinds of collaboration and participatory research with the traditional communities began. For instance, we have made audiovisual recordings of all the classes in all universities. And many masters of music are interested in having copies of their classes to use later in their communities as a support for the transmission of those musical traditions that now have very few masters knowledgeable of them.

As a movement that began in Latin America, the Meeting of Knowledges has affinities with other approaches, theories, and methodologies that were also developed throughout the continent. For instance, the connection between academics and the network of popular cultures bears resemblance to Orlando Fals Borda's methodology of Participation Action Research, developed in the1960s, which led him to envisage a "conjunction of academic knowledge with popular knowledge" (Fals Borda 2009: 306).[32] As Samuel Araújo has pointed out, he anticipated the approach developed by applied ethnomusicology and other forms of participatory research in ethnomusicology, although in our case action and participation occurs not only in the communities, but also in the universities.[33]

The project is also close and at the same time symmetric and complementary to Paulo Freire's pedagogy of the oppressed because some of the poor illiterate people whom we usually teach how to read and write are now becoming temporary university professors, who teach our students as well as ourselves. On the other hand, as Freire stressed the defenselessness of peoples and communities based on orality in face of an oppressive literate society, we stress the limitations and epistemic violence of our academic literate knowledge when confronted with the depth and sophistication of oral traditions maintained by illiterates who have been unfairly excluded from the academy.[34]

In spite of having affinities with collaborative, participatory, and applied proposals in ethnomusicology, the Meeting of Knowledges differs from many of them in the sense that it not only addresses the problems of the masters' communities, but it also invites the masters to help enlarging our own epistemically limited academic community. In other words, it is a kind of collaborative practice that affects both the community and the university—or rather, both the traditional musician and the professor who researches and collaborates with that musician. In this sense, for the Meeting of Knowledges the equivalent of an external action or participation is the act of inviting masters of traditional knowledges to teach, research, take part in examination boards, and advise students in the same institutional environment that recognizes and promotes modern Western "higher" knowledge: the university. In fact, it proposes an equal exchange, through collaboration and participation, between the two communities: in the masters' community, which will benefit from the ethnomusicologists' knowledge; and in the ethnomusicologists' community (i.e., the university), which will benefit from the masters' knowledge.

This spatial shift in the focus of collaboration implies also an institutional rearrangement in order to change the established rules and protocols that define our academic disciplines and our role in them, and in all instances—as teachers, as researchers, as activists, and even as co-authors with masters of music.[35] And here, we must inquire more specifically about the kind of relationship the Meeting of Knowledges can have to ethnomusicology as an established academic discipline, with its bureaucracy to legitimize teaching and research as true science.

Meeting of Knowledges and the Transformation of Ethnomusicology

The establishment of ethnomusicology as an academic field in the arts and in the humanities bears great proximity with the establishment of anthropology as a central discipline of humanities, social sciences, arts, and biology, among other areas of knowledge. So close they are to one another that one of the main approaches to ethnomusicology is to regard this relatively new discipline as a special branch of anthropology called anthropology of music. Edward Tylor published his canonical book, *Anthropology*, in 1881, and he inaugurated the chair of anthropology in Oxford in 1896. Simultaneous to Tylor's efforts, Guido Adler's founding essay was published in 1885. In order to clarify the significance of the academic and political movement we call Meeting of Knowledges, it is possible to identify three epistemological turns in the transformations which happened to both disciplines since their foundations until now.

The first epistemic turn, still alive today, takes ethnomusicology as an instantiation of Guido Adler's comparative musicology, especially in the systematic side of his chart, where he placed "Musicology (Examination and Comparison for ethnographic purposes)"; in other words, he refers to the study of musical systems that do not belong to the Western erudite spectrum, or the anthropological/musicological study of that spectrum.[36] This approach is the same developed earlier by anthropology and is marked by a clear subject-object relation: the academic studies of cultural/musical expressions of the non-Western peoples is realized by treating them as natives, or informants. Of course, the researchers can be sympathetic and lovable to the people they study, but their scientific approach is based on a separation between the people's specific interests as a society and the specific interests of the scientific corporation (always isolated from the people being studied).[37]

The chart of musicology as a science inaugurated by Adler was confirmed in the second half of the last century by two luminaries of (ethno)musicology: Charles Seeger, who commented on it extensively and took it as the inspiration for his own Unitary Field Theory of Musicology (Seeger 1970), in which he presented a rearrangement of practically the same set of disciplines present in Adler's chart; and John Blacking, who expanded the "ethnographic purpose" of the chart with his own cultural analysis, and also added the biological approach to music to the list of "auxiliary sciences" of the systematic study of "tonal art." As late as 1989, Blacking expressed his agreement with Adler's founding essay: "Adler's concept of *Tonkunst* is to my mind perfect to cope with the variety of conceptualizations of music throughout the world" (1991: 73). Of course, other colleagues have reaffirmed, with different perspectives, the *logos* of the study of music unified by Adler, which can be properly taken as an interdiscipline.

Both Seeger and Blacking questioned the necessity of the objectifying prefix "ethno-" for musicology as an academic science.[38] In sum, with or without the prefix, (ethno)musicology is an established field of academic research where the (ethno)musicologist (the subject of science) studies the music of other peoples (the object of a science of music as well as of the people who perform that music). Of course, no human being is an object; but a human being, or a human expression like music, can be treated as such, in theory and in method, if the scientist uses a subject-object epistemology. Putting it another way, even without the prefix, the objectified otherness of the musician and the musical community is implicit in the epistemological turn that founded the academic discipline of (ethno)musicology.

In spite of the effect of this dualist epistemology during the entire twentieth century, the political debate of decolonization, which began mainly outside academia,[39] had a great impact on academic anthropology (and soon thereafter, in ethnomusicology),[40] resulting in an epistemological shift, from the established subject-object relation to a new one, based on subject-subject encounters that leads to collaboration, participation, engagement, and commitment, as a response to social movements and other political demands placed by the communities to the ethnomusicologists. This shift in intention and attitude helped to put academic knowledge at the service of the communities which were previously treated (by the followers of the first epistemic model) only as object of study.[41]

To amplify these contrasts, in the first epistemological model of subject-object relations, the ethnomusicologist produces an interpretation of the music of the people he or she studies, who usually don't know what it means and to what purpose it was done, because that interpretation circulates mainly inside the academic space. On the other hand, in the second epistemological turn, based on a subject-subject relation, the ethnomusicologist's knowledge, as well as his or her social and cultural capital, is put at the service of the community, which then becomes aware (even if partially) of the types of analysis and interpretations he or she has developed about its traditions. Instead of the previous confinement within academia, which marked the first turn, this second turn works more like a back-and-forth movement for the ethnomusicologist, part of the time in the university and part of the time in the community.

Moreover, the second turn puts the community in various types of partnership with the academic world and therefore starts a process of transition to finally transform the overt objectification present in the first turn into a full subject-subject relation. However, it is probable that some collaborative and participatory projects are still in a stage of transition because the relationship of collaboration and participation is marked mainly by the ethnomusicologist's knowledge, which helps solve problems put forward by the community. On the other hand, it is not common to establish a collaboration on the basis that members of the community will help us solve our problems (one of them being the crisis of our epistemic model) with their knowledge.[42] So far, it is safe to say that we have moved from a modern academic discipline founded on a supposed political neutrality and a real distance from the communities to a politically engaged ethnomusicology.

The next step is to overcome entirely one of the colonial foundations of the discipline, namely, monologism, which keeps the academic subject in an exclusive and segregated world from the communities he or she studies or does collaborative work with. Certainly, there have been already many projects of epistemic collaboration; what the Meeting of Knowledges is bringing as a contribution to our field is sharing one's position as academic authority inside the university with the masters of music.[43] The ethnomusicological subject-subject relation realizes itself fully when we are able to exercise entirely our abilities as scholars and com-mitted individuals; and when the masters of music are also able to exercise, in front of us and of our students, their entire abilities as masters and as committed individuals. This, in short, is the aim of the Meeting of Knowledges in Music.

Taking advantage of another pair of Bakhtinian terms, we can say that col-laboration appears as the centrifugal force of the ethnomusicological episteme operating in the context of the ethnomusicologist's personal and political en-gagement with the community; on the other hand, scientific monologue is a cen-tripetal force that is constitutive of the modern academic identity, allowing no place equal to the ethnomusicologist as professor or researcher for any member of the community, even if he or she is a master of knowledge.[44]

Following the wealth of projects and practices of collaborative and applied ethnomusicology that marked the second epistemic turn in the discipline, I be-lieve the Meeting of Knowledges can contribute to the appearance of a third turn, on the way to realize a full subject-subject relation: one that is political, personal, and epistemic at the same time. With its intervention in the institutional rules of university teaching, the movement ceases to be unilateral and becomes a mu-tual and reciprocal epistemic collaboration: the academy helps the community with the knowledge it has accumulated, and the community helps the academy to widen its epistemic horizon by sending its masters to perform as teachers. Moreover, this new mode of collaboration places the (ethno)musicologist, who up to now is seen as the sole master of academic musical knowledge, in the role of a disciple of the master of traditional music—not a disciple in the master's community, which is the standard relationship developed during fieldwork, but a disciple who listens to the master in front of the students in the university's classroom.[45]

Furthermore, the Meeting of Knowledges offers two complementary aspects as a contribution to accomplish a full epistemic turn based on a subject-subject pursuit of musical knowledge. The first aspect is the centrality, for (ethno)mu-sicology as the *logos* about music, not only of the musical tradition with its genres, but of the music masters.[46] If they are not present in classrooms or in research groups, then the *logos* will continue to be exercised with the centripetal force of the unitary academic language, that is, as a theory and a method typ-ical of a monological episteme. Without the participation of masters of music, the departments of music and ethnomusicology will hardly be able to teach the fullness of non-Western erudite musical traditions for the students, with their multiple dimensions and expressive power. Professors of music and (ethno) musicologists may understand and perform well those non-Western erudite musical genres, but usually very few reach the condition of masters of those musical traditions.

The second aspect is the predicament of (ethno)musicology as an academic discipline dedicated to understand other musics and musicians and whose epistemology has not allowed the presence of the other (traditional, or non-Western) musician as an academic partner. Taking ethnomusicology as a narrative genre of modern Western science, its epistemology centered on the role of individual consciousness reinforces monologism. As Mikhail Bakhtin defines it:

> Monologism denies the existence outside itself of another consciousness with equal rights and equal responsibilities, another I with equal rights (thou). With a monologic approach another person remains wholly and merely an object of consciousness, and not another consciousness. Monologue pretends to be the ultimate word. It closes down the represented world and represented persons. (1984: 292–293)

We are here confronting a crisis of representation. If the ethnomusicologist can claim to represent a musical tradition in teaching and in research and accepts the exclusion of the masters of music of that tradition from the academic space, then he or she is implicitly declaring they are epistemically subaltern to us, as if they are incapable of representing themselves. We can here apply a lemma used by many social movements in Brazil, such as those of women, people with disabilities, and Blacks, among others: "nothing about us without us." In sum, masters are unrepresentable.

In order to overcome this crisis of representation, both epistemically and politically, the Meeting of Knowledges opens the space for dialogism as a new epistemic paradigm for the study, promotion, and sharing of musical knowledge and experience. By bringing them as professors of recognized Higher Knowledge, the masters of music will finally gain access to and interpret our own interpretations of their music—not as an interview or a dialogue in the field, but rather in the university classroom, where both the (ethno)musicologist as professor and the master will be sitting together on an equal basis, with teaching conducted by the master having the professor as an assistant. Epistemic exotopy (or outsidedness, as it is translated) will make possible a full subject-subject relation in our academic world:

> In the realm of culture, outsideness is a most powerful factor in understanding. It is only in the eyes of another culture that foreign culture reveals itself fully and profoundly. A meaning only reveals its depths once it has encountered and come into contact with another, foreign meaning: they engage in a kind of dialogue, which surmounts the closedness and one-sidedness of these particular meanings, these cultures. We raise new questions for a foreign culture,

ones that it did not raise itself; we seek answers to our own questions in it; and the foreign culture responds to us by revealing to us its new aspects and new semantic depths. Such a dialogic encounter of two cultures does not result in merging or mixing. Each retains its own unity and open totality, but they are mutually enriched. (1986: 7)

A question frequently asked about the Meeting of Knowledges is why such a bold step was taken in Brazil that seems unlikely to occur in other countries, namely, that illiterate masters of traditional knowledges are able to teach in universities, even to teach graduate students. I believe the political demand for academic change that gave birth to the project is a contemporary evidence in favor of the externalist approach to the understanding of epistemic transformations in the history of science. A great example of externalism still is, in my view, Boris Hessen's original reading of the scientific choices made by Isaac Newton in the production of his famous *Principia*. As he argued in his landmark essay, Newton's choices were due much more to the demands of the mercantile economy of England in his time than to his supposedly free and autonomous scientific intuitions.[47] Hessen analyzed and revealed, perhaps for the first time, the threefold sphere of agency of knowledge behind Newton's scientific revolution: the mercantile corporations, with an intercontinental presence; state institutions (which controlled Cambridge University), whose interests were heavily influenced by those corporations; and academics, such as Newton, also influenced by the interests of the state and of the corporations.

In our present case, somewhat similar to that moment of consolidation of modern Western science (and modern Eurocentrism and epistemic exclusion), what appears to have made the Meeting of Knowledges possible was less a theoretical discussion on decolonization, confined exclusively to academic debates,[48] than a very specific conjuncture that allowed the articulation, not of a threefold, but of a fourfold agency I already mentioned, all operating at the same time and in the same direction: state institutions, academics, communities, and masters; and all of them demanding together the presence of traditional knowledges and their representatives inside universities. The experience of the Meeting of Knowledges allows us to conclude, even if temporarily, that, in order to transcend our epistemic monologism and decolonize our academic institutions it is not enough to have arguments and theories developed by academics; it is also necessary to count on the simultaneous demand coming from the masters, as they claim the right to be recognized as people of high knowledge on equal terms with the doctors who are professors.

We can only understand fully the ethical, political, and intellectual implications of our academic study of music when we take into account the reactions of the masters of music to our theories, interpretations, and performances, when they come to our universities as our fellow teachers. With their presence, it will be possible to create specific protocols of epistemic dialogue between academics and masters for all areas of knowledge and disciplines, in sciences and in humanities. In this sense, the Meeting of Knowledges proposes to build a university environment based not only on shared *praxis* and collaboration but also on shared *logos*, in teaching and in research. This way, we may open the way for a pluriepistemic and dialogical interdiscipline of (ethno)musicology—always collaborative, open-ended, and sensitive to the contexts of the immense variety of musical traditions and of masters of music in the world.

Notes

1. I thank Samuel Araújo, Salwa El-Shawan Castelo-Branco, and Beverley Diamond for their kind support and suggestions during the production of this chapter. I also thank Felipe Oliveira for the help with the typing of it.
2. My basic references for applied ethnomusicology and similar projects are the extensive readers organized by Harrison, MacKinley, and Pettan (2010), and by Pettan and Todd (2015), as well as Araújo (2008), Hemetek (2010), Averill (2003), Dirksen (2012), and Seeger (2013), among others; and especially the comprehensive introductory essay for the present volume written by Diamond and Castelo-Branco.
3. I have developed this theme of epistemic exclusion in Latin American universities in other articles. See Carvalho (2018 and 2019a), Carvalho and Flores (2014a and 2014b).
4. For the effects of the Napoleonic and Humboldtian reforms in the constitutive epistemic exclusion of Brazilian universities, see Carvalho (2014, 2018b).
5. To clarify matters, I shall discuss issues of social and political commitment that affect mainly ethnomusicologists who are university professors; those who work in other kinds of institutions may find different problems and issues regarding the colonial background of the discipline.
6. For a description of Brazil's racial inequality as well as a detailed account of the system of quotas in Brazil, see Carvalho (2006).
7. In order to provide a synthesis of all the models of affirmative action implemented in Brazilian universities, I conceived the *Map of Affirmative Action in Brazil* (2016a), published together with a descriptive and analytical book on the Map (Carvalho 2016b).
8. I thank Beverley Diamond for calling my attention to the American, Canadian, and Australian cases.
9. Another example of epistemic racism is told in the recent tribute to the late Kwabena Nketia made by Kwasi Ampene: professors and students of the University of Ghana reacted negatively against the presence of master drummers, invited by Nketia to teach and perform, by insulting their non-Western musical art as "dondology" (Ampene 2019).

10. For a general description and analysis of these Afro-Brazilian genres, see Carvalho (2000).
11. I gave keynote speeches in both seminars and also wrote the founding documents of the second and the third one. See Carvalho (2008: 164).
12. See Carvalho (2005: 50). My own translation from the Portuguese text.
13. See Seminário Nacional de Políticas Públicas para as Culturas Populares (2005).
14. This theory of the fourfold agency will be presented in the last section.
15. I have elaborated extensively on the concept of *mestre* in another article: "Definition and Habilities of *Mestres* and *Mestras* of the Meeting of Knowledges" (Carvalho, Flórez and Ramos 2017: 189–192). George Steiner has elaborated on the decline of the figure of the master in modern Western society, finding problems with the English word "master" and its correlates in German, French, and Italian. Unfortunately, he didn't comment on the Portuguese *mestre* (Steiner 2005). As to master musicians, specifically, James Kippen has discussed the figure of the *ustad* in India (2012), and Meki Nzewi elaborated on the role of the "mother musician" in traditional Igbo drum ensembles (2008a).
16. See Lacan (1977: 177).
17. For a good discussion of popular culture in the Anglo-Saxon academy, see Hall (1998).
18. This distinction may be less pronounced in the digital era, although the oral transmission continues to be absent from it.
19. Obviously, this same universe of traditional cultures is still quite alive in many non-Western countries worldwide, with probable close affinities with the Latin American situation I am here describing.
20. See the official decree (2007).
21. For a detailed account of the first edition of the Meeting of Knowledges, see Carvalho (2010, 2011).
22. As I will elaborate on the last section, I am taking the concept of monologism and dialogism from Bakhtin (1984).
23. A special issue of the journal *Arts and Culture* of the University of Pará is entirely dedicated to the Meeting of Knowledges there: *Tucunduba*, no. 5 (2016); see also the introductory article (Carvalho et al. 2016).
24. Meki Nzewi (2008b) has offered a definition, similar to his concept of "total drama," which is quite appropriate for most performance traditions called "music" in Brazil.
25. It will be worthwhile, in another study, to compare musical diversity in music schools worldwide. For example, the University of Music and Performing Arts Vienna is an example of an integrative teaching institution. Meki Nzewi has also proposed and integrative curriculum for African schools of music (Nzewi 2017); and A. O. Nwamara and S. K. I. Chukwu (2016) proposed an intercultural musical arts education. In Brazil, this process is just beginning, provoked by the Meeting of Knowledges. Valéria Bittar of the State University of Santa Catarina (UDESC) is now proposing a total reformulation of the BA in music, and will be the first to include courses of Indigenous and Afro-Brazilian musics, together with courses in Meeting of Knowledges in music. Samuel Araújo and I are also helping the creation of similar BAs, including the

Meeting of Knowledges, both in the Pedro II College and in the School of Music of the Federal University of Rio de Janeiro.

26. For a discussion of these genres, see Carvalho (2000), and Carvalho et al (2016).

27. As I speak from the Afro-American diaspora, the connection with African performing arts must be made evident. For instance, Meki Nzewi has argued strongly about the centrality of the spiritual dimension in traditional African musical genres (see Nzewi 2008b).

28. For the cartography, see Carvalho, Vianna, and Salgado (2016).

29. Just to give an idea of the scale of the Indigenous musical (and overall cultural) diversity that is excluded from our universities, there are 305 different Indigenous nations in Brazil, speaking at least 165 different languages.

30. For a basic memorandum on the conceptual, political, and decolonizing aspects of *Notório Saber* for masters of traditional knowledges, see Carvalho (2016c).

31. The Institute of Inclusion made a documentary on the ceremony of award of *Notório Saber* for the masters in Ceará, which can be watched via the web site of the Institute of Inclusion: www.inctinclusao.com.br. Also, the Federal University of Minas Gerais has approved, on August 6, 2019, a resolution that grants the same title to the masters of the Meeting of Knowledges that taught there.

32. For a presentation of his theory and method, see Fals Borda (1979 and 2009) and Fals Borda and Rahman (1991).

33. See Araújo (forthcoming).

34. See Freire (1993). The Meeting of Knowledges has also affinities with other projects, such as the Intercultural Undergraduate Courses for Indigenous Teachers, which exist in many Latin American countries. For the pedagogic proposal of Amawtay Wasi, an Intercultural Indigenous University in Ecuador, see Sarango (2004).

35. An example within the ethnomusicologist's own tradition is Meki Nzewi, who published a book in co-authorship with other Igbo "mother musicians" (2008b); another is Rosângela de Tugny, colleague in the Meeting of Knowledges movement, who published books with Maxakali Indian masters (Tugny 2009a, 2009b); and I have also co-authored a new theory developed by one of our maroon masters (Carvalho 2019b).

36. See Erica Mugglestone and Guido Adler (1991).

37. Very often those peoples under study are trying to survive the plights of imperialism, injustice, class inequality, work exploitation, and the like, all provoked by the societies that produced the anthropologist/ethnomusicologist professional.

38. Seeger criticized the artificial polarity implicit in the prefix (1970: 188); and Blacking stated: "I believe we may be able to take the 'ethno' out of ethnomusicology before long (1991: 73).

39. Discussions of this theme began especially with the decolonization of African countries. We can think here of the powerful works and struggles of Frantz Fanon, Kwame Nkrumah, Julius Nyerere, Amílcar Cabral, and Aimé Césaire in the Caribbean.

40. Discussions of decolonization seem to be relatively recent in ethnomusicology, with a few exceptions, such as Agawu (2003), and more recently Solomon (2012), Anthony Seeger (2013), and Susana Sardo (2018), among others. I participated in

the Symposium on the Decolonisation of Knowledges in the University of Music and Performing Arts Vienna, hosted by Ursula Hemetek in May 2019.

41. Surely, disposition for collaborative work is not new in the discipline: as Anthony Seeger has remarked, Charles Seeger proposed the term "Applied Musicology" in 1939 (Seeger 1944).

42. A critical reading of the role of the university under neoliberal ideology is made by Ana Hofman (2010).

43. Ethnomusicology in Brazil has developed a strong political engagement with the communities, and an example of this trend is the book edited by Angela Lühning and Rosângela Tugny (Lühning and Tugny 2016).

44. Bakhtin affirms the centrifugal forces of the popular classes, constantly generating heteroglossia: "The centripetal forces of language, embodied in a 'unitary language,' operates in the midst of heteroglossia. . . . At any given moment of its evolution, language is stratified not only into linguistic dialectics in the strict sense of the word . . . but also . . . into languages that are socio-ideological: languages of social groups, 'professional' and 'generic' languages, and so forth" (1981: 271–272). Academic language is an example of the centripetal force of the "professional" or "unitary language."

45. Of course, there is continuity between the second and the third turn. For example, the ICTM Study Group on Applied Ethnomusicology defines its approach not only for solving concrete problems, but also "working inside and beyond typical academic contexts" (www.inctmusic.org). Klisala Harrison (2012) mentions "epistemic communities" of applied ethnomusicologists, which I believe can be transformed into a link between the second and the third turn, in the case it expands to include masters of music. The difference I propose is mainly of emphasis on epistemic equality inside academy.

46. In the case of musical traditions that are completely collective and do not seem to recognize the figure of the master, a group of musicians from that collective could be invited to occupy the same position of higher knowledge that the Meeting of Knowledges grants to music masters.

47. See Hessen's essay (1971), which was reproduced recently (2009). For a discussion of Hessen's epoch-making analysis and the confrontation between internalist and externalist approaches to the history of science, see Needham (1971).

48. The internalist position, which Hessen challenged radically with his study, believes precisely in the transforming capacity of the pure and autonomous academic debate—a perspective that was not able to overcome epistemic colonization and racism in Latin American universities until now.

Contributors' and Editors' Personal Statements

Samuel Araújo

In the late 1970s, while pursuing a university music degree with concomitant experience as a political militant under a civil-military dictatorship (1964–1985), I progressively became acquainted with the work of older generations in Brazil and elsewhere, which had laid the paths to forms of scholarship deeply grounded on local realities and epistemologies while maintaining horizontal partnerships with knowledge-producing collectives and individuals acting beyond the university walls. If many of such currents had derived from a left-leaning political field aimed at changing the status quo, that is, the one field that I have committed myself to from the beginning, others had ties with Humboldtian traditions of science-centered, liberal universities as key institutions in addressing crucial problems implicit in nation-building efforts, aiming at reforming the social structures rather than actually transforming them. From 1981 through 1985, when the dictatorship started showing signs of exhaustion after failing to cope with issues such the 1970s oil crisis, skyrocketing external debt, and soaring inflation, I had the opportunity to work as a teacher (1981–1985) at the Federal University of Paraíba, a Northeastern state holding extreme inequality indicators, at the time run by Lynaldo Cavalcanti, a liberal rector, who gave strong support to experiments integrating research, teaching, and outreach, which included some of the left-leaning projects previously relegated to extra-academic or even clandestine initiatives. This capacity of learning how to work out a transforming praxis from the bottom up through the breaches of an antagonistic state of affairs has become one of the fundamental principles of and challenges to the research work I have been involved with since then.

Samuel Araújo is Professor of Ethnomusicology at the Music Department of the Federal University of Rio de Janeiro (Brazil). He is past member of the Executive Board of the International Council for Traditional Music and past President of the Brazilian Ethnomusicology Association (ABET). He founded the pioneering Grupo Musicocultura, a collaborative project between the Ethnomusicology Laboratory of the University of Rio de Janeiro and the Center for Solidary Action of the Maré neighborhood of Rio de Janeiro, involving Maré's students and residents in collaborative research.

José Jorge de Carvalho

I earned my MA and PhD in Ethnomusicology and Anthropology at Queen's University of Belfast with John Blacking, who was a militant against apartheid. After Belfast, I became Professor of Anthropology at the University of Brasília and soon realized it was a quasi-apartheid neocolonial academic environment, with no Blacks or Indigenous people around, and an entirely Eurocentric curriculum. In 1998, the first Black student ever to enter our PhD program, and whose thesis I supervised, suffered discrimination from another professor. That racial incident led us both into a highly traumatic academic and legal struggle. As a political response to what became known as the Ari Affair (taken from his name and from the famous Dreyfus Affair of exactly one century before), I proposed quotas (affirmative action) for Black and Indigenous students. Starting in the University of Brasília, quotas became a national struggle, finally adopted by all federal universities. In 2010, I started the Meeting of Knowledges, a movement that is similar to epistemic quotas: masters of non-Western traditional knowledges (Indigenous, Afro-Brazilian, and other traditional peoples) are invited as visiting professors to teach regular courses in universities, even if they do not have school or academic titles.

Overcoming the subject-object, researcher-researched, Eurocentric colonial epistemology, now I study and research with and for the traditional peoples and communities, and not about them; they are co-researchers, co-authors, and colleagues. Courage balanced with prudence are two necessary resources as a professor with political and epistemic engagements inside academia.

José Jorge de Carvalho is Professor of Anthropology and Ethnomusicology at the University of Brasília (Brazil). He is also coordinator of the National Institute of Science and Technology and Inclusion in Higher Education and Research of the Brazilian Ministry of Science and Technology and the National Research Council (CNPq).

Rona Charles

My bush name is Goonginda, I am a Jun.gurn from the Anawurrngarri (Praying Mantis) clan in the area of Munja in Ngarinyin country. I grew up in the 1960s and 1970s in a community called Mowanjum. When I was a child, language, Culture, and Law, whether it was Junba, Wangga, or Wolungarri, was my classroom. My peers and I fit in to another world at school—the Australian world—but we still had our cultural world and education at home.

New social issues caused by the government in the late 1960s and into the 1970s impacted our families, languages, and culture, and my children and grandchildren live with these impacts today. I have a passion to bring Culture back to these generations, because I grew up in Culture and am part of Culture. There is a spirit talking to me, telling me to "keep going, don't let it die away"; I can feel the

Country telling me this. I sit down and can picture Jodba (our elder singer who passed in recent years) talking about trees, plants, medicine, and art. She is constantly teaching me, reminding me, sitting with me, especially when we are on Country. This is a gift that I am offered and I have to hold it. I think the old people who put down their songs and knowledge with Sally Treloyn years ago might have also seen that she had character to hold their gift as they came to the ends of their lives. We have worked to bring culture back and today we have young people coming through to hold it, as dancers, singers and, I hope, composers.

Rona Charles is an artist, ranger, cultural and conservation consultant, and community leader based in the Yumurlun (Pandanus Park) Community near Mowanjum in Western Australia.

Mudzunga Junniah Davhula

I was born in Sophiatown in Johannesburg, South Africa, and, thanks to a drive by my father to provide me with the best possible education, I went on to train as a primary school teacher. However, under the colonial/apartheid government, male and female teachers with the same qualifications would receive different salary packages, which raised my awareness of how education was not an equalizer. I continued on to study music education because music is life, in which the vocabulary of life is embedded. Through rhymes, poems, children, and folk songs, I found that there was more for me to learn. Like an injection, music seems to have found a place in me and has quite an inexplicable influence within my blood. Dynamic as life is, so is music. Things keep changing by day—so is music as it is part of human growth and development.

Growing up and knowing that the Christian church believed we were all heathens due to our cultural belief of ancestral gods provoked me to question the ethnicity, customary, and cultural setting of my people (the Vhavenda) with regard to their religion in all its parameters. Now living in a democratic state, the fear we used to have that Christians would laugh at us if we were to conduct research among our traditional practitioners has largely disappeared. Our research makes us understand more than just the background of our ancestral and cultural religious beliefs. Understanding my culture on a deeper level through research is where my eyes started to see things differently—to see that my people are philosophical in nature. It is this love of my culture and my commitment to making sure all children continue to have access to their music and culture that bonded me with the collaborative work I have been pursuing with Andrea Emberly and it is our hope that this continued work will positively impact Venda children now and into the future.

Mudzunga Junniah Davhula is a Creative Arts curriculum advisor for the Vhembe District, Limpopo Province Department of Education, South Africa. She is a practicing Venda musician and community leader.

Aileen Dillane

Growing up 1980s Ireland, in an ostensibly homogenous and economically de-pressed society where emigration was a feature of daily life, profoundly shaped me. Ireland went through radical changes from the late 1990s onward, during the "Celtic Tiger" economic boom, when inward migration from all over the world increased dramatically. At the time, I was studying for my doctorate in Chicago and on trips home witnessed the societal transformations, the increasing levels of diversity, and the concomitant cultural enrichments, all of which excited me as an ethnomusicologist-in-training. But I was also troubled by xenophobic discourses that began to circulate in this post-colonial nation that for centuries, especially since the Great Famine, had "exported" its citizens across the globe in search of a better life. Among my extraordinary University of Chicago mentors and peers, I found a vocabulary and means to contest these discourses, gaining an understanding into their historical and ideological underpinnings and structures of feeling. Since the global financial crash of 2008 and the extended period of Irish government-sponsored austerity that intensified and helped to transform these discourses into negative practices and policies, I have worked with sociologists at the University of Limerick (and with my colleague Tony Langlois in MIC) on topics relating to migrants and asylum seekers, and class and social disenfranchisement, especially in urban contexts. These projects have copper-fastened for me the importance of applied research and of finding ways to facilitate the bringing of people from different walks of life into a space in a shared task of doing, knowing, and simply being (the subject of my contribu-tion to this volume). Researching popular musics coming out of Ireland today that sonically and politically challenge hegemonic notions of "Irishness" through articulate expressions of plural and hybrid identities is a more recent, related interest.

Aileen Dillane is Lecturer in Music at the Irish World Academy of Music and Dance of the University of Limerick (Ireland). She is a founding member of the International Council for Traditional Music Ireland.

Andrea Emberly

Khombela—please share with me. This question/statement that I hear children in Venda singing loudly to each other throughout the day is always met with a careful distribution of whatever is at hand, a single lollipop, a package of sweets or a fizzy drink. What has always struck me is that no child is ever turned away empty-handed, no matter how small the sweet has to be divided into. This cul-ture of sharing and equity among children (with the acknowledgement that this is not a universal part of children's cultures around the world) is what has drawn me to understand how children's music and culture functions within this system of sharing and how, as an academic, I can integrate children's diverse knowledge into my work. Collaboration has always been key in this because the distribution equity that is embedded within a single word, *khombela*, seems significantly important to me in acknowledging that any of my academic work is just a tiny piece of a bigger whole and relies solely on the generosity of those I have had the fortune of working/living/creating/sharing with over the span of my academic career and in particular, the endless generosity that stems from my collaboration with Mudzunga Junniah Davhula. I have found that these collaborations cross many borders, from generational, to cultural, to community and beyond. This has led to my work in the field of children's studies, crossing academic boundaries in an attempt to integrate the ideas, theories, and cultures of children into an academic culture that has rarely acknowledged their contribution to our understanding of the world.

Andrea Emberly is Associate Professor at the Department of Humanities of York University, Canada. She currently heads a multi-year, international research project on Connecting Culture and Childhood.

Michael Frishkopf

Until 2007 I was an ethnomusicologist of a fairly traditional sort: an ethnographer aiming to *understand* the power of music for those who use it; a teacher hoping to develop a critical understanding of ethnomusicology in my students. In the spring of that year, I first led a study abroad trip to Ghana, where we encountered refugees from the horrific Liberian civil war, re-establishing their lives in a stable, bustling, but squalid refugee camp near Accra. I asked myself—and them: What could ethnomusicology do? How could we support refugee musicians? How could students get involved, and how might such an experience transform hem? How could we increase awareness and instill compassion back home? The answer was an interactive participatory action research project, culminating in a music CD, *Giving Voice to Hope* (http://bit.ly/buducd). Afterwards, I continued to question: How can music—broadly construed as all the discourses, practices, and experiences of musicking (including ethnomusicology itself)—support empathetic connection and rehumanization, reweaving a frayed social fabric in the face of the world's big problems? A series of project-answers ensued, centered (thus far) in Liberia, Ghana, Egypt, Ethiopia, and Canada, aiming not merely to understand, but to *apply* music as a powerful humanizing technology for positive social change, locally and globally. In parallel, I began to theorize these projects, synthesizing eclectic ideas from Habermasian theory, social phenomenology, the anthropology of emotion, social network theory, musical cybernetics, theories of (re)humanization and human development, and participatory action research. Gradually, over the following decade, I developed a theory and method for what I now call "music for global human development" (m4ghd.org), toward the musical development of the global human. This form of applied ethnomusicology has become increasingly central to my work—and my life.

Michael Frishkopf is Professor of Music and Director of the Canadian Center for Ethnomusicology at the University of Alberta.

Chad S. Hamill/ čnaq'ymi

Under the persistent weight of the colonial legacy, Spokane cultural heritage is at risk of being consigned to books and anthologies like this one. As a Spokane academic, I am increasingly preoccupied with guarding against the erasure of the Spokane people, not so much on my computer, but in our sláq'ist (sweat house), our ussneɫxʷ (longhouse), and the *Spokane Language House*, a nonprofit dedicated to reclaiming the Spokane language. Like the rest of our human and non-human relatives across mother earth, we are also facing a climate crisis fueled by human excesses. My contribution to this volume addresses these overlapping concerns, suggesting that for the Spokane, other tribes in the region, and our brothers and sisters around the world, cultural and environmental sustainability go hand in hand. Some might say "It's too late," too late for the language, too late for the stories, too late to reverse the disastrous effects of climate change. We can't give in to despair. If my ancestors had, Spokane traditional knowledge would have been consigned to books and anthologies a long time ago.

Chad S. Hamill/ čnaq'ymi is Professor of Applied Indigenous Studies at Northern Arizona University (USA) where he also serves as Vice President of the Office for Native American Initiatives.

Ana Hofman

Conclusion of the first draft of my chapter encompassed a personal note, which I tendentiously did not want to put in the acknowledgment section: "the time-management of my early career precarious position and the mother of a five-year-old, made this contribution far from the text I would be satisfied with." The idea behind this intervention was to make hearable usually silenced conditions of academic labor marked by everyday experience of precarity, vulnerability, and uncertain forms of existences. I like to think of this intervention as a small act of resistance, a fragment of much wider tactics of disobediences and fractures I attempt to address in my work on music and sound in what can be called frustrating social reality of the postsocialist neoliberal periphery of Central and Southeastern Europe. In my work, I address shared struggles over paid and unpaid labor that are deeply inscribed into my life and the everyday lives of people I live, perform, listen to, and research with. In doing that, I put an emphasis on the firsthand experience of state-socialism and current post-socialist neoliberal reality with an attempt to offer a view beyond Western liberal thought.

Ana Hofman is Senior Research Fellow and Assistant Professor at the Institute of Culture and Memory Studies, ZRC SAZU (Research Center of the Slovenian Academy of Sciences and Arts) in Ljubljana (Slovenia).

Tony Langlois

Tony Langlois received his PhD in 1997 from the Queen's University, Belfast, for his thesis on the Rai Music of Algeria and Morocco. He has since taught at the University of Ulster, Trinity College, Dublin; the Open University and University College, Cork. He has also worked in the cultural diversity section of the Northern Ireland Community Relations Council.

Andy McGraw

I come from a line of Scotch-Irish farmers and miners who migrated from Appalachia to Central Missouri in the early nineteenth century. After serving in World War II my grandfathers moved up to a lower-middle-class life in Kansas City. Coming of age in the late 1960s, my parents rejected both the Southern Baptism and overt racism of their parents. My father became an investigative journalist focusing on mining and farming. A picture of a miner hung over a light switch in our house, reminding us that the lights came on only because of people after the ground, breathing in the earth. In the early 1990s he won a Pulitzer Prize for exposing the government's systematic oppression of Black farmers. He also studied incarceration and collaborated with many prisoners, one of whom lived at our house after being released. I grew up in a home in which I heard many stories about how the "average Joe" often got "shafted" by power, in ways both overt and subtle. This is why I became fascinated with music's potential to empower. Ethnomusicologists stand in a privileged position to proclaim that power, and bear the responsibility of ensuring that their practice does not subtlety entrench forms of oppression.

Andy McGraw is Associate Professor at the Department of Music at the University of Richmond (USA).

Rhoda Roberts

A member of the Bundjalung nation, Widjabul and Gidabul clans, of Northern New South Wales and South East Queensland, Australia, Rhoda Roberts has been at the heart of contemporary Aboriginal artistic production. An actor and entrepreneur, she was the founder and Artistic Director of the annual International Festival The Dreaming and co-founder of Australia's first national Aboriginal theater company, the Aboriginal National Theatre Trust (ANTT), among others. She coined the term "Welcome to Country," establishing protocol manuals and welcomes by local custodians for the arts industry. She has been involved with a number of large events in varying roles including Creative Director, *Awakening* segment of the Sydney Olympic Games Opening Ceremony and Rugby World Cup 2003, among others. Roberts was the Creative Director for *Songlines*—the lighting of the Sydney Opera House sails, which opened Vivid Festival Sydney 2016, and she serves as an Aboriginal advisor to the Opera House. She often serves as a consultant for events throughout the Pacific.

Rhoda Roberts is head of Indigenous Programming at the Sydney Opera House. She is also producer of Vibe Australia, Creative Director of Rhoda Roberts Gallery & Events, and Director of the Boomerang Festival.

Jeff Titon

I was a peace and social justice activist before I was an ethnomusicologist. The folk music revival coupled with my parents' progressive political orientation led me to participate in the US civil rights movement, SDS, community organizing, the anti–Vietnam War movement, and the environmental movement. When I began to study ethnomusicology in graduate school, I already was a member of the blues music culture as a professional musician and advocate, giving back to the African American musicians who were giving so much to me. These reciprocities brought me into ethnographic fieldwork as a visitor, friend, and collaborative partner, rather than as an investigative reporter or objective scientist. When I began teaching ethnomusicology in the 1970s, I also started working as an applied ethnomusicologist within the US public folklore infrastructure, which led to my championing, within SEM, an ethnomusicology of social responsibility in the public interest. Reciprocity, advocacy, and musical and cultural sustainability have characterized my longitudinal field research with music cultures for the past fifty years, as well as my definition of ethnomusicology as "the study of people making music," my commitment to applied ethnomusicology, and my current project theorizing a sound ecology for economic, environmental, and social justice (see Jeff Todd Titon, *Toward a Sound Ecology: New and Selected Essays* [Indiana University Press, 2020]).

Jeff Titon is Professor of Music, Emeritus, at Brown University (USA). He is a founding Member and Current Co-Chair of the Applied Ethnomusicology Section of the Society for Ethnomusicology.

Sally Treloyn

Between 2000 and 2002 as a PhD student I lived and worked with elder Ngarinyin dance- and song-masters of Junba. These elders were born in the bush in the 1920s and 1930s, and lived through brutal histories of frontier colonial violence, World War II, new regimes of government and religious intervention, and displacements that fractured their own lives and those of younger generations around them. I served as documenter and scribe to these elders, supported by generous grants from the Australian Institute of Aboriginal and Torres Strait Islander Studies and the University of Sydney, and emerged with extensive knowledge of the histories and mechanisms of Junba stretching back to the early twentieth century.

The inequity in this was obscene, as I—in my mid-twenties, a non-Indigenous person of relative privilege, and an outsider to the region—was filling myself with knowledge of songs, while Ngarinyin peers and their children died around me. My training and background little equipped me to reconcile this in the moment or in writing up my doctoral research and it remained a painful lacuna that cross-sectioned my sense of self in ways that only years later could I begin to approach. As my colleague Rona Goonginda Charles notes in her personal statement, the old people who put down their songs and knowledge with me were equipped: looking around them—across generations past and present—they hoped that I and this research could play a role to bridge knowledge across generations. As I enter mid-career on faculty at the University of Melbourne, my research, service, and teaching addresses the sustainability of Junba, the complexities of intercultural collaboration around cultural heritage research, and bringing Indigenous philosophies of arts practice and practitioners into the academy.

Sally Treloyn is an Australia Research Council Future Fellow and Principal Research Fellow in the Faculty of Fine Arts and Music at the University of Melbourne.

Editors' Personal Statements

Salwa El-Shawan Castelo-Branco

My life has been divided between three very diverse geographical and cultural spaces that marked me personally and intellectually: Cairo, New York, and Lisbon. This experience provided me with a cosmopolitan worldview, a respect for and interest in engaging with individuals and groups who are very different from myself, and a capacity to recognize and respect multiple identities, values, and lifeways. I grew up in post-colonial Cairo. Yet, the legacies of colonialism and the resulting cosmopolitan formation were part of my family's history and my education at the English Mission College and in piano at the Cairo National Conservatory where I studied with the Italian Ettore Puglisi. The "discovery" of ethnomusicology in New York where I completed my master's degree in piano at Manhattan School of Music and my doctorate at Columbia University represented a major change in my personal and professional outlook and career. My move to Lisbon to take up a teaching position at the Faculty of Social Sciences and Humanities of the Nova University of Lisbon (UNL) represented a new challenge. It involved teaching and engaging in collaborative research with musicians and communities on their musical practices, heritage, memory, and other issues that are of concern to practitioners and that have been on the political and cultural agendas. It also entailed activism in academia and in the public sector: institutionalizing ethnomusicology at the UNL as a collaborative and socially engaged discipline, promoting its integration in other institutions of higher education, fighting for the creation of a National Sound Archive, and producing and promoting knowledge about and respect for diverse musics among specialists and the general public.

Salwa El-Shawan Castelo-Branco is Professor of Ethnomusicology at the Department of Musicology of the Nova University of Lisbon (Portugal), President of the Ethnomusicology Institute—Center for Studies in Music and Dance based at the same institution. She is current President of the International Council for Traditional Music (ICTM), and past Vice President of the ICTM and the Society for Ethnomusicology.

Beverley Diamond

I grew up in a farming community in rural Ontario where neighborly collaboration was the only way to get the heavy work done.. It would only be much later that I considered how our farm (and the cities where I would subsequently live) were on unceded First Nations land. During early fieldwork, I heard stories from Indigenous families whose children had been taken away to the now infamous Indian residential schools, children who suffered abuse, lost their language and culture as well as intergenerational love and nurturing, I sympathized but didn't see a way to fight the larger structures that perpetuated abuse. It took a Truth and Reconciliation Commission decades later to uncover the whole story and to initiate action in social institutions. The activist culture of York University in Toronto where I taught in the late 1980s and 90s was another eye-opener. Social justice issues were argued and acted upon in and beyond the classroom. "Research" became increasingly local engagement. What troubled me, however, were the many ways that the paradigm of "helper" and "helped" reinforced structures of discrimination rather than dismantling them. In Indigenous and other contexts, the strength, good sense, and resilience of people with whom I worked belied that paradigm. Upon moving to Newfoundland in 2002, I had the opportunity to create a public facing research centre that collaborates in a variety of ways with both settler and Indigenous communities.

Beverley Diamond is Professor Emerita at Memorial University, St. John's, Newfoundland (Canada). She held the first Canada Chair in Traditional Music at Memorial University, where she established and headed the research center for Music Media and Place.

Bibliography

Abdi, Ali. 2002. *Culture, Education, and Development in South Africa: Historical and Contemporary Perspectives.* Westport, CT: Bergin & Garvey.

Abrahams, Frank, Miranda M. Rowland, and Kristian C. Kohler. 2012. "Music Education behind Bars: Giving Voice to the Inmates and the Students Who Teach Them." *Music Educators Journal* 98 (4): 67–73.

Acker, Sandra, and Carmen Armenti. 2004. "Sleepless in Academia." *Gender and Education* 16 (1): 3–24.

Adair-Toteff, Christopher. 1995a. "Ferdinand Tönnies: Utopian Visionary." *Sociological Theory* 13 (1): 58–65.

Adorno, Theodor, and Richard Leppert. 2002. *Essays on Music.* Berkeley: University of California Press.

Agamben, Giorgio. 1998. *Homo Sacer: Sovereign Power and Bare Life.* Stanford, CA: Stanford University Press.

Alarcón-Jiménez, Ana-María. 2016. "Student Voices: A Student Union Column, Finding Paths on the Job Market." *SEM Students News* 12: 3–5.

Agawu, Kofi. 2003. *Representing African Music.* London: Routledge

Allen, Aaron & Kevin Dawe, eds. 2016. *Current Directions in Ecomusicology: music, culture, nature.* London: Routledge.

Almeida, Mauro W. B. 2003. "Marxismo e antropologia." In Armando Boito Jr. and Caio N. de Toledo (eds) *Marxismo e Ciências Humanas.* 75–85. São Paulo, Xamã/FAPESP/ CEMARX.

Amado, André. 2008. "IRB Regulations: An Intrusion into the Field?" *SEM Newsletter* 42 (3): 6.

Americans for the Arts. 2013. "Arts and Economic Prosperity IV." Washington, DC: Americans for the Arts. https://www.americansforthearts.org/by-program/ reports-and-data/research-studies-publications/arts-economic-prosperity-5/ arts-economic-prosperity-iv

Ampene, Kwasi. 2019. "On the Way Home with Dondology: A Tribute to Professor Emeritus J. H. Kwabena Nketia." *SEM Newsletter* 53, no. 3: 3–6.

Andrighetto, Luca, and Chiara Volpato. 2015. "Dehumanization." In *International Encyclopedia of the Social and Behavioral Sciences*, edited by James Wright, 2nd ed. Amsterdam: Elsevier

ANZ-ICTM. 2011. "Statement on Indigenous Music and Dance." ictmusic.org/sites/default/files/documents/IAMD_statement.pdf.

Araújo, Samuel and members of Grupo Musicultura. 2006. "Conflict and Violence as Conceptual Tools in Present-day Ethnomusicology. Notes from a Dialogical Experience in Rio de Janeiro." Ethnomusicology 50 (2): 287–313.

Araújo, Samuel. 2008. "From Neutrality to Praxis: The Shifting Politics of Ethnomusicology in the Contemporary World." Musikoloski Sbornik/ Musicological Annual 44(1):13–30.

Araújo, Samuel. 2009a. "Ethnomusicologists Researching Towns They Live In: Theoretical and Methodological Queries for a Renewed Discipline." *Journal of the Institute of Musicology of the Serbian Academy of Sciences and Arts* 9: 33–50.

Araújo, Samuel. 2009b. "From Neutrality to Praxis: The Shifting Politics of Ethnomusicology in the Contemporary World." *Muzikološki Zbornik/Musicological Annual* 44 (1): 13–30.

Araújo, Samuel, and Vinceno Cambria. 2013. "Sound Praxis, Poverty, and Social Participation: Perspectives from a Collaborative Study in Rio de Janeiro." *Yearbook for Traditional Music* 45: 28–42.

Araújo, Samuel, and Grupo Musicultura. 2006. "Conflict and Violence as Conceptual Tools in Present-Day Ethnomusicology: Notes from a Dialogical Experience in Rio de Janeiro." *Ethnomusicology, Estados Unidos* 50: 287–313.

Araújo, Samuel, and Grupo Musicultura. 2010. "Sound Praxis: Music, Politics, and Violence in Brazil." In *Music and Conflict*, edited by John Morgan O'Connell and Salwa El-Shawan Castelo-Branco, 217–231. Urbana: University of Illinois Press.

Arendt, Hannah. 1998. *The Human Condition*. Chicago: University of Chicago Press.

Armano, Emiliano, and Annalisa Murgia. 2013. "The Precariousnesses of Young Knowledge Workers: A Subject-Oriented Approach." *Global Discourse* 3 (3–4): 486–501.

Armstrong, Robert. 1975. *Wellspring: On the Myth and Source of Culture*. Berkeley: University of California Press.

Australian Council for the Arts. 2014. *Arts in Daily Life: Australian Participation in the Arts*. Final Report, Commonwealth of Australia, Canberra.

Australian Institute for Aboriginal and Torres Strait Islander Studies (AIATSIS). 2012. *Guidelines for Ethical Research in Australian Indigenous Studies*. 2nd ed. Canberra: AIATSIS.

Averill, Gage. 2003. "Ethnomusicologists as Public Intellectuals: Engaged Ethnomusicology in the University." *Folklore Forum* 34 (1/2): 49–59.

Bakan, Michael B. 2015. "'Don't Go Changing to Try and Please Me': Combating Essentialism through Ethnography in the Ethnomusicology of Autism." *Ethnomusicology* 59 (1): 116–144.

Bakan, Michael B., Benjamin Koen, Fred Kobylarz, Lindee Morgan, Rachel Goff, Sally Kahn, and Megan Bakan. 2008. "Following Frank: Response-Ability and the Co-Creation of Culture in a Medical Ethnomusicology Program for Children on the Autism Spectrum." *Ethnomusicology* 52 (2): 163–202.

Bakan, Michael B. 2015. "Being Applied in the Ethnomusicology of Autism." In *The Oxford Handbook of Applied Ethnomusicology*, edited by Svanibor Pettan and Jeff Todd Titon, 278–316. New York: Oxford University Press.

Bakhtin, Mikhail. 1981. *The Dialogical Imagination*. Edited by Michael Holquist. Austin: University of Texas Press.

Bakhtin, Mikhail. 1984. *Problems of Dostoevsky's Poetics. 1963.* Translated by C. Emerson. Minneapolis: University of Minnesota Press.

Bakhtin, Mikhail. 1986. "Response to a Question from the Novy Mir Editorial Staff." In *Speech Genres and other Late Essays*, 1–9. Austin: University of Texas Press.

Baldwin, John W. 1959. "The Medieval Theories of the Just Price." *Transactions of the American Philosophical Society, NS* 49 (4): 1–92.

Baldy, Cutcha Risling. 2013. "Why We Gather: Traditional Gathering in Native Northwest California and the Future of Bio-Cultural Sovereignty." *Ecological Processes* 2 (1): 1–10.

Bankert, Elizabeth A, and Robert J. Amdur. 2006. *Institutional Review Board: Management and Function*. Sudbury, MA: Jones & Bartlett Publishers.

Baron, Robert. 2016. "Public Folklore Dialogism and Critical Heritage Studies." *International Journal of Heritage Studies* 22: 588–606.

Barry, Jim, John Chandler, and Heather Clark. 2001. "Between the Ivory Tower and the Academic Assembly Line." *Journal of Management Studies* 38 (1): 87–101.

Barz, Gregory, and Judah Cohen. 2011. *The Culture of AIDS in Africa: Hope and Healing through Music and the Arts.* Oxford: Oxford University Press.

Barz, Gregory F., and Timothy J. Cooley. 2008. *Shadows in the Field: New Perspectives for Fieldwork in Ethnomusicology.* Oxford: Oxford University Press.

Bauman, Zygmunt. 1999. *Culture as Praxis.* London: Sage.

"The Belmont Report: Ethical Principles and Guidelines for the Protection of Human Subjects of Research." n.d. Washington, DC: The National Commission for the Protection of Human Subjects of Biomedical and Behavioral Research.

Bendix, Regina. 2013. "The Power of Perseverance. Exploring Negotiation Dynamics at the World Intellectual Property Organization." In *The Gloss of Harmony: The Politics of Policy Making in Multilateral Organisations,* edited by Birgit Muller, 23–49. London: Pluto.

Bendix, Regina, et al., eds. 2012. *Heritage Regimes and the State.* Göttingen: Universitätsverlag Göttingen.

Bendix, Regina, and Valdimar Tr. Hafstein. 2009. "Culture and Property. An Introduction." *Ethnologia Europaea: Journal of European Ethnology* 39(2): 5–10.

Bendrups, Dan. 2015. "Transcending Researcher Vulnerability through Applied Ethnomusicology." In *The Oxford Handbook of Applied Ethnomusicology,* edited by Svanibor Pettan and Jeff Todd Titon, 71–92. New York: Oxford University Press.

Bennett, Andy. 2018. "Popular Music Scenes and Aging Bodies." *Journal of Aging Studies* 45: 49–53.

Berger, Harris with Jocelyne Guilbault, Maureen Mahon, Jayson Beaster-Jones, Henry Spiller and Deborah Wong. 2014. "Call and Response: Music, Power and the Ethnomusicological Study of Politics and Culture." *Ethnomusicology* 58/2: 314–353.

Berger, Harris and Ruth Stone, eds. 2019. *Theory for Ethnomusicology. Histories, Coversations, Insights.* New York: Routledge.

Berlin, Gabriele, and Artur Simon, eds. 2002. *Music Archiving in the World: Papers Presented at the Conference on the Occasion of the 100th Anniversary of the Berlin Phonogramm-Archiv.* Berlin: Verlag für Wissenschaft und Bildung.

Bigenho, Michelle, and Henry Stobart. 2016. "The Devil in Nationalism: Indigenous Heritage and the Challenges of Decolonization." *International Journal of Cultural Property* 23 (2): 141–166.

Bird Rose, Deborah. 1986. "Passive Violence." *Australian Aboriginal Studies,* no. 1: 24.

Bird Rose, Deborah. 1992. *Dingo Makes Us Human: Life and Land in an Australian Aboriginal Culture.* Cambridge, UK: Cambridge University Press.

Bird Rose, Deborah. 1996. "Land Rights and Deep Colonising: The Erasure of Women." *Aboriginal Law Bulletin* 3 (85): 6.

Blacking, John. 1964. *Black Background: The Childhood of A South African Girl.* New York: Abelard-Schuman.

Blacking, John. 1967. *Venda Children's Songs: A Study in Ethnomusicological Analysis.* Johannesburg: Witwatersrand University Press.

Blacking, John. 1969a. "Initiation and the Balance of Power—The Tshikanda Girl's Initiation of the Venda of the Northern Transvaal." In *Ethnological and Linguistic*

Studies in Honour of N. J. van Warmelo, edited by the Ethnological Section, 21–38. Pretoria: Government Printer.

Blacking, John. 1969b. "Songs, Dance, Mimes and Symbolism of Venda Girls' Initiation Schools." *African Studies* 28 (28–35): 266.

Blacking, John. 1970. "Tonal Organizations in the Music of Two Venda Initiation Schools." *African Studies* 14 (1): 1–56.

Blacking, John. 1973. *How Musical Is Man?* Seattle: University of Washington Press.

Blacking, John. 1985. "Movement, Dance, Music, and the Venda Girls' Initiation Cycle." In *Society and the Dance: The Social Anthropology of Process and Performance*, edited by P. Spencer, 64–91. Cambridge, UK: Cambridge University Press.

Blacking, John. 1987. *"A Commonsense View of All Music": Reflections on Percy Grainger's Contribution to Ethnomusicology and Music Education*. Cambridge, UK: Cambridge University Press,

Blacking, John. 1988. "Dance and Music in Venda Children's Cognitive Development." In *Acquiring Culture: Cross Cultural Studies in Child Development*, edited by G. Jahoda and I. M. Lewis, 91–112. London: Croom Helm.

Blacking, John. 1990. "Music In Children's Cognitive and Affective Development." In *The Biology of Music Making: Music and Child Development*, edited by F. L. Roehmann and F. R. Wilson, 68–78. St. Louis: MMB Music Inc.

Blacking, John. 1991. "John Blacking: An Interview Conducted and Edited by Keith Howard," *Ethnomusicology* 35 (1): 55–76.

Blacking, John, John Baily, and Andrée Grau. 2002. *Domba, 1956–1958: A Personal Record of Venda Initiation Rites*. Audio-Visual Series. Bloomington: Society for Ethnomusicology.

Blacking, John, and Tom Huffman. 1985. "The Great Enclosure and Domba." *Man London* 20 (3): 542–545.

Blesser, Barry, and Linda Ruth Salter. 2007. *Spaces Speak, Are You Listening? Experiencing Aural Architecture*. Cambridge, MA: MIT Press.

Boff, Leonardo. 1987. *Introducing Liberation Theology*. Maryknoll, NY: Orbis Books.

Bohlman, Philip V. 2004. *The Music of European Nationalism: Cultural Identity and Modern History*. Vol. 1. Santa Barbara, CA: ABC-Clio.

Bohlman, Philip V. 2011. *Music, Nationalism and the Making of the New Europe*. New York: Routledge.

Bohlman, Philip V., Sebastian Klotz, and Lars-Christian Koch. 2007. "'Tale of Three Cities—Berlin, Chicago, and Kolkata at the Metropolitan Musical Crossroads." In *Cultural Diversity in the Urban Area: Explorations in Urban Ethnomusicology*, edited by Ursula Hemetek and Adelaida Reyes, 27–50. Berlin and Chicago: Institut für Musik und Darstellende Kunst.

Bok, Derek. 2003. *Universities in the Marketplace: The Commercialization of Higher Education*. Princeton: Princeton University Press.

Booth, Philip. 1996. *Trying to Say It: Outlooks and Insights on How Poems Happen*. Ann Arbor: University of Michigan Press.

Bowman, Paul, and Richard Stamp, eds. 2011. *Reading Rancière*. London and New York: Continuum. https://www.wipo.int/publications/en/details.jsp?id=4195.

Breen, Marcus, C. Schultz, L. Rankine, M. Brunton, D. Petherick, R. Ryan, and G. Tunstill. 1989. *Our Place, Our Music: Aboriginal Music: Australian Popular Music in Context*. Vol. 2. Canberra: Aboriginal Studies Press.

Brewer, John D. 2013. *The Public Value of the Social Sciences: An Interpretive Essay*. London, Oxford, New York, New Delhi, Sydney: Bloomsbury.

Brown, Michael F. 2004. *Who Owns Native Culture?* Cambridge, MA: Harvard University Press.

Brown, Reuben Jay. 2016. "Following Footsteps: The Kun-Borrk/Manyardi Song Tradition and Its Role in Western Arnhem Land Society." PhD thesis. University of Sydney.

Bryan, Joe. 2009. "Where Would We Be without Them?: Knowledge, Space and Power in Indigenous Politics." *Futures* 41 (1): 24–32.

Buber, Martin. 1958. *I and Thou*. New York: Scribner.

Buchanan, Donna A. 2006. *Performing Democracy: Bulgarian Music and Musicians in Transition*. Chicago: University of Chicago Press.

Bull, Michael, and Les Black. 2003. *The Auditory Culture Reader*. Oxford: Berg.

Bulled, Nicola. 2016. *Prescribing HIV Prevention: Bringing Culture into Global Health Communication*. New York: Routledge.

Butler, Judith. 1990. *Gender Trouble: Feminism and the Subversion of Identity*. New York and London: Routledge.

Butler, Judith. 2014. "Rethinking Vulnerability and Resistance." https://www.sussex.ac.uk/webteam/gateway/file.php.

Cajete, Gregory. 2000. *Native Science: Natural Laws of Interdependence*. Santa Fe, NM: Clear Light Publishers.

Cambria, Vincenzo. 2008. "Diferença: Uma questão (re) corrente na pesquisa etnomusicológica." *Revista Musica & Cultura*. Vol 3. file:///Users/scb/Downloads/3.%20vincenzo%20cambria.pdf.

Campbell, Genevieve. 2012. "Ngariwanajirri, the Tiwi 'Strong Kids Song': Using Repatriated Song Recordings in a Contemporary Music Project." *Yearbook for Traditional Music* 44: 1–23.

Campbell, Genevieve. 2014. "Song as Artefact: The Reclaiming of Song Recordings Empowering Indigenous Stakeholders—and the Recordings Themselves." In *Circulating Cultures: Exchanges of Australian Indigenous Music, Dance and Media*, Edited by Amanda Harris. 101–128. Canberra: ANU Press.

Carter, Paul. 2010. *Ground Truthing: Explorations in a Creative Region*. Perth: University of Western Australia Publishing.

Carvalho, José Jorge de. 2000. *Afro-Brazilian Music and Rituals. Part 1: From Traditional Genres to the Beginnings of Samba*. Working Paper Series 30. Durham, NC: Duke–University of North Carolina Program in Latin American Studies.

Carvalho, José Jorge de. 2005. "As artes sagradas Afro-Brasileiras e a preservação da natureza." In *Seminário Arte e Etnia Afro-Brasileira*, 41–59. Série Encontros e Estudos. Rio de Janeiro: Centro Nacional de Folclore e Cultura Popular/IPHAN/MEC.

Carvalho, José Jorge de. 2006. *Inclusão étnica e racial no Brasil*. 2nd ed. São Paulo: Attar Editorial.

Carvalho, José Jorge de. 2007. "Espetacularização e Canibalização Das Culturas Populares." In *Encontro Sul-Americano Das Culturas Populares e II Seminário Nacional de Políticas Públicas Para as Culturas Populares*. São Paulo: Instituto Polis; Brasília, DF: Ministério Da Cultura.

Carvalho, José Jorge de. 2010. "Los estudios culturales en América Latina: Interculturalidad, acciones afirmativas y encuentro de saberes." *Tabula Rasa*, no. 12: 229–251.

Carvalho, José Jorge de. 2011. "Universidades empobrecidas de conhecimento. Entrevista sobre o projeto encontro de saberes." *História da Ciência Online. Revista de História da Biblioteca Nacional,* 2011. www.revistadehistoria.com.br/historiadaciencia/2011/01/%E2%80%9Cas-nossas-universidades-estao-empobrecidas-de-conhecimento%E2%80%9D.

Carvalho, José Jorge de. 2014. *Por um mundo pluriepistêmico: As quatro dimensões do encontro de saberes.* Cadernos de Inclusão 6. Brasília: Instituto de Inclusão no Ensino Superior e na Pesquisa.

Carvalho, José Jorge de, and Carla Águas. 2015. "Encontro de saberes: Um desafio teórico, político e epistemológico." Actas do Colóquio Internacional Epistemologias do Sul: Aprendizagens Globais Sul-Sul, Sul-Norte e Norte-Sul. *Vol. 1: Democratizar a Democracia,* 1017-1027. Coimbra: Universidade Coimbra/Centro de Estudos Sociais, 2015.

Carvalho, José Jorge de. 2016a. "Mapa das ações afirmativas no Brasil." Colored map. Brasília: CNPq/Ministério da Educação/Instituto de Inclusão no Ensino Superior e na Pesquisa.

Carvalho, José Jorge de. 2016b. *A política de cotas no ensino superior. Ensaio descritivo e analítico do mapa das ações afirmativas no Brasil.* Brasília: Ministério da Educação/ Instituto de Inclusão no Ensino Superior e na Pesquisa.

Carvalho, José Jorge de et al. 2016c Encontro de Saberes. Uma Experiência de Ensino e Aprendizagem no curso de Licenciatura em Música e no Programa de Pós-Graduação em Artes da Universidade Federal do Pará, *Tucunduba,* No. 5, 4-11, 2016.

Carvalho, José Jorge de. 2016d. "Metamorphoses of Afro-Brazilian Performance Traditions: From Cultural Heritage to the Entertainment Industry." In *A Latin American Music Reader,* edited by Javier León and Helena Simonett, 406–429. Urbana: University of Illinois Press

Carvalho, José Jorge de. 2020 <2016e>. "Notório Saber para os Mestres e Mestras dos Povos e Comunidades Tradicionais: Uma Revolução no Mundo Acadêmico Brasileiro." 2020, Belo Horizonte. Ensaios Mundos Possíveis. Belo Horizonte: DAC/UFMG, 2020. On-line text. https://issuu.com/culturaufmg.

Carvalho, José Jorge de. 2016f. "Transnational Interculturality in Music Education. An Original Contribution of Brazilian and Swedish Researchers." In *Music in an Intercultural Perspective,* edited by Antenor Ferreira Corrêa, 11–12. Brasília: Strong Edições.

Carvalho, José Jorge de. 2018. "Encontro de saberes e descolonização: Para uma refundação étnica, racial e epistêmica das universidades brasileiras." In *Decolonialidade e Pensamento Afrodiaspórico,* edited by Joaze Bernardino-Costa, Nelson Maldonado-Torres, and Ramón Grossfoguel, 79–106. Belo Horizonte: Autêntica.

Carvalho, José Jorge de. 2019a. "Transculturality and the Meeting of Knowledges." In *Transkulturelle Erkundungen. Wissenschaftlich-künstleriche Perspektiven,* edited by Ursula Hemetek, Daliah Hindler, Harald Huber, Therese Kaufmann, Isolde Malmberg, and Hande Sağlam, 79–94. Viena: Böhlau Verlag.

Carvalho, José Jorge de. 2019b. "Mais uma teoria de Bispo: o limite a fronteira." In *Colonização, Quilombos. Modos e Significações,* edited by Antonio Bispo, 91–93. 2nd ed. Brasília: Ayó/INCT de Inclusão.

Carvalho, José Jorge de, and Carla Águas. 2015. "Encontro de saberes: Um desafio teórico, político e epistêmológico." *Actas do Colóquio Internacional Epistemologias do Sul: Aprendizagens Globais Sul-Sul, Sul-Norte e Norte-Sul. Vol. 1: Democratizar a Democracia.* Coimbra: 1017-1027. Coimbra: Universidade de Coimbra.

Carvalho, José Jorge de, Liliam Barros Cohen, Antenor Ferreira Corrêa, Sonia Chada, and Paula Nakayama. 2016. "The Meeting of Knowledges as a Contribution to Ethnomusicology and Music Education." *The World of Music* n.s. 5 (1): 111–133.

Carvalho, Jose Jorge de, Liliam Barros Cohen, et al. 2016. "Uma experiência de ensino e aprendizagem no curso de licenciatura em música e no programa de pós-graduação em artes da Universidade Federal do Pará." *Tucunduba*, no. 5: 4–11.

Carvalho, José Jorge de, and Juliana Flórez Flórez. 2014a. "Encuentro de saberes: Proyecto para decolonizar el conocimiento universitario eurocéntrico." *Nómadas (Col)*, no. 41: 131–147.

Carvalho, José Jorge de, and Juliana Flórez Flórez. 2014b. "The Meeting of Knowledges: A Project for the Decolonization of Universities in Latin America." *Postcolonial Studies* 17 (2): 122–139.

Carvalho, José Jorge de, Juliana Flórez e Máncel Ramos. 2017. "El Encuentro de Saberes: Hacia una Universidad Pluriepistémica. Em: Nina Alejandra Cabra Ayala e Camila Aschner Restrepo. In *Saberes Nómadas: Derivas del Pensamiento Propio*, 183–208. Bogotá: Ediciones Universidad Central, 2017.

Carvalho, Jose Jorge de, Letícia Vianna, and Flávia Salgado. 2016. "Mapeando Mestres e Mestras dos Saberes Populares Tradicionais." *Políticas culturais: Fundação Casa Rui Barbosa*. Rio de Janeiro: Fundação Casa Rui Barbosa.

Carver, Mandy. 2014. *Understanding African Music*. Grahamstown, South Africa: International Library of African Music.

Cascone, Sarah. 2018. "Arts Industries Add $764 Billion Per Year to the US Economy, Says a New Landmark Study." *Artnet News*, March 27. https://news.artnet.com/art-world/arts-contribute-764-billion-us-economy-1254170

Castelo-Branco, Salwa El-Shawan. 2010. "Epilogue: Ethnomusicologists as Advocates." In *Music and Conflict*, edited by John O'Connell and Salwa El-Shawan Castelo-Branco, 243–52. Urbana: University of Illinois Press.

"CELP." 2015. Center for Environmental Law Policy. www.celp.org/tag/ralph-w-johnson-water-hero-award.

Ceribašić, Naila. 2000. "Defining Women and Men in the Context of War: Images in Croatian Popular Music in the 1990s." In *Music and Gender*, edited by Pirkko Moisala and Beverley Diamond, 219–238. Urbana: University of Illinois Press.

Ceribašić, Naila. 2013. "L'économie de la musique traditionnelle en Croatie postsocialiste." *Ethnologie Française* 43 (2): 255–265.

Ceribašić, Naila. 2015. "Povrh tekstualnog predstavljanja u etnomuzikoloiji: od epistemologije do angažmana i pragme." *ARMUD* 46 (2): 185–201.

Ceribašić, Naila. 2019. "Musings on Ethnomusicology, Interdiciplinarity, Intradisciplinarity and Decoloniality." *Etnološka tribina* 49 (42): 3-12.

Ceribašič, Naila. 2019. "On Engaging Up and Expertise in Ethnomusicology: The Example of Expert Services in the Programme for Safeguarding Intangible Cultural Heritage." *Ethnomusicology Matters. Influencing Social and Political Realities*. Edited by Ursula Hemetek, Marko Kölbl & Hande Sağlam. 233-256. Vienna: Böhlau Verlag.

Ceribašić, Naila, Ana Hofman, and Ljerka Vidić Rasmussen. 2008. "Post-Yugoslavian Ethnomusicologies in Dialogue." *Yearbook for Traditional Music* 40: 33–45.

Černič Istenič, Majda. 2017. "Bele lise v statistikah o kariernih poteh moških in žensk v akademskem okolju." In *Znanost(brez) mladihby*, edited by Ana Hofman, 51–72. Ljubljana: Založba ZRC.

Černič-Istenič, Majda. 2014. "Slovenia—a Report." In *Contextualizing Women's Academic Careers: Comparative Perspectives on Gender, Care and Employment Regimes in Seven European Countries (GARCIA Working Paper n. 1)*, edited by Nicky Le Feuvre, 185–242. Trento: University of Trento. http://garciaproject.eu/wp-content/uploads/2014/07/GARCIA_report_wp1D1.pdf.

Certeau, Michel de. 1984. *The Practice of Everyday Life*. Berkeley: University of California Press.

Cheliotis, Leonidas. 2014. "Decorative Justice: Deconstructing the Relationship between the Arts and Imprisonment." *International Journal for Crime, Justice and Social Democracy* 3 (1): 16–34.

Cheliotis, Leonidas, and Aleksandra Jordanoska. 2016. "The Arts of Desistance: Assessing the Role of Arts-Based Programmes in Reducing Reoffending." *The Howard Journal of Crime and Justice* 55 (1–2): 25–41.

China Culture. 2016. "China Increased Culture Spending in 2015." ChinaCulture.org.

Chrisholm, L. 2004. *Changing class: Education and social change, 1990-2002*. Cape Town: Compress.

Chwe, Michael Suk-Young. 2001. *Rational Ritual Culture, Coordination, and Common Knowledge*. Princeton: Princeton University Press.

Clayton, Martin, Rebecca Sager, and Udo Will. 2004. "In Time with the Music: The Concept of Entrainment and Its Significance for Ethnomusicology." *ESEM Counterpoint* 1 (1–45).

Clifford, James, and George E. Marcus. 1986. *Writing Culture: The Poetics and Politics of Ethnography*. Berkeley: University of California Press.

Cobussen, Marcel, and Nanette Nielsen. 2016. *Music and Ethics*. Routledge.

Cohen, Sara. 1995. "Sounding Out the City: Music and the Sensuous Production of Place." *Transactions of the Institute of British Geographers* 20 (4): 434–446.

Cohen, Sara. 2012. "Bubbles, Tracks, Borders and Lines: Mapping Music and Urban Landscape." *Journal of the Royal Musical Association* 137 (1): 135–170.

Corn, Aaron. 2012. "Now and in the Future: The Role of the National Recording Project for Indigenous Performance in Australia in Sustaining Indigenous Music and Dance Traditions." *MUSICultures* 39 (1): 231–250.

Cornett, Elwood. 1990. Interviewed by Jeff Todd Titon and John Wallhausser, April 1, Blackey, Kentucky. S-VHS videorecording. A copy of the recording is on deposit at the Berea Sound Archives, Hutchins Library, Berea College, Berea, Kentucky.

Costanza, Robert, John H. Cumberland, Herman E. Daly, Robert Goodland, Richard B. Norgaard, Ida Kubiszewski and Carol Franco. 2015. *Introduction to Ecological Economics*. 2nd edition. Boca Raton, FL: Taylor & Francis.

Coulthard, Glen S. 2007. "Subjects of Empire: Indigenous Peoples and the 'Politics of Recognition' in Canada." *Contemporary Political Theory* 6 (4): 437–460.

Coulthard, Glen S. 2014. *Red Skin, White Masks: Rejecting the Colonial Politics of Recognition*. Minneapolis: University of Minnesota Press.

Cronon, William. 1991. *Natures Metropolis: Chicago and the Great West*. New York: W. W. Norton.

Crossik, G., and Patrycja Kaszynska. 2016. *Understanding the Value of Arts & Culture: The AHRC Cultural Value Project*. London: Arts and Humanities Research Council.

Cusick, Suzanne G. 1994. "On a Lesbian Relationship with Music: A Serious Effort Not to Think Straight." In *Queering the Pitch*, edited by Philip Brett, Elizabeth Wood, and Gary C. Thomas, 67–84. London: Routledge.

Cusick, Suzanne G. 2008. "Musicology, Torture, Repair." *Radical Musicology* 3 (1): 1–9.

Daily Mail. 2016. "The Modern-Day Poverty of Kentucky Where People Live with No Running Water or Electricity." https://www.dailymail.co.uk/news/article-2134196/ Pictured-The modern-day-poverty-Kentucky-people-live-running-water-electricity. html.

Dallaire, Roméo, and Brent Beardsley. 2005. *Shake Hands with the Devil: The Failure of Humanity in Rwanda*. Edited by Distributed Graf. New York; Berkeley, CA: Carroll & Graf.

Daly, Herman, and Joshua Farley. 2010. *Ecological Economics*. 2nd ed. Washington, DC: Island Press.

Data Team. 2016. "Ebola in Africa: The End of a Tragedy?" *The Economist*, January. https://www.economist.com/graphic-detail/2016/01/14/ebola-in-africa-the-end-of-a-tragedy.

Daughtry, J. Martin. 2015. *Listening to War: Sound, Music, Trauma, and Survival in Wartime Iraq*. New York: Oxford University Press.

DeCesari, Chiara. 2012. "Thinking Through Heritage Regimes." In *Heritage Regimes and the State*, edited by Regina Bendix, Aditya Eggert, and Arnika Pesselman, 399–413. Göttingen: University of Göttingen.

Deem, Rosemary. 2003. "Gender, Organisational Cultures and the Practices of Manager-Academics in UK Universities." *Gender, Work and Organisation* 10 (2): 239–259.

Deleuze, Gilles, and Félix Guattari. 1980. *Mille Plateaux*. Paris: Editions Minuit.

Delhanty, Gerald. 2003. *Community*. London: Routledge.

DeNora, Tia. 2015. *Music Asylums. Wellbeing Through Music in Everyday Life*. Farnham: Ashgate.

Department of Education. 2002. "Revised National Curriculum Statement Grades R-9 (Schools)." Pretoria: The Department of Education of South Africa.

Department of Education. 2012. "Curriculum and Assessment Policy Statement (CAPS)." Music. Republic of South Africa: Department of Education.

Devereux, Eoin, Martin J. Power, and Amanda Haynes. 2011. "Tarring Everyone with the Same Shorthand?: Journalists, Stigmatization & Social Exclusion." *Journalism: Theory, Practice & Criticism* 3 (4): 500–517.

Diamond, Peter, and Hannu Vartiainen. 2007. *Behavioral Economics and Its Applications*. Princeton: Princeton University Press.

Dillane, Aileen. 2014. "Review of 'Sonor-Cities—Learning Culture through City Soundscapes.'" *World of Music* 3 (1): 174–175.

Dillane, Aileen, and Tony Langlois. 2012. "Considering the Cultural Mapping of a City: Explorations in LimerickSoundscapes." Unpublished paper delivered to the European Seminar on Ethnomusicology. Bern, Switzerland.

Dillane, Aileen, and Tony Langlois. 2015. "Our Sounds, Our City: Urban Soundscapes, Critical Citizenship and the LimerickSoundscapes Project." *Journal of Urban Cultural Studies* 2 (2): 135–150.

Dillane, Aileen, Tony Langlois, Martin J. Power, and Orfhlaith Ní Bhriain. 2015. "Urban Soundscapes and Critical Citizenship: Explorations in Activating a 'Sonic Turn' in Urban Cultural Studies." *Journal of Urban Cultural Studies* 2 (2): 89–106.

Dirksen, Rebecca. 2012. "Reconsidering Theory and Practice in Ethnomusicology: Applying, Advocating, and Engaging beyond Academia." *Ethnomusicology Review* 17: 1–35.

Dove, Mourning, and Jay Miller. 1990. *Mourning Dove: A Salishan Autobiography*. Lincoln: University of Nebraska Press.

Dubois-Shaik, Farah, and Bernard Fusulier. 2016. "Experiences of Early Career Researchers/Academics: A Qualitative Research on the Leaky Pipeline and Interrelated Phenomena in Six European Countries." GARCIA working paper n. 11. Trento: University of Trento. http://garciaproject.eu/wp-content/uploads/2016/10/GARCIA.

Dubois-Shaik, Farah, and Bernard Fusulier, eds. 2015. "Academic Careers and Gender Inequality: Leaky Pipeline and Interrelated Phenomena in Seven European Countries." GARCIA working paper. Trento: University of Trento. http://garciaproject.eu/wp-content/uploads/2015/12/GARCIA_working_paper_5.pdf.

Durkheim, Émile. 1964 <1933>. *The Division of Labor in Society*. New York: Free Press of Glencoe.

Durkheim, Émile. 1995. *The Elementary Forms of Religious Life*. Edited by Karen E. Fields. New York: Free Press.

Durkheim, Émile. 2002. *Suicide: A Study in Sociology*. Translated by George Simpson. London: Routledge.

Edgar, Andrew. 2006. *Habermas : The Key Concepts*. London and New York: Routledge.

Edwards, James Rhys. 2015. "Critical Theory in Ecomusicology." In *Current Directions in Ecomusicology*, edited by Aaron S. Allen and Kevin Dawe, 153–164. London: Routledge.

Ekelund, Robert Burton, and Robert D. Tollison. 2000. *Economics: Private Markets and Public Choice*. Reading, MA: Addison-Wesley.

Ellis, Catherine. 1968. "Integration and Disintegration." *Australian Society for Education through the Arts Bulletin* 3 (5): 3–5.

Emberly, Andrea. 2015. "Repatriating Childhood: Issues in the Ethical Return of Venda Children's Musical Materials from the Archival Collection of John Blacking." In *Records, Research, and Responsibility*, edited by N. Thieberge, A. Harris, L. Barwick, and A. Harris, 163–186. Sydney: Sydney University Press.

Emberly, Andrea, and Lusani Davhula. 2016. "My Music, My Voice: Musicality, Culture and Childhood in Vhavenda Communities." *Childhood* 23 (3): 438–454.

Emberly, Andrea, and Lusani Davhula. n.d. "Looking Back, Looking Forward: Vhavenda Musical Life as Documented by John Blacking 1956–1958." In *Africa: International Library of African Music (ILAM). Exhibition Catalogue*. Grahamstown, South Africa: ILAM.

Emberly, Andrea, and Mudzunga Davhula. 2018. "Legacies of Research for Children, Collaboration and Connection: Supporting the Sustainment of Musical Arts Practices in Contemporary Vhavenda Children's Culture." In *John Blacking and the Current African Musicology: Reflections, Reviews, Analyses and Prospects*, edited by Geoff Maypaya. Cape Town: CASAS. https://casaspubs@casas.co.za.

Emberly, Andrea, and Jane Davidson. 2011. "From the Kraal to the Classroom: Shifting Musical Arts from the Community to the School with Special Reference to Learning Tshigombela in Limpopo, South Africa." *International Journal of Music Education* 29 (3): 265–282.

Emberly, Andrea, and Jennifer Post. 2019. "Sharing John Blacking: The Development of Archival Practices to Support the Repatriation and Reunification of a Historical Ethnomusicological Collection." In *The Oxford Handbook of Musical Repatriation*, edited by Frank Gunderson and Brett Woods. New York: Oxford University Press. https://www.oxfordhandbooks.com/view/10.1093/oxfordhb/9780190659806.001.0001/oxfordhb-9780190659806-e-12.

Emberly, Andrea, and Sally Treloyn. 2013. "Sustaining Cultures, Sustaining Collections: Accessing Australia and Its Ethnomusicological Records." *Musicology Australia Special Issue: Music, Culture and Sustainability* 35 (2): 159–177.

Erlmann, Veit, ed. 2004. *Hearing Cultures: Essays on Sound, Listening and Modernity.* Oxford: Berg.

Escobar, Arturo. 1991. "Anthropology and the Development Encounter: The Making and Marketing of Development Anthropology." *American Ethnologist* 18 (4): 658–682.

Escobar, Arturo. 1995. *Encountering Development: The Making and Unmaking of the Third World.* Princeton: Princeton University Press.

Escobar, Arturo. 2007. "Worlds and Knowledges Otherwise: The Latin American Modernity/Coloniality Research Program." *Cultural Studies* 21 (2–3): 179–210.

Etzkowitz, Henry. 1998. "The Norms of Entrepreneurial Science: Cognitive Effects of the New University-Industry Linkages." *Research Policy* 27 (8): 823–33.

Etzkowitz, Henry. 2004. "The Triple Helix and the Rise of the Entrepreneurial University." In *The Science-Industry Nexus: History, Policy, Implications*, edited by K. Grandin and S. Widmalm, 69–91. Sagamore Beach, MA: Science History Publications.

European Parliament. 2010. "Report on Atypical Contracts, Secured Professional Paths, Flexicurity and New Forms of Social Dialogue [2009/2220(INI)]." *European Parliament. Brussels: Committee on Employment and Social Affairs.* www.europarl.europa.eu.

Fakin Bajec, Jasna, and Polona Sitar. 2017. "Neoliberalna politika in konstruiranje znanstvene odličnosti v slovenskem prostoru." In *Znanost (brez) mladih*, edited by Ana Hofman . 99–126. Ljubljana: Založba ZRC.

Fals Borda, Orlando. 1979. "Investigating Reality in Order to Transform It: The Colombian Experience." *Dialectical Anthropology* 4 (1): 33–55.

Fals Borda, Orlando. 1987. "The Application of Participatory Action-Research in Latin America." *International Sociology* 2 (4): 329–47.

Fals Borda, Orlando. 2005. "Participatory Action Research." In *Fundamentals of Action Research Volume II, Varieties and Workplace Applications of Action Research*, edited by Julie Wolfram Cox and Bill Cooke, 3–9. London: Sage.

Fals Borda, Orlando. 2006. "Participatory (Action) Research in Social Theory: Origins and Challenges." In *Handbook of Action Research: Participative Inquiry and Practice*, edited by Peter Reason and Hilary Bradbury, 27–37. London and Thousand Oaks, CA: Sage.

Fals Borda, Orlando. 2010. *Antología Orlando Fals Borda.* Universidad Nacional de Colombia.

Fals Borda, O., and V. Moncayo. 2009. "Una sociología sentipensante para América Latina." *Consejo Latinoamericano de Ciencias Sociales-CLACSO.* Colombia: Siglo del Hombre.

Fals Borda, Orlando, and Muhammad Anisur Rahman. 1991. *Action and Knowledge: Breaking the Monopoly with Participatory Action-Research.* New York: Apex Press.

Feld, Steven. 1982. *Sound and Sentiment: Birds, Weeping, Poetics and Song in Kaluli Expression.* Durham, NC: Duke University Press.

Feld, Steven. 2000. "The Politics and Poetics of Pygmy Pop." In *Western Music and Its Others*, edited by David Hesmondhalgh and Georgina Born, 254–279. Berkeley: University of California Press.

Feld, Steven, and Keith Basso, eds. 1996. *Senses of Place.* Santa Fe, NM: School of American Research Press.

Finn, Daniel R. 2003. "The Moral Ecology of Markets: On the Failure of the Amoral Defense of Markets." *Review of Social Economy* 6 (2): 135–162.

Finnegan, Ruth. 1989. *The Hidden Musicians: Music-Making in an English Town.* Middletown, CT: Wesleyan University Press.

Finney, Jack. 1955. *The Body Snatchers.* New York: Dell.

Foster, George M. 1971. "Contribution to 'Anthropology on the Warpath: An Exchange.'" *New York Review of Books.* April 8: 43–44.

Foster, Michael Dylan, and Lisa Gilman. 2015. *UNESCO on the Ground: Local Perspectives on Intangible Cultural Heritage.* Bloomington: Indiana University Press.

Fox, Aaron A. 2004. *Real Country: Music and Language in Working-Class Culture.* Durham, NC: Duke University Press.

Fox, Aaron A. 2013. "Repatriation as Animation through Reciprocity." In *The Cambridge History of World Music,* edited by Philip Bohlman, 522–554. Cambridge, UK: Cambridge University Press.

France 24. 2016. "Poll Finds Xenophobia on the Rise in France." France24. September 6, 2016. www.france24.com/en/20140121-france-poll-finds-xenophobia-rise-racism-muslims-islam-hollande-death-penalty.

Freedom House. 2016. "Freedom House." https://freedomhouse.org/report/freedom-world/freedom-world-2016.

Freire, Paulo. 1970. *Pedagogy of the Oppressed.* Translated by M. B. Ramos. New York: Continuum.

Freire, Paulo. 1993. *Pedagogy of the Oppressed.* rev. ed. New York: Continuum.

Freire, Paulo. 2005. *Education for Critical Consciousness.* New York: Continuum.

Frishkopf, Michael. 1999. "Sufism, Ritual, and Modernity in Egypt: Language Performance as an Adaptive Strategy." PhD diss., Los Angeles: UCLA.

Frishkopf, Michael ed. 2010. *Music and Media in the Arab World.* Cairo: The American University.

Frishkopf, Michael. 2017. "Popular Music as Public Health Technology: Music for Global Human Development and 'Giving Voice to Health' in Liberia." *Journal of Folklore Research* 54 (1–2): 41–86.

Frishkopf, Michael, Sulemana Abu, David Zakus, Ibrahim Abukari Zukpeni, and Alhassan Mubarak. 2016. "'Singing and Dancing for Health: Traditional Music and Dance for Health Education and Promotion in Rural Northern Ghana.' Health Education and Promotion in Rural Northern Ghana." Website. http://bit.ly/sngdnc4h.

Frishkopf, Michael, Hasan Hamze, Mubarak Alhassan, Ibrahim Abukari Zukpeni, Sulemana Abu, and David Zakus. 2016. "Performing Arts as a Social Technology for Community Health Promotion in Northern Ghana." *Family Medicine and Community Health* 4 (1): 22–36. https://doi.org/doi:10.15212/FMCH.2016.0105.

Frishkopf, Michael, and Samuel Morgan. 2013a. *Sanitation and Safe Water in Liberia (Music Video).* http://www.youtube.com/watch?v=AmCk4WHPfSU&feature=youtube_gdata_player.

———. 2013b. *Sanitation and Safe Water in Liberia (Documentary).* http://www.youtube.com/watch?v=5eDal4NaYbw&feature=youtube_gdata_player.

Galtung, Johan. 1996. *Peace by Peaceful Means: Peace and Conflict, Development and Civilization.* Oslo; London; Thousand Oaks, CA: International Peace Research Institute; Sage Publications. http://site.ebrary.com/id/10369641.

Garma Forum on Indigenous Performance Research (GFIPR). 2002. "Garma Statement on Indigenous Music and Performance." www.aboriginalartists.com.au/NRP_statement.htm.

Gautier, Ana María Ochoa. 2015. *Aurality: Listening and Knowledge in Nineteenth-Century Colombia*. Durham, NC: Duke University Press.

Gaver, William, Tony Dunne, and Elena Pacenti. 1999. "Design: Cultural Probes." *Interactions* 6 (1): 21–29.

Gilbert, Shirli. 2005. *Music in the Holocaust: Confronting Life in the Nazi Ghettos and Camps*. Oxford: Oxford University Press.

Gilman, Lisa. 2016. *My Music, My War: The Listening Habits of US Troops in Iraq and Afghanistan*. Middletown, CT: Wesleyan University Press.

Goffman, Erving. 1959. *The Presentation of the Self in Everyday Life*. New York: Doubleday.

Goffman, Erving. 1961. *Asylums: Essays on the Social Situation of Mental Patients and Other Innates*. New York: Doubleday.

Grant, Catherine. 2014. *Music Endangerment*. New York: Oxford University Press.

Gray, Judith. 1997. "Returning Music to the Makers: The Library of Congress, American Indians, and the Federal Cylinder Project." *Cultural Survival Quarterly* 20 (4): 42.

Grinnell, Frederick. 1983. "The Problem of Intersubjectivity: A Comparison of Martin Buber and Alfred Schutz." *Human Studies* 6 (2): 185–95.

Grupo Musicultura, Universidade Federal do Rio de Janerio, Alexandre Dias da Silva, Alice Emery, Elza Maria Cristina Laurentino de Carvalho, Jaqueline Calazans, Juliana Catinin, et al. 2015. "É permitido proibir: a práxis sonora da pacificação." *Revista Vórtex* 3 (2): 149–158.

Gržinić, Marina, and Šefik Tatlić. 2014. *Necropolitics, Radialization, and Global Capitalism: Historicization of Biopolitics and Forenseics of Politics, Art, and Life*. Lanham, Boulder, New York, and London: Lexington Books.

Gunsalus, C. Kristina, Edward M. Bruner, Nicholas C. Burbules, Leon Dash, Matthew Finkin, Joseph P. Goldberg, William T. Greenough, Gregory A. Miller, Michael G. Pratt, and Masumi Iriye. 2007. "The Illinois White Paper: Improving the System for Protecting Human Subjects: Counteracting IRB 'Mission Creep.'" *Qualitative Inquiry* 13 (5): 617–649.

Guy, Nancy. 2002. "Governing the arts, governing the state: Peking opera and political authority in Taiwan." *Ethnomusicology* 46 (1): 96–119.

Guy, Nancy. 2002. "Trafficking in Taiwan Aboriginal Voices." Edited by Sjoerd R. Jaarsma. 195–209. *Handle with Care: Ownership and Control of Ethnographic Materials.* Pittsburgh: University of Pittsburg Press.

Habermas, Jürgen. 1984. *The Theory of Communicative Action*. Vol. 2. Boston: Beacon Press.

Hafstein, Valdimar. 2014. "Protection as Dispossesion: Government in the Vernacular." In *Cultural Heritage in Transit: Cultural Rights as Human Rights*, edited by Deborah Kapchan, 25–57. Philadelphia: University of Pennsylvania Press.

Hagedorn, Katherine J. 2001. *Divine Utterances: The Performance of Afro-Cuban Santería*. Washington, DC: Smithsonian Institution Press.

Hahn, Tomie. 2007. *Sensational Knowledge: Embodying Culture through Japanese Dance*. Middletown, CT: Wesleyan University Press.

Hahnel, Robin. 2015. "Participatory Economics and the Commons." *Capitalism Nature Socialism* 26 (3): 31–43.

Halberstam, Jack. 1998. *Female Masculinity*. Durham, NC: Duke University Press.

Hale, Charles. 2007. "In Praise of 'Reckless Minds': Making a Case for Activist Anthropology." In Les Field and Richard Fox (eds.), *Anthropology Put to Work*; 103–127 Oxford: Berg.

Hall, Patricia, ed. 2018. *The Oxford Handbook on Music Censorship*. New York: Oxford University Press.

Hall, Stuart. 1998. "Notes on Deconstructing 'The Popular.'" In *Cultural Theory and Popular Culture*, edited by John Storey. London and New York: Prentice Hall.

Hallgren, Claes. 2010. "Eric Mjöberg and the Rhetorics of Human Remains." In *The Long Way Home: The Meaning and Values of Repatriation*, edited by Paul Turnbull and Michael Pickering, 134–143. New York: Berghahn Books.

Hamari, Juho, Mimmi Sjöklint, and Antti Ukkonen. 2015. "The Sharing Economy: Why People Participate in Collaborative Consumption." *Journal of the Association for Information Science and Technology*. https://doi.org/doi:10.1002/asi.23552.

Hamburger, Philip. 2004. "The New Censorship: Institutional Review Boards." *The Supreme Court Review* 2004: 271–354.

Hamill, Chad Stephen. 2008. *Songs from Spirit: Power and Prayer in the Columbia Plateau*. PhD diss., University of Colorado at Boulder.

Hamill, Chad S. 2012. *Songs of Power and Prayer in the Columbia Plateau: The Jesuit, the Medicine Man, and the Indian Hymn Singer*. Corvallis: Oregon State University Press.

Hanley, Cationa. 2019. "Theory and Praxis in Aristotle and Heidegger." September 24, 2019. https://www.bu.edu/wcp/Papers/Acti/ActiHanl.htm.

Hannerz, Ulf. 1980. *Exploring the City. Inquiries Towards An Urban Anthropology*. New York: Columbia University Press.

Hanson, Bradley. 2014. "Tuned Our Way: Music, Memory and Heritage in East Tennessee." Ph.D diss., Brown University.

Haq, Mahbub ul. 1995. *Reflections on Human Development: How the Focus of Development Economics Shifted from National Income Accounting to People-Centered Policies, Told by One of the Chief Architects of the New Paradigm*. New York: Oxford University Press.

Harbert, Benjamin Jason. 2010. *Doing Time: The Work of Music in Louisiana Prisons*. PhD diss., University of California, Los Angeles.

Harrison, Klisala. 2012. "Epistemologies of Applied Ethnomusicology." *Ethnomusicology* 56 (3): 505–29.

Harrison, Klisala. 2013. "The Relationship of Poverty to Music." *Yearbook for Traditional Music* 45: 1–12.

Harrison, Klisala. 2014. "The Second Wave of Applied Ethnomusicology." *MUSICultures* 41 (2): 15–33.

Harrison, Klisala. 2016. "Why Applied Ethnomusicology." In *Applied Ethnomusicology in Institutional Policy and Practice*, 1–22. Helsinki: Collegium.

Harrison, Klisala, and Svanibor Pettan. n.d. "Introduction." In *Applied Ethnomusicology: Historical and Contemporary Approaches*, edited by Klisala Harrison, Elizabeth Mackinlay, and Svanibor Pettan. Newcastle upon Tyne: Cambridge Scholars Publishing.

Harrison, Klisala, Elizabeth Mackinlay, and Svanibor Pettan, eds. 2010. *Applied Ethnomusicology: Historical and Contemporary Approaches*. Newcastle upon Tyne: Cambridge Scholars Publishing.

Harvey, David. 1973. *Social Justice and the City*. London: Edward Arnold.

Haslam, Nick. 2006. "Dehumanization: An Integrative Review." *Personality and Social Psychology Review* 10 (3): 252–264.

Hassan, Robert. 2003. "Network Time and the New Knowledge Epoch." *Time & Society* 12 (2–3): 225–241.

Hawes, Bess Lomax. 1992. "Practice Makes Perfect: Lessons in Active Ethnomusicology." *Ethnomusicology* 36 (3): 337–343.

Hayes, Eileen M. 2010. *Songs in Black and Lavender: Race, Sexual Politics, and Women's Music*. Urbana: University of Illinois Press.

Haynes, Amanda, Martin J. Power, Eoin Devereux, Aileen Dillane, and James Carr. 2016. *Public and Political Discourses of Migration: International Perspectives*. London: Rowman & Littlefield.

Heatherington, Tracey, and Filippo M Zerilli, eds. 2016. "Anthropologists in/of the Neoliberal Academy." *ANUAC* 5 (1): 41–90.

Helbig, Adriana N. 2014. *Hip Hop Ukraine: Music, Race, and African Migration*. Bloomington: Indiana University Press.

Hemetek, Ursula. 2010. "The Music of Minorities in Austria: Conflict and Intercultural Strategies." In *Applied Ethnomusicology: Historical and Contemporary Approaches*, edited by Klisala Harrison, Elizabeth Mackinlay, and Svanibor Pettan, 182–199. Newcastle upon Tyne: Cambridge Scholars Publishing.

Hemetek, Ursula, and Adelaida Reyes, eds. 2007. *Cultural Diversity in the Urban Area: Explorations in Urban Ethnomusicology*. Vienna: Institut für Musik und Darstellende Kunst.

Herbst, Andre, Meki Nzewi, and Kofi Agawu. 2003. *Musical Arts in Africa: Theory, Practice and Education*. Pretoria: Unisa Press.

Hernandez, Deborah Pacini. 1995. *Bachata: A Social History of Dominican Popular Music*. Philadelphia: Temple University Press.

Hertzman, Marc A. 2013. *Making Samba: A New History of Race and Music in Brazil*. Durham, NC: Duke University Press.

Hesmondhalgh, David. 2017. "Capitalism and the Media: Moral Economy, Well-Being and Capabilities." *Media, Culture & Society* 39 (2): 202–218.

Hesmondhalgh, David, and Sarah Baker. 2011. *Creative Labour: Media Work in Three Cultural Industries*. London and New York: Routledge.

Hessels, Laurens K., and Harro van Lente. 2008. "Re-Thinking New Knowledge Production: A Literature Review and a Research Agenda." *Research Policy* 37 (4): 740–760.

Hessen, Boris. 1971. "The Social and Economic Roots of Newton's *Principia*." In *Science at the Crossroads*, edited by Nikolai Bukharin et al., 147–203. London: Frank Cass & Co.

Hessen, Boris. 2009. "The Social and Economic Roots of Newton's *Principia*." In Boris Hessen and Henryk Grossman, *The Social and Economic Roots of the Scientific Revolution*, edited by Gideon Freudenthal and Eric McLaughlin, 41–101. Boston: Springer.

Hilder, Thomas. 2012. "Repatriation, Revival and Transmission: The Politics of a Sámi Musical Heritage." *Ethnomusicology Forum* 21 (2): 161–79. Taylor & Francis.

Hilder, Thomas. 2014. *Sámi Musical Performance and the Politics of Indigeneity in Northern Europe*. Vol. 17. Rowman & Littlefield.

Hilder, Thomas R., Henry Stobart, and Shzr Ee Tan. 2017. *Music, Indigeneity, Digital Media*. Vol. 6. Boydell & Brewer.

Hofman, Ana. 2010. "Maintaining the Distance, Othering the Subaltern: Rethinking Ethnomusicologists' Engagement in Advocacy and Social Justice." In *Applied Ethnomusicology: Historical and Contemporary Approaches*, edited by Klisala Harrison, Elizabeth Mackinlay, and Svanibor Pettan, 22–35. Newcastle upon Tyne: Cambridge Scholars Publishing.

Hofman, Ana. 2015. "Music (as) Labour: Professional Musicianship, Affective Labour and Gender in Socialist Yugoslavia." *Ethnomusicology Forum* 24 (1): 28–50.

Hofman, Ana. 2017. "Na začetku znanstvene kariere skozi perspektivo spola—izkušnje in izzivi." In *Znanost (brez) mladih*, edited by Ana Hofman, 99–126. Ljubljana: Založba ZRC.

Hofman, Ana. 2019. "Ethnomusicology and Decoloniality: Perspectives from the Post-Socialist Fringe." *Etnološka tribina* 49 (42): 16–19.

Horkheimer, Max. 1972. *Critical Theory: Selected Essays*. Vol. 1. Bloomsbury: A&C Black.

Howard, Keith. 2012. *Music as Intangible Cultural Practice: Policy, Ideology and Practice in the Preservation of East Asian Traditions*. London and New York: Routledge.

"Human Development Index." 2014. UNDP. http://hdr.undp.org/en/content/human-development-index-hdi.

Hunter, Justin R. 2016. "The State of the Field: Your Views, Your Visions, Your Voices." *SEM Students News* 12: 5–7.

ICPHR. 2013. *What Is Participatory Health Research?* Berlin: ICPHR.

ICTM. 2015. https://ich.unesco.org/en/accredited-ngos-00331?accredited_ngos_name=ICTM&accredited_ngos_countryAddress=all&accredited_ngos_geo=all&accredited_ngos_ga=all&accredited_ngos_domain=all&accredited_ngos_inscription=all&accredited_ngos_safe_meas=all&accredited_ngos_term=all&accredited_ngos_full_text=&pg=00331.

IFPRI. 2016. https://www.ifpri.org/news-release/hunger-levels-remain-%E2%80%9Cserious%E2%80%9D-or-%E2%80%9Calarming%E2%80%9D-52-developing-countries.

Ingold, Tim. 2000. *The Perception of the Environment*. Routledge: London.

Intergovernmental Panel on Climate Change. 2014. *Climate Change 2014—Impacts, Adaptation and Vulnerability: Regional Aspects*. Cambridge, UK: Cambridge University Press.

Irwin, John. 2013. *The Jail: Managing the Underclass in American Society*. Berkeley: University of California Press.

Jäncke, Lutz. 2008. "Music, Memory and Emotion." *Journal of Biology* 7 (6): 21. https://doi.org/doi:10.1186/jbiol82.

Johnson, Bruce, and Martin Cloonan. 2008. *Dark Side of the Tune: Popular Music and Violence*. Aldershot: Ashgate.

Johnson, Laura, and Paul Morris. 2010. "Towards a Framework for Critical Citizenship Education." *The Curriculum Journal* 21 (1): 77–96.

Jordan, Jennifer, Marijke C. Leliveld, and Ann E. Tenbrunsel. 2015. "The Moral Self-Image Scale: Measuring and Understanding the Malleability of the Moral Self." *Frontiers in Psychology* 6 (December). https://www.frontiersin.org/search/journal.

Jurková, Zuzana, ed. 2012. Urban People Special Edition: Listening to the Music Of the City. *Urban People* 14 (2). https://urbanpeople.cuni.cz/LMENG-45.html.

Kahunde, Samuel. 2012. "Repatriating Archival Sound Recordings to Revive Traditions: The Role of the Klaus Wachsmann Recordings in the Revival of the Royal Music of Bunyoro-Kitara, Uganda." *Ethnomusicology Forum* 21 (2): 197–219.

Kapchan, Deborah. 2014. *Cultural Heritage in Transit. Intangible Rights as Human Rights*. Philadelphia: University of Pennsylvania Press.

Karush, Matthew B. 2017. *Musicians in Transit: Argentina and the Globalization of Popular Music*. Durham, NC: Duke University Press.

Kearney, Amanda. 2009. "Intangible Cultural Heritage: Global Awareness and Local Interest." In *Intangible Heritage*, edited by Laurajane Smith and Natsuko Akagawa, 209–226. New York: Routledge.

Kemmis, Stephen, and Robin McTaggart. 2005. "Participatory Action Research: Communicative Action and the Public Sphere." In *The SAGE Handbook of Qualitative Research*, edited by Norman K Denzin and Yvonna S Lincoln, 559–603. Thousand Oaks, CA: Sage Publications.

Kemmis, Stephen, Robin McTaggart, and Rhonda Nixon. 2014. *The Action Research Planner: Doing Critical Participatory Action Research*. Singapore: Springer.

Kheshti, Roshanak. 2015. *Modernity's Ear. Listening to Race and Gender in World Music*. New York: New York University Press.

Kippen, James. 2008. "Working with the Masters." In *Shadows in the Field. New Perspectives for Fieldwork in Ethnomusicology*, edited by Gregory Barz and Timothy J. Cooley, 125–140. Oxford: Oxford University Press.

Kirkaldy, Alan. 2007. "Capturing the Soul: The Vhavenda and the Missionaries, 1870–1900." *Histories* 52 (1): 272–274.

Kirksey, Eben. 2015. *Emergent Ecologies*. Durham, NC: Duke University Press.

Kirshenblatt-Gimblett, Barbara. 1988. "Mistaken Dichotomies." *The Journal of American Folklore* 101 (400): 140–155.

Kisliuk, Michelle. 1998. *Seize the Dance: BaAka Musical Life and the Ethnography of Performance*. New York: Oxford University Press.

Knežević Hočevar, Duška, Tanja Petrović, and Ana Hofman. 2015. "Slovenia." In *Constructing Excellence: The Gap between Formal and Actual Selection Criteria for Early Career Academics (GARCIA Working Paper n. 2)*, edited by Channah Herschberg, Yvonne Benschop, and Marieke van den Brink, 241–273. Trento: University of Trento. http://garciaproject.eu/wp-.

Koen, Benjamin D. 2017. "Medical Ethnomusicology and Psychological Flexibility in Healing, Health, and Wellness." In *Ethnomusicology: A Contemporary Reader, Volume II*, edited by Jennifer Post, 111–123. New York: Routledge.

Kolšek, Katja, and Tomaž Gregorc. 2011. *Prihodnost znanosti: Neoliberalizem, univerza in politika sodobnega znanstvenega raziskovanja (Zbirka Anagoga)*. Novo Mesto: GOGA.

Koshul, Basit. 2005. *The Postmodern Significance of Max Weber's Legacy: Disenchanting Disenchantment*. New York: Palgrave Macmillan.

Koskoff, Ellen. 2000. *Music in Lubavitcher Life*. Urbana: University of Illinois Press.

Koskoff, Ellen. 2014. *A Feminist Ethnomusicology: Writings on Music and Gender*. Urbana: University of Illinois Press.

Kowal, Emma. 2008. "The Politics of the Gap: Indigenous Australians, Liberal Multiculturalism, and the End of the Self-Determination Era." *American Anthropologist* 110 (3): 338–348.

Krause, Bernie. 2012. *The Great Animal Orchestra: Finding the Origins of Music in the World's Wild Places*. London: Profile Books.

Kricher, John. 2009. *The Balance of Nature: Ecology's Enduring Myth*. Princeton: Princeton University Press.

Krims, Adam. 2002. "The Hip-Hop Sublime as a Form of Commodification." In *Music and Marx*, edited by Regula Qureshi, 63–80. London: Routledge.

Krims, Adam. 2003. "Marxist Music Analysis without Adorno: Popular Music and Urban Geography." *Analyzing Popular Music*, 131–157.

Krims, Adam. 2007. *Music and Urban Geography*. London: Routledge.

Krimsky, Sheldon. 2003. *Science in the Private Interest: Has the Lure of Profits Corrupted Biomedical Research?* New York: Rowman & Littlefield Publishers.

Kruger, Jaco. 1999. "Singing Psalms with Owls: A Venda Twentieth-Century Musical History." *African Music* 7 (4): 122–146.

Kun, Josh. 2005. *Audiotopia: Music, Race, and America.* Berkeley: University of California Press.

Kurin, Richard. 2017. "A Conversation with Richard Kurin." In *The Routledge Companion to Intangible Cultural Heritage,* edited by Michelle Stefano and Peter Davis, 40–46. New York and London: Routledge

Lacan, Jacques. 1977. *The Four Fundamental Concepts of Psycho-Analysis.* London: Hogarth Press.

Lancefield, Robert C. 1998. "'Musical Traces' Retraceable Paths: The Repatriation of Recorded Sound." *Journal of Folklore Research* 35 (1): 47–68.

Langlois, Tony. 2013. "LimerickSoundscapes: A People's Soundscape." Paper presented at the *Technology Association National Conference.* Dublin.

Lassiter, Luke E. 2005. *The Chicago Guide to Collaborative Ethnography.* Chicago: University of Chicago Press.

Latour, Bruno. 2017. *Facing Gaia: Eight Lectures on the New Climatic Regime.* London: Polity.

Laurence, Felicity. 2008. "Music and Empathy." In *Music and Conflict Transformation: Harmonies and Dissonances in Geopolitics,* edited by Olivier Urbain, 13–25. London and New York: I. B. Tauris.

Lazzarato, Maurizio. 2009. "Neoliberalism in Action Inequality, Insecurity and the Reconstitution of the Social." *Theory, Culture & Society* 26 (6): 109–133.

León, Javier. 2009. "National Patrimony and Cultural Policy: The Case of the Afroperuvian Cajón." In *Music and Cultural Rights, edited by* Andrew N. Weintraub and Bell Yung, 110–139. Urbana: University of Illinois Press.

Lerner, Neil and Joseph N. Straus. 2006. *Sounding Off: Theorizing Disability in Music.* New York: Routledge.

Levin, Theodore Craig. 1999. *The Hundred Thousand Fools of God: Musical Travels in Central Asia (and Queens, New York).* Bloomington: Indiana University Press.

Levine, Victoria Lindsay, and Dylan Robinson. 2019. *Music and Modernity among First Peoples of North America.* Middletown, CT: Wesleyan University Press.

Lewey, Jamie Bissonnette. 2016. "For the Penobscot Nation, the Water in the River Is the Blood in Their Veins." *Bangor Daily News,* June 21, 2016. http://bangordailynews.com/2016/01/05/opinion/contributors/for-the-penobscot-nation-the-water-in-the-river-is-the-blood-in-their-veins.

Lewin, Kurt. 1946. "Action Research and Minority Problems." *Journal of Social Issues* 2 (4): 34–46.

Loewenson, R., A. C. Laurell, C. Hogstedt, L. D'Ambruoso, and Z. Shroff. 2014. *Participatory Action Research in Health Systems: A Methods Reader.* Harare: EQUINET.

Lomax, Alan. 1972. "Appeal for Cultural Equity." *The World of Music* 14 (2): 3–17.

Lowery, Wesley. 2011. "Aren't More White People Than Black People Killed by Police? Yes, but No." *Washington Post,* July 11. https://www.washingtonpost.com/news/post-nation/wp/2016/07/11/arent-more-white-people-than-black-people-killed-by-police-yes-but-no.

Lühning, Angela, and Rosângela Pereira de Tugny. 2016. "Ethnomusicology in Brazil: Introductory Reflections." *The World of Music* 5 (1): 7–21.

Lykes, M. Brinton, and Erzulie Coquillon. 2007. "Participatory Action Research and Feminisms." In *Handbook of Feminist Research: Theory and Praxis,* edited by Sharlene Hesse-Biber, 297–326. London: Sage.

Lykes, M. Brinton, and Rachel M. Hershberg. 2012. "Participatory Action Research and Feminisms: Social Inequalities and Transformative Praxis." In *Handbook of Feminist Research: Theory and Praxis*, edited by Sharlene Nagy Hesse-Biber, 331–367. 2nd ed. Thousand Oaks, CA: Sage.

Lynn, Kathy, John Daigle, Jennie Hoffman, Frank Lake, Natalie Michelle, Darren Ranco, Carson Viles, Garrit Voggesser, and Paul Williams. 2013. "The Impacts of Climate Change on Tribal Traditional Foods." *Climatic Change* 120 (3): 545–556.

Mackey, Eva. 2016. *Unsettled Expectations: Uncertainty, Land and Settler Decolonization.* Winnipeg: Fernwood Publishing.

Mackinlay, Elizabeth, and Katelyn Barney. 2014. "Unknown and Unknowing Possibilities: Transformative Learning, Social Justice, and Decolonising Pedagogy in Indigenous Australian Studies." *Journal of Transformative Education* 12 (1): 54–73.

Mackinlay, Elizabeth, and Gordon Chalmers. 2014. "Remembrances and Relationships: Rethinking Collaboration in Ethnomusicology as Ethical and Decolonising Practice." In *Collaborative Ethnomusicology: New Approaches to Music Research between Indigenous and Non-Indigenous Australians*, edited by Katelyn Barney, 63–79. Melbourne: Lyrebird Press.

Magrini, Tullia. 2003. *Music and Gender: Perspectives from the Mediterranean.* Chicago: University of Chicago Press.

Mahon, Maureen. 2014. "Music, Power, and Practice." *Ethnomusicology* 58 (2): 327–333.

Mahon, Maureen. 2019. "Constructing Race and Engaging Power through Music: Ethnomusicology and Critical Approaches to Race." In *Theory for Ethnomusicology. Histories, Conversations, Insights*, edited by Harris M. Berger and Ruth M. Stone, 99–113. 2nd ed. New York: Routledge.

Manathunga, Catherine. 2009. "Research as an Intercultural 'Contact Zone.'" *Discourse: Studies in the Cultural Politics of Education* 30 (2): 165–177.

Manuel, Peter. 1993. *Cassette Culture: Popular Music and Technology in North India.* Chicago: University of Chicago Press.

Manuel, Peter. 2002. "Modernity and Musical Structure: Neo-Marxist Perspectives on Song Form and Its Successors." In *Music and Marx*, edited by Regula Qureshi, 45–62. New York: Routledge.

Manuel, Peter. 2019. "Marxist Approaches to Music, Political Economy, and the Culture Industries: Ethnomusicological Perspectives." In *Theory for Ethnomusicology. Histories, Conversations, Insights*, edited by Harris M. Berger and Ruth M. Stone, 51–70. 2nd ed. New York: Routledge.

Marcus, George E., and Michael M. J. Fischer. 2014. *Anthropology as Cultural Critique: An Experimental Moment in the Human Sciences.* Chicago: University of Chicago Press.

Marcuse, Herbert. 2002. *One-Dimensional Man: Studies in the Ideology of Advanced Industrial Society.* London: Routledge.

Marett, Allan. 2010. "Vanishing Songs: How Musical Extinctions Threaten the Planet." *Ethnomusicology Forum* 19 (2): 249–262.

Marett, Allan, and Linda Barwick. 2003. "Endangered Songs and Endangered Languages." In *Maintaining the Links: Language Identity and the Land*, edited by J. Blythe and R. M. Brown, 144–151. Bath, UK: Foundation for Endangered Languages.

Massumi, Brian. 2002. *Parables for the Virtual: Movement, Affect, Sensation.* Durham, NC: Duke University Press.

Mathivha, Regina. 1986. "The Berlin Missionary Venture in Education at Tshakhuma, Venda, 1872." PhD diss., Polokwane: University of North Limpopo.

Matsue, Jennifer Milioto. 2013. "Stars to the State and Beyond: Globalization, Identity, and Asian Popular Music." *Journal of Asian Studies* 72 (1): 5–20.

McCann, Anthony. 2001. "All That Is Not Given Is Lost: Irish Traditional Music, Copyright, and Common Property." *Ethnomusicology* 45 (1): 89–106.

McCann, Anthony. 2003. *Beyond the Commons: The Expansion of the Irish Music Rights Organisation, the Elimination of Uncertainty, and the Politics of Enclosure.* Published by the author and available through Amazon.com.

McCartney, Andra. 2016. "Journées Sonores, canal de Lachine". https://concordia.academia.edu/AndraMcCartney.

McCullough, David. 1992. *Truman.* New York: Simon & Schuster.

McIntosh, Jonathan. 2013. "'Seeing the Bigger Picture': Experiential Learning, Applied Ethnomusicology and the Use of Gamelan Music in Adult Literacy Education." *International Journal of Music Education* 31 (1): 16–25.

McNeill, Fraser. 2011. *AIDS, Politics, and Music in South Africa.* Cambridge, UK: Cambridge University Press.

Mead, Margaret. 1969. "Research with Human Beings: A Model Derived from Anthropological Field Practice." *Daedalus,* 361–86.

Meintjes, Louise. 2003. *Sound of Africa!: Making Music Zulu in a South African Studio.* Durham, NC: Duke University Press.

Melaney, William D. 2006. "Arendt's Revision of Praxis: On Plurality and Narrative Experience." In *Logos of Phenomenology and Phenomenology of the Logos. Book Three,* 465–479. Dordrecht: Springer.

Meštrović, Stjepan Gabriel. 1992. *Durkheim and Postmodern Culture.* New York: A. de Gruyter.

Minnevich, Pauline, Ellen Waterman, and James Harley, eds. 2013. *Art of Immersive Soundscapes.* Regina: University of Regina Press.

Mill, John Stuart. 1844. *Essays on Economics and Society, Part 1.* In *The Complete Works of John Stuart Mill.* https://oll.libertyfund.org/titles/mill-the-collected-works-of-john-stuart-mill-volume-iv-essays-on-economics-and-society-part-i

Mills, Sherylle. 1996. "Indigenous Music and the Law: An Analysis of National and International Legislation." *Yearbook for Traditional Music* 28: 57–86.

Mitchell, Tony. 2001. *Global Noise: Rap and Hip-Hop Outside the USA.* Middletown, CT: Wesleyan University Press.

Mjöberg, Eric. 2012. *Among Wild Animals and People in Australia (Bland vilda djur och folk i Australien).* Translated by Margareta Luotsinen and Kim Akerman. Western Australia: Hesperian Press.

Moi, Toril. 2003 <1985>. *Sexual/Textual Politics: Feminist Literary Theory.* London: Routledge.

Moisala, Pirkko, and Beverley Diamond eds. 2000. *Music and Gender.* Urbana: University of Illinois Press.

Monson, Ingrid Tolia, ed. 2003. *The African Diaspora: A Musical Perspective.* Critical and Cultural Musicology 3. New York: Routledge.

Montero-Diaz, Fiorella. 2017. "YouTubing the 'Other': Lima's Upper Classes and Andean Imaginaries." In *Music, Identity, Digital Media,* edited by Thomas Hilder, 74–94. Rochester, NY: University of Rochester Press.

Montgomery, Kathleen, and Amalya L. Oliver. 2009. "Shifts in Guidelines for Ethical Scientific Conduct: How Public and Private Organizations Create and Change Norms of Research Integrity." *Social Studies of Science* 39 (1): 137–155.

Morcom, Anna. 2013. *Illicit Worlds of Indian Dance: Cultures of Exclusion*. London: Hurst.

Móricz, Klára. 2008. *Jewish Identities. Nationalism, Racism and Utopianism in 20th-Century Music*. Berkeley: University of California Press.

Morton, Timothy. 2013. *Hyperobjects: Philosophy and Ecology after the End of the World*. Minneapolis: University of Minnesota Press.

Mouton, N., G. Louw, and Strydom G. 2012. "A Historical Analysis of the Post-Apartheid Dispensation Education in South Africa (1994–2011)." *International Business & Economics Research Journal* 11 (11): 1211–1222.

Mugglestone, Erica. 1981. "Guido Adler's 'The Scope, Method, and Aim of Musicology' (1885): An English Translation with an Historico-Analytical Commentary." *Yearbook for Traditional Music* 13: 1–21.

Mulaudzi, Phalandwa Abraham. 2001. "The Domba Variety: An Initiation Language for Adulthood." *South African Journal of African Languages* 21 (1): 9–15.

Munk, Nina. 2013. *The Idealist: Jeffrey Sachs and the Quest to End Poverty*. New York: Knopf Doubleday.

Murphy, Clifford. 2015. "The Applied Ethnomusicologist as Public Folklorist: Ethnomusicological Practice in the Context of a Government Agency in the United States." In *The Oxford Handbook of Applied Ethnomusicology*, edited by Svanibor Pettan and Jeff Todd Titon. 709–734. New York: Oxford University Press.

Muthivhi, Azwihangwisi. 2010. "Ploughing New Fields of Knowledge: Culture and the Rise of Community Schooling in Venda." *Journal of Education* 48: 137–154.

Mydlarz, Charlie. 2013. "Exploring Soundscapes: Cutting-Edge Data Collection by Citizen Scientists Maps a World of Sonic Diversity." *Perspectives Magazine* 1 (1). www.salford.ac.uk/research/perspectives-magazine/volume-1/issue-1/exploring-soundscapes.

Nannyonga-Tamusuza, Sylvia, and Andrew N. Weintraub. 2012. "The Audible Future: Reimagining the Role of Sound Archives and Sound Repatriation in Uganda." *Ethnomusicology* 56 (2): 206–233.

National Endowment for the Arts. 2015. "APSCA Issue Brief #1: The Arts and GDP." Washington, DC: National Endowment for the Arts, Office of Research and Analysis.

National Science Foundation. n.d. "Frequently Asked Questions and Vignettes: Interpreting the Common Rule for the Protection of Human Subjects for Behavioral and Social Science Research." www.nsf.gov/bfa/dias/policy.

Needham, Joseph. 1971. "Foreword." In Nikolai Bukharin et al., *Science at the Crossroads*, vii–x. London: Frank Cass & Co.

Nell, Ian. 2012. "Exploring Notions of Critical Citizenship at Stellenbosch." http://stbweb02.stb.sun.ac.za/sotl/SOTL_previous/SOTL_2012/presentations/Day2/SOTL2012_Day2_INell_etal.pdf

Nelson, Cary. 2015. "Dystopia Is Now: The Threats to Academic Freedom." *Ethics in Science and Environmental Politics* 15: 17–22.

Nettl, Bruno. 1983. *Eight Urban Musical Cultures: Tradition and Change*. Urbana: University of Illinois Press.

Neuenfeldt, Karl, ed. 2007. *Indigenous Peoples, Recording Techniques, and the Recording Industry*. Special Issue of *The World of Music* 49 (1).

Nikolaidis, Evangelos, and Leonidas Maroudas. 2013. "Institutional Changes and the Expansion of Flexible Forms of Employment in Higher Education: The Case of Greek Universities." *Journal for Critical Education Policy Studies* 11 (3): 127–145.

Norvor, Kwasi and Michael Frishkopf. 2007. *Kinka: Traditional Songs from Avenorpedo*. Alberta: s.n.

Noyes, Dorothy. 2014. "Policy in Practice: The Unintended Consequences of ICH." In *The Fifth Forum on China-US Folklore and Cultural Heritage*, 16–19. Santa Fe, NM: Museum of International Folk Art. www.afsnet.org/page/FICH2

Nussbaum, Martha C. 1995. "Objectification." *Philosophy & Public Affairs* 24 (4): 249–291.

Nwamara, A. O., and S. K. I. Chokwu. 2016. "The Retrieval Research Strategy Approach to Intercultural Musical Arts Education in Contemporary Africa." *West African Journal of Musical Arts Education (WAJMAE)* 3 (1): 5–16.

Nzewi, Meki. 2007. "A Contemporary Study of Musical Arts Informed by African Indigenous Knowledge Systems: Illuminations, Reflections, and Explorations." Vol. 4. Pretoria: Centre for Indigenous Instrumental African Music and Dance.

Nzewi, Meki. 2008a. "The Igbo Concept of Mother Musicianship." In Meki Nzewi, Israel Anyahuru and Tom Ohiarahumunna. *Musical Sense and Musical Meaning: An Indigenous African Perception*. Pretoria: UNISA Press.

Nzewi, Meki. 2008b. "African Musical Arts Creativity and Performance: The Science of the Sound." *African Musicology Online* 2 (1): 1–7.

Nzewi, Meki. 2017. "Reinstating the Soft Science of African Indigenous Musical Arts for Humanity-Sensed Contemporary Education and Practice.", *FAEEBA* 26 (48): 61–78.

O'Connell, John Morgan, and Salwa El-Shawan Castelo-Branco. 2010. *Music and Conflict*. Urbana: University of Illinois Press.

Oja, Carol J. 2009. "*West Side Story* and *The Music Man*: Whiteness, Immigration and Race in Music during the 1950s." *Studies in Musical Theatre* 3 (1): 13–30.

Oliveros, Pauline. 2005. *Deep Listening: A Composer's Sound Practice*. New York: iUniverse.

Pacini Hernandez, Deborah. 2004. *Rockin' las Americas*. Pittsburgh: University of Pittsburgh Press.

Peat, F. David, and F. David Peat. 2005. *Blackfoot Physics: A Journey into the Native American Universe*. Boston: Weiser Books.

Peck, Jamie, and Adam Tickell. 2002. "The Urbanization of Neoliberalism: Theoretical Debates Neoliberalizing Space." *Antipode* 34 (3): 380–404.

Pels, Dick. 2003. *Unhastening Science: Autonomy and Reflexivity in the Social Theory of Knowledge*. Liverpool: Liverpool University Press.

Perrone, Charles A., and Christopher Dunn, eds. 2002. *Brazilian Popular Music and Globalization*. New York and London: Routledge.

Petri, Helmut. 1954. *Sterbende Welt in Nordwest-Australien*. Carlisle, WA: Hesperion Press.

Pettan, Svanibor. 2003. "Male, Female and Beyond in the Culture and Music of Roma in Kosovo." In *Music and Gender. Perspectives from the Mediterranean*, edited by Tullia Magrini, 287–306. Chicago: University of Chicago Press.

Pettan, Svanibor. 2010. "Music in War, Music for Peace: Experiences in Applied Ethnomusicology." In *Music and Conflict*, edited by John Morgan O'Connell and Salwa El-Shawan Castelo-Branco, 177–192. Urbana: University of Illinois Press.

Pettan, Svanibor. 2015. "Applied Ethnomusicology in the Global Arena." In *The Oxford Handbook of Applied Ethnomusicology*, edited by Svanibor Pettan and Jeff Todd Titon, 4–53. New York: Oxford University Press.

Pettan, Svanibor, ed. 2008. "Special Issue on Applied Ethnomusicology, A Festschrift for Kjell Skyllstad." *Muzikološki Zbornik/Musicological Anual* 44 (1).

Pettan, Svanibor, and Jeff Todd Titon, eds. 2015. *The Oxford Handbook of Applied Ethnomusicology*. New York: Oxford University Press.

"Physician Density." 2016. *The World Factbook*. https://www.cia.gov/library/publications/the-world-factbook/fields/2226.html.

Pieslak, Jonathan. 2015. *Radicalism and Music: An Introduction to the Music Cultures of al-Qa'ida, Racist Skinheads, Christian-Affiliated Radicals, and Eco-Animal Rights Militants*. Middletown, CT: Wesleyan University Press.

Plato. 2007. *The Republic, Book III*. Translated by Benjamin Jowett. Charleston, SC: Bibliozaar.

Polanyi, Michael. 1962. *Personal Knowledge: Towards a Post-Critical Philosophy*. London: Routledge.

Post, Jennifer C. 2018. *Ethnomusicology: A Contemporary Reader*. Vol. 2. New York and London: Routledge.

Povinelli, Elizabeth. 2002. *The Cunning of Recognition. Indigenous Alterities and the Making of Australian Multiculturalism*. Durham, NC: Duke University Press.

Pratt, Mary Louise. 1992 (2008). *Imperial Eyes: Travel Writing and Transculturation*. New York: Routledge.

Pynes, Patrick Gordon. 2000. *Erosion, Extraction, Reciprocation: An Ethno/Environmental History of the Navajo Nation's Ponderosa Pine Forests*. PhD diss., University of New Mexico.

Qureshi, Regula. 2002. *Music and Marx: Ideas, Practice, Politics*. New York and London: Routledge.

Racy, Ali Jihad. 1991. "Creativity and Ambience: An Ecstatic Feedback Model from Arab Music." *The World of Music* 33 (2): 7–26.

Radano, Ronald M., Philip V. Bohlman, and Houston A. Baker. 2000. *Music and the Racial Imagination*. Chicago: University of Chicago Press.

Radder, Hans. 2010. *The Commodification of Academic Research: Science and the Modern University*. Pittsburgh: Pittsburgh University Press.

Ragot, Richard, et al. 2002. "Time, Music and Aging." *Psychomusicology* 18 (1–2): 28–45.

Rahman, Muhammad Anisur. 2005. "The Theory and Practice of Participatory Action Research." In *Fundamentals of Action Research Volume II, Varieties and Workplace Applications of Action Research*, edited by Julie Wolfram Cox and Bill Cooke, 11–24. London: Sage.

Ramabulana, Vusani. 1988. "Domba Yesterday and Today." PhD diss., Thohoyandou, Limpopo: University of Venda.

Ramos, Silvia, and Ana Maria Ochoa. 2009. "Music and Human Rights. The AfroReggae Cultural Group and the Youth from the *Favelas* as Responses to Violence in Brazil." In *Music and Cultural Rights*, edited by Andrew Weintraub and Bell Yung, 219–240. Urbana: University of Illinois Press.

Rancière, Jacques. 1999. *Disagreement: Politics and Philosophy*. Translated by J. Rose. Minneapolis: University of Minnesota Press.

Rector, John M. 2014. *The Objectification Spectrum: Understanding and Transcending Our Diminishment and Dehumanization of Others*. New York: Oxford University Press.

Redmond, Anthony. 2005. "Strange Relatives: Mutualities and Dependencies between Aborigines and Pastoralists in the Northern Kimberley." *Oceania* 75 (3): 234–246.

Redmond, Anthony, and Fiona Skyring. 2010. "Exchange and Appropriation: The Wurnan Economy and Aboriginal Land and Labour at Karunjie Station, North-Western Australia." In *Indigenous Participation in Australian Economies*, edited by Ian Keen, 73–90. Acton, Australia: ANU E Press.

Redmond, Anthony. 2012. Tracking Wurnan: Transformations in the trade and exchange of resources in the northern Kimberley. *Indigenous participation in Australian economies II: Historical engagements and current enterprises*, edited by Natasha Fijn, Ian

Keen, Christopher Lloyd and Michael Pickering, 57–72. Canberra: Australian National University E Press.

Reed, Trevor. 2009. "Returning Hopi Voices: Redefining Repatriation through Community Partnership." Paper presented at the Native American and Indigenous Studies Association Conference, Minneapolis, Minnesota, May 21.

Reed, Trevor. 2019. "Pu'ltaaqatsit Aw Tuuqayta (Listening to Our Modern Lives)." In *Music and Modernity among First Peoples of North America*, edited by Victoria Lindsay Levine and Dylan Robinson, 258–264. Middletown, CT: Wesleyan University Press.

Rees, Helen. 2012. "Intangible Cultural Heritage in China Today: Policy and Practice in the Early Twenty-First Century." In *Music as Intangible Cultural Heritage,* edited by Keith Howard, 23–54. Farnham: Ashgate.

Reigersberg, E. Muriel Swijghuisen. 2016. "Policy Formation, Ethics Statement and Ethics in Ethnomusicology: The Need for Increased and Sustained Engagement." Helsinki: Helsinki Collegium for Advanced Studies.

Reily, Suzel, and Lev Weinstock, eds. 1998. *Venda Girls' Initiation Schools by John Blacking.* Belfast: Queen's University of Belfast.

Resnik, David. 2007. *The Price of Truth: How Money Affects the Norms of Science.* New York: Oxford University Press.

Rice, Timothy. 1987. "Toward the Remodeling of Ethnomusicology." *Ethnomusicology* 31 (3): 469–488.

Rice, Timothy. 2014. "Ethnomusicology in Times of Trouble." *Yearbook for Traditional Music* 46: 191–209.

Rifkin, Mark. 2011. "Settler States of Feeling: National Belonging and the Erasure of Native American Presence." In *A Companion to American Literary Studies*, edited by Caroline F. Levander and Robert S. Levin, 342–355. Malden, MA: Blackwell.

Rizman, Rudi. 2014. *Čas (brez) alternative: Sociološke in politološke refleksije.* Ljubljana: Znanstvena knjižnica—Refleksije.

Robinson, Dylan and Keavy Martin, eds. 2016. *Arts of Engagement. Taking Aesthetic Action In and Beyond the Truth and Reconciliation Commission of Canada.* Waterloo: Wilfrid Laurier University Press.

Rojas Guerra, Jose Maria. 2010. "Perfacio." In *Antologia*, edited by Orlando Fals Borda, ix–liii. Bogotá: Universidad Nacional de Colombia.

Rollefson, J. Griffith. 2017. *Flip the Script. European Hip Hop and the Politics of Postcoloniality.* Chicago: University of Chicago Press.

Rose, Tricia. 1994. *Black Noise: Rap Music and Black Culture in Contemporary America.* Middletown, CT: Wesleyan University Press.

Rosenberry, William. 1997. "Marx and Anthropology." *Annual Review of Anthropology* 26 (1): 25–46.

Ross, Alex. 2016. "When Music Is Violence." *The New Yorker*, July 4, 2016. https://www.newyorker.com/magazine/2016/07/04/when-music-is-violence

Ross, John Alan, Steven M. Egesdal, and George Hill. 2011. *The Spokan Indians.* Spokane, WA: Michael J. Ross.

Sabido, Miguel. 2004. "The Origins of Entertainment-Education." In *Entertainment-Education and Social Change: History, Research, and Practice*, edited by Arvind Singhal, Michael J. Cody, Everett M. Rogers, and Miguel Sabido, 61–74. Mahwah, NJ: Lawrence Erlbaum Associates.

Sachs, Jeffrey D. 2005. *The End of Poverty: Economic Possibilities for Our Time.* London: Penguin.

Said, Edward. 1978. *Orientalism.* New York: Vintage.

Sakakeeny, Matt. 2013. *Roll with It: Brass Bands in the Streets of New Orleans*. Durham, NC: Duke University Press.

Sakakeeny, Matt. 2015. *Playing for Work: Music as a Form of Labor in New Orleans*. London and New York: Oxford University Press.

Samson, Guillaume. 2015. "Maloya Music as World Cultural Heritage: The Cultural, Political and Ethical Fallout of Labelling." *Translingual Discourse in Ethnomusicology* 1: 27–43.

Samson, Guillaume, and Carlos Sandroni. 2013. "The Recognition of Samba de Roda and Reunion Maloya as Intangible Cultural Heritage of Humanity." *Vibrant* 10 (1): 530–551.

Sandroni, Carlos. 2010. "Samba de roda: Intangible Heritage of Humanity." *Estudos Avançados* 24 (69): 373–387.

Sanghani, Radhika. 2014. "UN: Britain's Sexism More 'Pervasive' Than Any Other Country." *The Telegraph*, April 15, 2014. www.telegraph.co.uk/women/womens-politics/10767784/UN-Britains-sexism-more-pervasive-than-any-other-country.html.

Sarango, Luis Fernando. 2004. *Aprender en la sabiduría y el buen vivir*. Quito: Universidad Intercultural de las Nacionalidades y Pueblos Indígenas Amawtay Wasi.

Sardo, Susana. 2018. "Shared Research Practices On and About Music: Toward Decolonizing Colonial Ethnomusicology." In *Making Music, Making Society*, edited by Josep Martí and Sara Revilla Gútiez, 217–238. Cambridge, UK: Cambridge Scholars Publishing

Scales, Christopher A. 2012. *Recording Culture: Powwow Music and the Aboriginal Recording Industry on the Northern Plains*. Durham, NC: Duke University Press.

Schafer, R. Murray. 1977. *The Tuning of the World*. New York: Knopf.

Schafer, R. Murray. 1994. *The Soundscape: Our Sonic Environment and the Tuning of the World*. Rochester, VT: Destiny Books.

Schippers, Huib, and Dan Bendrups, eds. 2015. "Sound Futures: Exploring Contexts for Music Sustainability." Special Issue of *The World of Music* (New Series) 4 (1).

Schippers, Huib, and Catherine Grant. 2016. *Sustainable Futures for Music Cultures*. New York: Oxford University Press.

Schrag, Z. 2010. *Ethical Imperialism*. Baltimore: Johns Hopkins University Press.

Schütz, Alfred. 1951. "Making Music Together: A Study in Social Relationship." *Social Research* 18 (1): 76–97.

Schütz, Alfred. 1967a. *Collected Papers II: Studies in Social Theory*. Edited by Arvid Brodersen. The Hague: M. Nijhoff.

Schütz, Alfred. 1967b. *The Phenomenology of the Social World*. Evanston, IL: Northwestern University Press.

Schütz, Alfred. 1970. *On Phenomenology and Social Relations*. Edited by Helmut R. Wagner. Chicago: University of Chicago Press.

Schütz, Alfred, and I. Schutz. 1967. *Collected Papers III: Studies in Phenomenological Philosophy*. The Hague: M. Nijhoff.

Scott, John. 2000. *Social Network Analysis: A Handbook*. London and Thousand Oaks, CA: Sage Publications.

Seeger, Anthony. 1992. "Ethnomusicology and Music Law." *Ethnomusicology* 36 (3): 345–359.

Seeger, Anthony. 1996. "Ethnomusicologists, Archives, Professional Organizations and the Shifting Ethics of Intellectual Property." *Yearbook for Traditional Music* 28: 87–105.

Seeger, Anthony. 2006. "Lost Lineages and Neglected Peers: Ethnomusicologists Outside Academia." *Ethnomusicology* 50 (2): 214–235.

Seeger, Anthony. 2008. "Theories Forged in the Crucible of Action." In *Shadows in the Field: New Perspectives for Fieldwork in Ethnomusicology*, edited by Gregory Barz and Timothy J Cooley, 271–288. London and New York: Oxford University Press.

Seeger, Anthony. 2009. "Lessons Learned from the ICTM (NGO) Evaluation of Nominations for UNESCO's *Masterpieces of the Oral and Intangible Heritage of Humanity, 2001–5.*" In Intangible *Heritage*, edited by *Laurajane Smith and Natsuko Akagawa*, 112–128. New York: Routledge.

Seeger, Anthony. 2013. "On Epistemology and Applied Ethnomusicology in a Postcolonial World." Interview with Maurice Mengel. *El Oído Pensante* 1 (2). http://ppct.caicyt.gov. ar/index.php/oidopensante/issue/view/188.

Seeger, Anthony, and Shubha Chaudhury, eds. 2004. *Global Perspectives on Audiovisual Archives in the 21st Century*. Calcutta: Seagull Books.

Seeger, Charles. 1944. "Music and Government: Field for Applied Musicology." In *Papers Read at the International Congress of Musicology Held at New York, September 11–18, 1939*, 12–20. New York: Music Educators National Conference for the American Musicological Society.

Seeger, Charles. 1970. "Toward a Unitary Field Theory for Musicology." *Selected Reports* I: 171–210. Los Angeles: Institute of Ethnomusicology, UCLA.

Seitel, Peter. 2001. Safeguarding Traditional Cultures. A Global Assessment. Washington: Smithsonian Insitution.

Sen, Amartya. 1999. *Development as Freedom*. New York: Knopf.

Sennett, Richard. 1998. *The Corrosion of Character: Personal Consequence of Work in the New Capitalism*. New York: W. W. Norton.

Serafimovska, Stoijikova et al. 2016. "Safeguarding Intangible Cultural Heritage in the Republic of Macedonia." *Yearbook for Traditional Music* 48: 1-24.

Sereny, Gitta. 1974. *Into That Darkness from Mercy Killy to Mass Murder*. New York: McGraw-Hill.

Servaes, Jan. 1996. "Communication for Development in a Global Perspective: The Role of Governmental and Non-Governmental Agencies." *Communications* 21 (4): 407–418.

Sheehy, Daniel. 1992. "A Few Notions about Philosophy and Strategy in Applied Ethnomusicology." *Ethnomusicology* 36 (3): 323–336.

Shelemay, Kay Kaufman. 1991. *A Song of Longing. An Ethiopian Journey*. Urbana: University of Illinois Press.

Shelemay, Kay Kaufman. 1999. "The Impact and Ethics of Musical Scholarship." In *Rethinking Music*, edited by Nicholas Cook and Mark Everist, 531–544. Oxford: Oxford University Press.

Shelemay, Kay Kaufmann. 2006. *Soundscapes: Exploring Music in a Changing World*. London: Norton.

Shelemay, Kay Kaufman. 2013. "The Ethics of Ethnomusicology in a Cosmopolitan Age." In *The Cambridge History of World Music*, edited by Philip V. Bohlman, 786–806. Cambridge, UK: Cambridge University Press.

Shorrocks, Anthony, James B. Davies, and Rodrigo Lluberas. 2015. *Global Wealth Databook 2015*. Zurich: Credit Suisse.

Simonett, Helena 2016. Yoreme Cocoon Leg Rattles: An Eco-organological Perspective. *TRANS. Revista Transcultura de Musica/Transcultural Music Review*, 20: 1-33.

Simpson, Audra and Andrea Smith, eds. 2014. *Theorizing Native Studies*. Durham, NC: Duke University Press.

Singhal, Arvind. 2004. *Entertainment-Education and Social Change: History, Research, and Practice*. Mahwah, NJ: Lawrence Erlbaum Associates.

Slaughter, Sheila, and Larry L. Leslie. 1997. *Academic Capitalism: Politics, Policies, and the Entrepreneurial University*. Baltimore: Johns Hopkins University Press.

Slaughter, Sheila, and Gary Rhoades. 2004. *Academic Capitalism and the New Economy: Markets, State, and Higher Education*. Baltimore: Johns Hopkins University Press.

"Slavery Today." 2016. Endslaverynow. 2016. http://endslaverynow.org/learn/slavery-today.

Slobin, Mark. 1992. "Ethical Issues." In *Ethnomusicology: An Introduction*, edited by Helen Myers, 329–336. London: Macmillan.

Slovic, Paul. 2007. "'If I Look at the Mass I Will Never Act': Psychic Numbing and Genocide." *Judgment and Decision Making* 2 (2): 79–95.

Small, Christopher. 1998. *Musicking: The Meanings of Performing and Listening*. Hanover, NH: University Press of New England.

Smith, Adam. 1759. *The Theory of Moral Sentiments*. https://www.gutenberg.org/files/58559/58559-h/58559-h.htm.

Smith, Adam. 1776. *An Inquiry into the Nature and Causes of the Wealth of Nations*. https://www.gutenberg.org/files/3300/3300-h/3300-h.htm.

Smith, Linda Tuhiwai. 1999. Decolonizing methodologies : research and indigenous peoples. Dunedin: University of Otago Press.

Society for Ethnomusicology. 2008. "SEM Policy Guidelines for Institutional Review Boards." *www.ethnomusicology.org*.

Society for Ethnomusicology. 2013. "Statement Regarding Review of Ethnographic Research by Institutional Review Boards or Ethics Committees." *www.ethnomusicology.org*.

Solomon, Thomas. 2012. "Where Is the Postcolonial in Ethnomusicology?" In *Ethnomusicology in East Africa: Perspectives from Uganda and Beyond*, edited by Sylvia Nannyonga-Tamusuza and Thomas Solomon, 216–251. Kampala, Uganda: Fountain.

Somerville, Margaret, and Tony Perkins. 2003. "Border Work in the Contact Zone: Thinking Indigenous/Non-Indigenous Collaboration Spatially." *Journal of Intercultural Studies* 24 (3): 253–266.

Sontag, Susan. 1977. *On Photography*. Picador: New York.

Spinney, Ann Morrison. 2006. "Medeolinuwok, Music, and Missionaries in Maine." In *Music in American Religious Experience*, edited by Philip V. Bohlman, Edith L. Blumhofer, and Maria M. Chow, 57–82. New York: Oxford University Press.

Stahl, Matt, and Leslie M. Meirer. 2012. "The Firm Foundation of Organizational Flexibility: The 360 Contract in the Digitalizing Music Industry." *Canadian Journal of Communication* 37 (3): 441–458.

Stayt, Hugh. 1931. *The Bavenda*. London: Oxford University Press for the International Institute of African Languages and Cultures.

Steiner, George. 2005. *Lessons of the Masters*. Cambridge, MA: Harvard University Press.

Stergiou, Konstantinos, and Stylianos Somarakis. 2016. "Academic Freedom and Tenure: Introduction." *Ethics in Science and Environmental Politics* 15: 1–5.

Stobart, Henry. 2010. "Rampant Reproduction and Digital Democracy: Shifting Landscapes of Music Production and 'Piracy' in Bolivia." *Ethnomusicology Forum* 19: 27–56.

Stoever, Jennifer Lynn 2016. *The Sonic Color Line*. New York: New York University Press.

Stojikova Serafimovska, Velikova, Dave Wilson, and Ivona Opetčeska Tatarčeska. 2016. "Safeguarding Intangible Cultural Heritage in the Republic of Macedonia." *Yearbook for Traditional Music* 48: 1–24.

Stokes, Martin. 1994. *Ethnicity, Identity and Music: The Musical Construction of Place*. Oxford: Berg.

Stokes, Martin. 2002. "Marx, Money, and Musicians." In *Music and Marx: Ideas, Practice, Politics*, edited by Regula Burkhard Qureshi, 139–166. New York and London: Routledge.

Strauss, Joseph N. 2011. *Extraordinary Measures. Disability in Music*. New York: Oxford University Press.

Subramanian, Ram, Ruth Delaney, Stephen Roberts, Nancy Fishman, and Peggy McGarry. 2015. *Incarceration's Front Door: The Misuse of Jails in America*. Brooklyn, NY: Vera Institute of Justice.

Sugarman, Jane C. 1997. *Engendering Song: Singing and Subjectivity at Prespa Albanian Weddings*. Chicago: University of Chicago Press.

Sugarman, Jane C. 2019. "Theories of Gender and Sexuality: From the Village to the Anthropocene." In *Theory for Ethnomusicology. Histories, Conversations, Insights*, edited by Harris M. Berger and Ruth M. Stone, 71–98. New York: Routledge.

Sunardi, Christina. 2015. *Stunning Males and Powerful Females: Gender and Tradition in East Javanese Dance*. Urbana: University of Illinois Press.

Sweers, Britta. 2015. "Music and Conflict Resolution: The Public Display of Migrants in National(ist) Conflict Situations in Europe: An Analytical Reflection on University-Based Ethnomusicological Activism." In *The Oxford Handbook of Applied Ethnomusicology*, edited by Svanibor Pettan and Jeff Todd Titon, 511–552. New York: Oxford University Press.

"Syrian Refugees." 2016. http://syrianrefugees.eu/.

Tacchi, Jo. 2002. "Radio Texture: Between Self and Others." In *The Anthropology of Media: A Reader*, edited by Kelly Askew and Richard R. Wilk, 241–257. London: Blackwell.

Tax, Sol. 1975. "Action Anthropology." *Current Anthropology* 16 (4): 514–517.

Taylor, Timothy D. 2012. *The Sounds of Capitalism: Advertising, Music, and the Conquest of Culture*. Chicago: University of Chicago Press.

Teeuwen, Steffen, and Rudolphus Hantke, eds. 2007. *Gypsy Scholars, Migrant Teachers and the Global Academic Proletariat: Adjunct Labor in Higher Education*. Amsterdam and New York: Rodopi.

Thomas, Martin. 2014. "Turning Subjects into Objects and Objects into Subjects: Collecting Human Remains on the 1948 Arnhem Land Expedition." *Circulating Cultures: Indigenous Music, Dance and Media in Australia*, edited by Amanda Harris, 129–166. *Canberra: ANU Press ANU Press*.

Thoreau, Henry David. 1971. *Walden*. Princeton: Princeton University Press.

Throsby, David. 2010. *The Economics of Cultural Policy*. Cambridge, UK: Cambridge University Press.

Throsby, David, and Michael Hutter, eds. 2008. *Beyond Price: Value in Culture, Economics and the Arts*. Cambridge, UK: Cambridge University Press.

Tible, Jean. 2011. "Lutas contra o um: notas do diálogo entre uma antropologia e um Marx contra o estado." *Revista de Antropologia Social dos Alunos do PPGAS-UFSCar* 3 (1): 171–197.

Titon, Jeff Todd. 1992. "Music, the Public Interest, and the Practice of Ethnomusicology." *Ethnomusicology* 36 (3): 314–322.

Titon, Jeff Todd. 1999. "'The Real Thing: Tourism, Authenticity, and Pilgrimage among the Old Regular Baptists at the 1997 Smithsonian Folklife Festival," *The World of Music* 41 (3): 115–139.

Titon, Jeff Todd. 2009. "Music and Sustainability: An Ecological Viewpoint." *The World of Music* 51 (1): 119–138.

Titon, Jeff Todd. 2012. "A Sound Commons for All Living Creatures." *Smithsonian Folkways Magazine* Winter. www.folkways.si.edu/magazine-fall-winter-2012-sound-commons-living-creatures/science-and-nature-world/music/article/smithsonian.

Titon, Jeff Todd. 2014. "Applied Ethnomusicology and the University: A Fraught Relation." March 14. http://sustainablemusic.blogspot.si/2014/03/applied-ethnomusicology-and-university.html.

Titon, Jeff Todd. 2015a. "Applied Ethnomusicology: A Descriptive and Historical Account." In *The Oxford Handbook of Applied Ethnomusicology*, edited by Svanibor Pettan and Jeff Todd Titon, 4–29. New York: Oxford University Press.

Titon, Jeff Todd. 2015b. "Exhibiting Music in a Sound Community." *Ethnologies* 37 (1): 23–41.

Titon, Jeff Todd. 2015c. "Sustainability, Resilience, and Adaptive Management for Applied Ethnomusicology." In *The Oxford Handbook of Applied Ethnomusicology*, edited by Svanibor Pettan and Jeff Todd Titon, 157–95. New York: Oxford University Press.

Titon, Jeff Todd. 2016. "Orality, Commonality, Commons, Sustainability, Resilience." *Journal of American Folklore* 129 (514): 486–497.

Titon, Jeff Todd. 2019. "Ecojustice, Religious Folklife and a Sound Ecology." *Yale Journal of Music & Religion* 5 (2): Article 7. DOI: https://doi.org/10.17132/2377-231X.1142.

Titon, Jeff Todd. 2020. "Sustainability and a Sound Ecology." In Jeff Todd Titon, *Toward a Sound Ecology: New and Selected Essays*, 254–275. Bloomington: Indiana University Press.

Titon, Jeff Todd, and Svanibor Pettan. 2015. "An Introduction to Applied Ethnomusicology." In *The Oxford Handbook of Applied Ethnomusicology*, 4–67, edited by Svanibor Pettan and Jeff Todd Titon. New York: Oxford University Press.

Toner, Peter. 2003. "History, Memory and Music: The Repatriation of Digital Audio to Yolngu." In *Researchers, Communities, Institutions and Sound Recordings*, edited by Linda Barwick, Allan Marett, Jane Simpson, and Amanda Harris, 2–17. Sydney: University of Sydney Press.

Toynbee, Jason, and Byron Dueck, eds. 2011. *Migrating Music*. London and New York: Routledge.

Treasure, Julian. 2012. "Why Architects Need to Use Their Ears." TED Talks. www.ted.com/talks/julian_treasure_why_architects_need_to_use_their_ears.

Treloyn, Sally. 2016a. "Approaching an Epistemic Community of Applied Ethnomusicology in Australia: Intercultural Research on Australian Aboriginal Song." In *Studies across Disciplines in the Humanities and Social Sciences 21*, edited by Klisala Harrison, 23–39. Helsinki: Helsinki Collegium for Advanced Studies.

Treloyn, Sally. 2016b. "Music in Culture, Music as Culture, Music Interculturally: Reflections on the Development and Challenges of Ethnomusicological Research in Australia." *Voices: A World Forum for Music Therapy* 16 (2). https://doi.org/10.15845/voices.v16i2.877.

Treloyn, Sally, and Rona Googninda Charles. 2014. "How Do You Feel about Squeezing Oranges?: Reflections and Lessons on Collaboration in Ethnomusicological Research in an Aboriginal Australian Community." In *Collaborative Ethnomusicology: New Approaches to Music Research between Indigenous and Non-Indigenous Australians*, edited by Katelyn Barney, 169–186. Melbourne: Lyrebird Press.

Treloyn, Sally, and Rona Googninda Charles. 2015. "Repatriation and Innovation: The Impact of Archival Recordings on Endangered Dance-Song Traditions and Ethnomusicological Research." In *Research, Records and Responsibility: Ten Years of PARADISEC*, edited by Amanda Harris, Nick Thieberger, and Linda Barwick, 187–206. Sydney: Sydney University Press.

Treloyn, Sally, Rona Googninda Charles, and Sherika Nulgit. 2013. "Repatriation of Song Materials to Support Intergenerational Transmission of Knowledge about Language in the Kimberley Region of Northwest Australia." In *Endangered Languages beyond Boundaries: Proceedings of the 17th Foundation for Endangered Languages Conference*, edited by Mary Jane Norris, 18–24. Bath, UK: Foundation for Endangered Languages.

Treloyn, Sally, and Andrea Emberly. 2013. "Sustaining Traditions: Ethnomusicological Collections, Access and Sustainability in Australia." *Musicology Australia* 35 (2): 159–177.

Treloyn, Sally, Matthew Dembal Martin, and Rona Googninda Charles. 2016. "Cultural Precedents for the Repatriation of Legacy Song Records to Communities of Origin." *Australian Aboriginal Studies*, 2: 94–103.

Troutman, John W. 2009. *Indian Blues: American Indians and the Politics of Music 1879–1934*. Norman: University of Oklahoma Press.

Truax, Barry. 1999. *Handbook for Acoustic Ecology*. Burnaby, Canada: Cambridge Street Publishing.

Tuan, Yi-Fu. 2004. *Art, Place, Self*. Santa Fe, NM: Center for American Places.

Tuck, Eve, and K. Wayne Yang. 2012. "Decolonization Is Not a Metaphor." *Decolonization: Indigeneity, Education & Society* 1 (1):1–40.

Tucker, Joshua. 2016. "The machine of sonorous indigeneity: craftsmanship and sound ecology in an Andean instrument workshop." *Ethnomusicology Forum* 25 (3): 326–344.

Tugny, Rosangela Pereira, et al. 2009a. *Mõgmõka yõg kutex / Cantos do Gavião-Espírito*. Rio de Janeiro: Azougue.

Tugny, Rosangela Pereira, et al. 2009b. *Xunĩm yõg kutex xi ãgtux xi hemex yõg kutex / Cantos e Histórias do Morcego Espírito e do Hemex*. Rio de Janeiro: Azougue.

Turino, Thomas. 2008. *Music as Social Life: The Politics of Participation*. Chicago: University of Chicago Press.

Turino, Tom. 2009. "Four Fields of Music Making and Sustainable Living." *The World of Music* 51 (1): 95–118.

UNDP. 2014. "Human Development Reports." http://hdr.undp.org/en.

UNESCO. 2001. "Universal Declaration on Cultural Diversity." UNESCO. http://portal.unesco.org/en/ev.php-URL_ID.

UNESCO. 2013. "Intangible Cultural Heritage for Sustainable Development: A Virtual Exhibition." www.unesco.org/culture/ich/en/ich-for-sustainable-development-a-virtual-exhibition-2013-00693.

UNESCO. 2015. "Browse the Lists of Intangible Cultural Heritage and the Register of Best Safeguarding Practices." www.unesco.org/en/lists

UNESCO. 2016. "What Is Intangible Cultural Heritage?" www.unesco.org/culture/ich/en/what-is-intangible-heritage-00003.

"UNESCO Statistics." 2016. www.unesco.org/new/en/education/themes/education-building-blocks/literacy/resources/statistics.

UNHCR. 2006. *Liberia: Strategies and Programs*. Liberia: UNHCR.

United Nations. 2007. "Declaration on the Rights of Indigenous Peoples." https://www.un.org/development/desa/indigenouspeoples/declaration-on-the-rights-of-indigenous-peoples.html.

United Nations. 2016. "Global Issues." www.un.org/en/globalissues/briefingpapers.

Urbain, Olivier. 2007. *Music and Conflict Transformation: Harmonies and Dissonances in Geopolitics*. London: I. B. Tauris.

Usner, Eric Martin. 2010. "United States Ethnomusicology and the Engaged University." In *Applied Ethnomusicology: Historical and Contemporary Approaches*, edited by Harrison Klisala, Svanibor Pettan, and Elizabeth Mackinlay, 76–95. Newcastle upon Tyne: Cambridge Scholars Publishing.

Van Zanten, Wim. 2012. "Social Qualities of Time and Space Created in Performing Arts of West Java: The Implications for Safeguarding Living Culture." *Wacana* 14 (1): 121–144.

Van Gulik, R. H. 1969. *The Lore of the Chinese Lute*. Rutland, VT: Charles Tuttle.

Vasco Uribe, Luis Guillermo. 2002. "Entre selva y páramo, viviendo y pensando la lucha India." Bogotá: Instituto Colombiano de Antropología e Historia.

Vellend, Mark. 2015. "The Community Concept." Oxford Bibliographies. https://www.oxfordbibliographies.com/view/document/obo-9780199830060/obo-9780199830060-0011.xml.

Vidmar, Ičo. 2017. *Nova muzika v New Yorku. Neodvisni glasbeniki in pravica do mesta*. Ljubljana: Studia humanitatis.

Viveiros de Castro, Eduardo. 2013. "The Relative Native." *HAU: Journal of Ethnographic Theory* 3 (3): 473–502.

Voegelin, Salomé. 2010. *Listening to Noise and Silence: Towards a Philosophy of Sound Art*. New York: Continuum.

Walsh, Catherine E. 2009. *Interculturalidad, estado, sociedad: Luchas (de) coloniales de nuestra época*. Quito: Universidad Andina Simón Bolívar.

Warmelo, Nicolaas van. 1932. *Contributions towards Venda History, Religions and Tribal Ritual*. Vol. 3. Pretoria: Department of Native Affairs, Goverment Printer.

Wasserman, Stanley, and Katherine Faust. 1994. *Social Network Analysis: Methods and Applications*. Cambridge, UK: Cambridge University Press.

Waxer, Lise. 2013. *Situating Salsa: Global Markets and Local Meanings in Latin Popular Music*. Middletown, CT: Wesleyan University Press.

Weber, Max. 1930. *The Protestant Ethic and the Spirit of Capitalism*. Translated by Talcott Parsons. New York: Charles Scribner's Sons.

Weber, Max. 1978. *Economy and Society: An Outline of Interpretive Sociology*. Berkeley: University of California Press.

Weintraub, Andrew N. 2009. "Introduction." In *Music and Cultural Rights*, edited by Andrew N. Weintraub and Bell Yung, 1–18. Urbana: University of Illinois Press.

Weintraub, Andrew Noah, and Bell Yung. 2009. *Music and Cultural Rights*. Urbana: University of Illinois Press.

Wenner, Adrian M. 1964. "Sound Communication in Honey Bees." *Scientific American* 210: 116–124.

Wessman, R. 1908. *The Bawenda of the Spelonken (Transvaal): A Contribution towards the Psychology and Folk-Lore of African Peoples*. London: The African World Ltd.

Westerkamp, Hildegarde. 1974. "Soundwalking." *Sound Heritage* 3 (4): 18–27.

White, Bob W., ed. 2012. *Music and Globalization: Critical Encounters*. Tracking Globalization. Bloomington: Indiana University Press.

Whitely, Sheila. 2005. *Too Much, Too Young. Popular Music, Age and Gender*. New York: Routledge.

Wildcat, Daniel R. 2009. *Red Alert!: Saving the Planet with Indigenous Knowledge*. Golden, CO: Fulcrum.

Williams, Alan. 2015. "The Problem and Potential of Commerce." In *The Oxford Handbook of Applied Ethnomusicology*, edited by Svanibor Pettan and Jeff Todd Titon, 772–801. New York: Oxford University Press.

Williamson, John, and Martin Cloonan. 2016. *Players' Work Time. A History of the British Musicians' Union, 1893–2013*. Manchester: Manchester University Press.

Wilson, Shawn. 2008. *Research is Ceremony: Indigenous Research Methods*. Black Point, Nova Scotia: Fernwood Publishing.

Wong, Deborah. 2006. "Ethnomusicology and Difference." *Ethnomusicology* 50 (2): 259–279.

Wong, Deborah. 2014. "Sound, Silence, Music: Power." *Ethnomusicology* 58 (2): 347–353.

Wong, Deborah. 2015. "Ethnomusicology without Erotics." *Women and Music: A Journal of Gender and Culture* 19 (1): 178–185.

World Health Organization (WHO). 2016. "Urgent Call Available at https://web.archive. org/web/20160529035759/http://www.who.int/water_sanitation_health/sanitation/ action/en/, to Action on Sanitation." www.who.int/water_sanitation_health/sanita-tion/action/en.

World Intellectual Property Organization (WIPO). 2004. "What Is Intellectual Property?" Geneva: World Intellectual Property Organization. https://www.oxfordbibliographies. com/view/document/obo-9780199830060/obo-9780199830060-0011.xml

World Intellectual Property Organization (WIPO). 2006. "IP [Intellectual Property] Asset Development and Management: A Key Strategy for Economic Growth." Geneva: World Intellectual Property Organization. https://www.wipo.int/publications/en/details. jsp?id=293&plang=EN.

World Intellectual Property Organization (WIPO). 2016. "Intergovernmental Committee." IGC. https://www.wipo.int/publications/en/details.jsp?id=3861.

World Intellectual Property Organization (WIPO). 2017. "Protect and Promote Your Culture: A Practical Guide to Intellectual Property for Indigenous Peoples and Local Communities." Geneva: World Intellectual Property Organization. https://www.wipo. int/publications/en/details.jsp?id=4195.

Wrazen, Louise. 2016. "Spiraling to Redefine (Dis)Ability: A Case Study in Summer Music Programming for Children." *Yearbook for Traditional Music* 48: 167–185.

Wynecoop, Nancy Perkins, and N. Wynecoop Clark. 1985. *In the Stream: An Indian Story*. Spokane, WA: s.n.

WynSculley, Catherine. 2012. "Critical Citizenship Blogspot." Blog. https:// criticalcitizenship.wordpress.com/2012/01/17/hello-world.

Ylijoki, Oili-Helena. 2010. "Future Orientations in Episodic Labor: Short-Term Academics as a Case in Point." *Time Society* 19 (3): 365–386.

Yung, Bell. 2009. "Historical Legacy and the Contemporary World: UNESCO and China's Qin Music in the Twenty-First Century." In *Music and Cultural Rights*, edited by Andrew N. Weintraub and Bell Yung, 140–168. Urbana: University of Illinois Press.

Zemp Hugo. 1996. "The/An Ethnomusicologist and the Record Business." *Yearbook for Traditional Music* 28: 36–56

Ziman, J. 2000. *Real Science: What It Is, and What It Means*. Cambridge, UK: Cambridge University Press.

Index